DEATH
OF A
TYCOON

NICK DAVIES

DEATH
OF A
TYCOON

*An Insider's Account
of the Fall
of Robert Maxwell*

ST. MARTIN'S PRESS
NEW YORK

ACKNOWLEDGEMENTS

To all those friends and acquaintances in London, New York, Paris, Moscow and Jerusalem who co-operated so willingly and fully to help unravel the truth about Robert Maxwell and his many lives. Thank you.

And especial thanks to two people whose assistance and support were invaluable: Andrea Martin and Bob Cole.

Library of Congress Cataloging-in-Publication Data

Davies, Nicholas.
    Death of a tycoon / Nicholas Davies.
      p. cm.
    ISBN 0-312-09249-0
    1. Maxwell, Robert, 1923–1991. 2. Publishers and publishing—Great Britain—Biography. 3. Newspaper publishing—Great Britain—History—20th century.
I. Title.
Z325.M394D38   1993
070.5′092—dc20
    [B]   93-21742
                                                                      CIP

First published in Great Britain by Sidgwick & Jackson Limited as *The Unknown Maxwell*.

First U.S. Edition: May 1993
10 9 8 7 6 5 4 3 2 1

CONTENTS

ONE
'Sometimes I think I should just end it all.'
1

TWO
*'All I can remember of my childhood is the awful
feeling of hunger.'*
13

THREE
*'It looked as though the good life would never end.
But now it is about to.'*
34

FOUR
'Leave me alone, will you, woman!'
65

FIVE
'Something must be done. I can't go on like this.'
87

SIX
'I've decided to appoint myself Editor-in-Chief.'
120

SEVEN
*'I'm not like ordinary men; I don't have time
to take care of myself.'*
154

Contents

EIGHT
'You have my word that you can trust me.'
202

NINE
'Gorbachov treated me like a Head of State.'
246

TEN
'They'll wish they'd never been born.'
291

ELEVEN
'If there is a way back after death, then I will be the one to find it.'
312

ONE

'Sometimes I think I should just end it all.'

I t was a damp Sunday afternoon in the spring of 1990 when Robert Maxwell phoned and asked me to come and see him in his apartment. His voice sounded dreadful, heavy with a cold. He wanted to talk about the *European*, his pet project, which had been on sale for just a couple of weeks. I could tell he wasn't in a good humour. I had been involved with the *European* throughout the planning stages and we had often discussed the matter.

When I went to his tenth-floor apartment I was shown into his palatial bedroom by one of his Filipino maids. He was lounging on the bed, with a large white towelling robe around him, and watching television, flicking from channel to channel. He beckoned me to come in and sit down.

As he turned down the volume of the TV he said, in one of his most solemn voices, a voice he used when he was feeling particularly sorry for himself: 'It's not a very good paper, is it?' pointing dismissively to the *European* strewn out across the bed and looking at me from under his bushy eyebrows.

'You sound awful,' I said, 'are you ill?'

'No,' he replied, 'but I've had this cold for a long time; it's affecting my voice; I can't get rid of it.'

Colds were a common complaint for Maxwell, but, as he

1

only had one complete lung, colds could be more serious for him than most people, and he knew it.

For a while we went through the paper, page by page, and the more he talked the more dispirited he became. He wondered if it had been a mistake to start the *European*, a waste of money. He wondered why so many people were against it, why people weren't buying it, why the paper wasn't winning over advertisers. I tried in vain to reassure him, realizing that he was probably feeling sorry for himself because of his cold rather than anything being wrong with the *European*.

'You know you have to have patience with a new paper,' I said, 'so why not wait a little before condemning it out of hand? It has to find its feet; you have to give it a chance.'

His only reply to that was a dispirited grunt. He got off the bed and walked to the window overlooking the city. And he went on, talking to himself, not really to me: 'Sometimes I don't know why I go on. Everything I try, people turn against me . . . I've got no friends, no one I can turn to . . . no one to share my life with . . . sometimes I think I should just end it all, throw myself out of the window . . . I sometimes feel I can't go on.' And he stood staring out of the window at the grey skies.

After a moment's silence, and realizing there was nothing I could say to cheer him up, I said: 'Would you like a cup of coffee, because I would love a tea?'

He turned round, the conversation half-forgotten. 'Yes, order one.'

His moment of self-pity gone, he said: 'It's shit, isn't it? . . . It's no fucking good,' and he looked at me for a reply.

'I disagree,' I told him, 'You must give the paper a chance. You know everyone has been under great pressure down there and the journalists want it to be a success, the same as you do; their reputations are on the line as well.'

My reply only received another grunt and he lay down on

the bed again and flicked on CNN – Cable News Network – one of his favourite channels. So I left to order the tea and coffee.

It was the only time I ever remember Maxwell referring to suicide, or even mentioning it, and I took it all with a pinch of salt. I dismissed his speech as typical of Maxwell when he was unhappy, miserable, unwell and feeling sorry for himself. I had seen him on other occasions feeling down, but not as bad as that Sunday afternoon.

I had known Maxwell for the past five years. I had travelled the world with him, accompanying him in his private Gulfstream jets to twenty or more countries on many visits; taking notes on his behalf during private interviews with world leaders. During those five years we had spoken nearly every day on the phone whether he was in Britain or travelling abroad on his own. We had spent hours talking on Saturdays in his office or his apartment at the top of Maxwell House near London's Holborn Circus.

He would often call me up on a Saturday morning, usually after 8 a.m., and ask me to drop by and see him later in the morning because he had something he wanted to discuss. He knew Saturday was meant to be my day off. But that was Maxwell.

On arrival he would be most polite, apologizing for phoning me so early, apologizing for asking me to come in on my day off, and always there would be coffee and fresh orange juice. Maxwell was often a different man on Saturdays, more relaxed, more open to suggestion, happy to pass the time of day. He would usually be dressed casually in trousers and a short-sleeved, open-necked shirt. The topics we discussed would range from the *Daily Mirror* to the *European*; from editors to columnists; from Moscow to Washington; from Bonn to Paris; and sometimes we would

3

discuss MCC and Mirror Group finances. I would try to draw him on those subjects but he was always evasive, and would only speak in generalizations, never specifics. We might chat for twenty minutes or an hour. But I didn't fool myself; the main reason he asked me to call in was because he was bored. The workaholic Maxwell couldn't operate on Saturdays and the phones hardly ever rang.

I was foreign editor of the *Daily Mirror* and had been since 1976. I had never met Maxwell before he took over Mirror Group in July 1984, but knew of him, of course. When there was a danger of him taking over the Group I went to the *Mirror* library and read all I could find about him. I didn't like what I read.

Initially, I found Maxwell a challenge because of his approach to people. He would expect his employees to leap to attention, metaphorically speaking, whenever he entered a room; he would expect a silence to descend on a gathering whenever he approached; his mere presence should command attention and respect. It gave him confidence, made him feel superior. He always loved playing the boss, commanding respect, being treated like a superior by those he chose to have around him. And, in many ways, a great many of the subordinates he did have around him seemed to enjoy that role.

I watched him at so many meetings. He did behave like a dictator whenever he had his employees around him; he did treat them in any way he wished; he did seem to derive pleasure, perhaps sadistic pleasure, from seeing people squirm before him. But more than that, Maxwell liked others to see him performing; he seemed to enjoy ridiculing and bullying his employees, particularly in front of other members of staff. And usually, whenever Maxwell menaced and growled at some wretched employee, reducing him to a state of nervousness, he would immediately change his act and crack a joke, making others present respond with

4

forced laughter, and relief that they hadn't been the person under attack.

I was fortunate. He hardly ever caught me out. He would often fire questions at me, perhaps about the Soviet Union or French elections, or whatever, and most of the time I knew the answers. He liked that. After a while he stopped trying to wrong-foot me. And that was when our relationship changed. He stopped treating me like one of his employees to be bullied, but as someone who knew what he was talking about.

Sometimes, however, things would go wrong. I remember being in Paris with Maxwell in his car on one of our early trips together. I was trying to raise someone in London on the mobile phone. As always Maxwell was sitting in front with the chauffeur and I was in the back. Minutes went by as I tried in vain to contact London.

'What the fuck are you doing back there?' he asked in his threatening voice.

'If you must know,' I responded, 'I'm fucking everything up.'

He loved that and roared with laughter; and didn't say another word till I had made contact with London.

We had endlessly discussed world political situations, perhaps his favourite subject, and especially the dramatic events of the late 1980s – the collapse of Communism, Eastern Europe and the Soviet Union. It was probably one of the reasons we became close, since I spent hours reading and studying the ever-changing world political situation and could talk to him knowledgeably about the unfurling events.

Maxwell had taken me into his confidence, often discussing the most senior appointments throughout his newspaper empire, including the appointment of editors, who, officially, were my seniors. He discussed his newspapers with me, including their content, their foreign coverage, their direction, always asking for my opinion, which I willingly gave him. He told me that I was one of his 'very few friends', someone he could talk to, but I don't think Maxwell ever had real friends.

Nearly a year after his death, I still think of this extraordinary, larger-than-life man, this bully who could be so charming and minutes later so nasty and vicious; who could treat his wife and family so appallingly and leave thousands of pensioners with not a single penny, yet secretly pay out money to treat hundreds of children from Chernobyl who were suffering the dreadful effects of radiation.

In many ways Maxwell led a courageous life, his war record is testament to that; yet I wonder whether he had the courage to take his own life by silently slipping over the edge of the *Lady Ghislaine* and swimming until exhaustion overcame him. There was every reason for him to do so, although it was the coward's way out. Maxwell's life had been one of courage, bravery and stoic resilience in the face of daunting obstacles. Yet, would Maxwell have been able to face the hatred, the shame and the humiliation when the world discovered that he had stolen hundreds of millions of pounds from his companies, pushing them to the brink of bankruptcy, and plundered his own employees' pension funds?

I cannot believe that Maxwell fell overboard. It was a calm night, the Atlantic was still. It seems almost inconceivable that he could have simply fallen overboard. There are those, including an Israeli minister, bankers and brokers, who believe Maxwell was murdered. Throughout my research into this book I have come across influential people who don't know whether he jumped or was pushed. But very few think it was a genuine accident.

I was forever being given one piece of advice: 'Remember Watergate; remember that Deep Throat repeatedly gave Woodward and Bernstein [the two *Washington Post* reporters who uncovered the scandal] one piece of advice: "Follow the money trail."' Those who advised me added: 'When you find where the money is you will then know whether Maxwell was murdered or whether he suicided.'

And there is a case, many would suggest a strong case, to suggest that Maxwell was murdered.

In the last few months of his life Maxwell had gained two very powerful enemies, either of whom would have murdered him with very little, if any, fear of possible consequences. One was the KGB, and the other was the organized crime syndicate that controlled the *New York Daily News*, the American newspaper he bought with such jubilation in early 1991.

For decades Maxwell had been involved with the KGB, not, as far as is known, as an active agent or in spying activities, but according to KGB sources in Moscow, he acted as a conduit, a banker, 'laundering' the KGB's money outside the Soviet Union. He also acted as an 'agent of influence'. In 1991, the Soviet Communist Party in Moscow published confidential papers revealing that Pergamon was listed as a 'friendly firm'. The Communist Party of the Soviet Union identified a 'friendly firm' in three different categories: a Western firm which Moscow wanted to trade with for a particular reason; a firm that would always be paid first in hard currency; or a Western firm that had been given a privileged status by the KGB. Maxwell and Pergamon came in the third category, according to Moscow. And it was the reason why Maxwell was treated like a VIP whenever he visited the Soviet Union.

Through his bewildering myriad of companies, stiftungs (tax free trusts) and secret accounts in Liechtenstein, Maxwell had been 'laundering' US dollars on behalf of the KGB, taking a rake-off in the process and helping to build a fortune in the Maxwell Foundation in Liechtenstein. And Maxwell was also involved in spiriting money away on behalf of members of the Communist Party in 1990 when they saw the writing on the wall.

When senior directors of the KGB in Moscow realized the Soviet Union was close to collapse they decided it was time to call in their dues. They knew Maxwell had been creaming off a fortune for years with the money provided by Moscow, playing the foreign exchange market with their money, building substantial funds for himself. Simply by reading the Western press they knew every detail of his life, his billion-dollar companies: Maxwell Communications Corporation, Pergamon and Mirror Group Newspapers. They knew his lifestyle was that of a billionaire tycoon with his Gulfstream IV; his luxury ocean-going yacht, the *Lady Ghislaine*; his suites in the Ritz in Paris and the Helmsley Palace in New York.

Evidence from Moscow during the spring and summer of 1992 has revealed that Maxwell was 'invited' to pay back the money he had been making with the KGB's funds since the 1970s. It has been impossible to discover how much money was involved but, according to Moscow, it was 'tens of millions of US dollars'. Maxwell earned their enmity during 1991 when he failed to produce what the KGB demanded.

Secondly there was 'the Mob'. For years, if not decades, the printing and distribution of the *New York Daily News* had been controlled by one of America's organized crime syndicates, according to newspaper publishing authorities in New York.

And it was not the only newspaper. In June 1992, Robert M. Morgenthau, the Manhattan District Attorney, indicted a ring led by the Bonanno criminal family, alleging they 'exercised control' over the circulation of the the *New York Post*, the *Daily News'* main rival tabloid. The Manhattan DA said the racketeering was directed by an eighty-two-year-old Mafia *capo*, or captain, in the Bonanno family, Al Embarrato. Besides Al Embarrato, who is known as Al Walker, twelve men, including Robert Perrino, the *Post*'s superintendent of deliveries and alleged to be another member of the Bonanno family, and Anthony Michele, the *Post*'s circulation director, were accused of participating in Mafia crimes at the paper. The thirteen men faced ninety-nine counts of racketeering.

Aides to the District Attorney said the Bonanno gang, with the assistance of an official of the Newspaper and Mail Deliverers Union, stole newspapers from loading docks at the *Post*'s printing plant and compelled drivers from an independent wholesaler to sell them to vendors for twenty to thirty cents. The news-stand price of the *Post* is fifty cents.

At the same time, Robert Morgenthau confirmed that investigations were also underway into thefts of news-papers by organized crime groups at the *New York Times* and Maxwell's paper, the *New York Daily News*.

Michael G. Cherkasky, chief of Morgenthau's Investi-gation Division, said inquiries at the *Daily News* and at a major delivery wholesaler had revealed that another Mafia family, the Lucchese family, were involved in the racketeering. He estimated that racketeering at the *Daily News* had probably been netting the underworld about $5 million a year.

Before Maxwell took over the *Daily News* in February 1991, Ian Watson, editorial director of the *European*, accompanied Maxwell to New York for talks with the union leaders whom they were trying to persuade to accept redundancies and cutbacks, prior to buying the paper from the Chicago Tribune Group.

Watson reported later: 'After seven of the ten print unions had agreed to the cutbacks I went to see leaders of the remaining three who were holding out. I remember most vividly the conversation I had with one union official: He said to me, in a broad Brooklyn accent: "Are you a New Yorker?"'

Watson, a proud Scotsman with a strong Scots accent, replied, 'No. Why?'

'Do you know New Yorkers? Do you understand them?'

Watson again replied, 'No.'

The union boss then said: 'If you think you can push us into an agreement, you'll end up in the East River with your throats slit. All of you.'

Watson commented later: 'He was not play-acting; he was deadly serious.'

Maxwell believed he could tame the *Daily News* unions, and slash the workforce, in the same way he had reduced the number of print employees throughout Mirror Group Newspapers in the late 1980s. The Chicago Tribune Group wanted out at any cost, having lost $250 million in ten years. They tempted Maxwell by offering to hand over $60 million if he purchased the paper before March 15, 1991. He thought that was a gift from heaven. He knew the *Daily News* was suffering from overmanning, restrictive practices, a corrupt labour force, old printing machinery and weak management. He was arrogant enough to believe he could deal with all that. But he was a stranger to New York's newspaper industry. What he didn't realize at the time was that the print unions were controlled by the Mafia.

He was ecstatic when he won control of the *Daily News* and was fêted throughout New York for saving an American institution. But within weeks he was to learn that the deals he had thrashed out with the print unions were worthless, for the Mafia controlled the unions; and they called the shots – not the newspaper owners.

Maxwell was told that the Mafia controlled the print run of the *Daily News* and the entire distribution network, down to and including the street vendors. He was told that for years the Mob had taken part of the nightly print run as their own, over and above the normal print run; and no employer had been able to break their hold.

10

However, Maxwell also knew that during the past few years organized crime syndicates in New York and other major US cities had been on the run as the authorities had decided their power had to be ended. He also realized that the only way he would ever make the *Daily News* profitable was to cut the workforce and introduce new technology, as in the UK newspaper industry. And the only way was to see off the Mafia. He asked the Manhattan District Attorney's office to investigate.

That was the reason why in the months prior to his death he became more and more nervous whenever he visited New York. Many people noted his anxiety in 'the Big Apple', so very different from the swashbuckling, beaming Maxwell who won the hearts of New Yorkers when he rescued the *Daily News* only months previously. That was also why, just days before his death, he called in America's most prestigious security agency and private investigators, Kroll Associates, and held talks with Jules Kroll, the Chief Executive Officer.

Maxwell told Kroll he was convinced that there were people out to kill him, to get him, to destroy his life and his business, and asked him to investigate. He named businessmen and political enemies. At the end of the two-hour meeting Maxwell agreed to compile a memo listing the strange events which had led him to this conclusion. He was never to write that memo. Within a week he was dead.

Finally, just two weeks before his death, there was the explosive story that burst across the newspapers when the highly respected Pulitzer Prize-winning American author Seymour Hersh accused Maxwell and myself in his book *The Samson Option* of being Mossad agents and dealing in arms for Israel. He also accused both Maxwell and myself of being responsible for betraying the Israeli nuclear technician, Mordechai Vanunu, to Mossad agents in Britain. As a result, Vanunu, who had blown the whistle on Israel's nuclear secrets to *The Sunday Times* in 1986, had been kidnapped by Mossad agents and secretly flown back to Israel where, after a trial, he was sentenced to eighteen years in jail.

In the days and weeks following Maxwell's death many claimed that it was his involvement with Mossad that had led to his death. I don't believe for a moment that Maxwell was working for Mossad. He had direct access to Israeli government ministers. Why would Maxwell have bothered talking to the boys in the engine room when he could talk to the officers on the bridge, simply by picking up a phone? He was avowedly pro-Israel and made no pretence of the fact, openly boasting of his involvement in Israel and his business enterprises there.

TWO

'All I can remember of my childhood is the awful feeling of hunger.'

Robert Maxwell stood in the ornate salon of the Vendôme suite in the Ritz in Paris dressed in an open-necked shirt, a pair of bright blue trousers, but no shoes or socks. He was in an expansive mood, happy with the world. He had just taken a call from one of his London stockbrokers.

He turned to his personal valet, Simon Grigg. 'Get some champagne and bring out some caviare. Mr Davies and I deserve it.'

It was in the spring of '89 just prior to the glorious July celebrations observing the bicentenary of the French Revolution. Maxwell was spending a few days in Paris organizing in his inimitable way the exhibition he was funding as his offering to his friend, President Mitterrand, towards the great event.

The champagne was brought into the room, two bottles of Dom Perignon, and placed in the ornate silver ice-coolers the Ritz always provides. Simon, helped by two French waiters, placed a large saucer of the caviare on a bed of crushed ice in another silver salver, alongside the Matzos plain water biscuits which Maxwell always liked to eat with his favourite delicacy.

There was no pretension, no feeling that this was an event out of the ordinary. It was seven o'clock in the evening and the right time for a man of Maxwell's position, privilege and power to indulge in one of his favourite pastimes, eating, his passion in life, and to indulge in what he liked most, Beluga caviare, the very best Russian caviare that money could buy.

He walked over to the table, scooped up a large dollop of the pale black eggs with a silver tablespoon and put it on the biscuit. And in one movement the biscuits and the caviare disappeared in a second into his open mouth. Some dribbled out around his mouth and spilled down his shirt as he happily munched away and, at the same time, scooped another large spoonful of the stuff on to another biscuit and into his eager mouth. Hardly able to speak, he wiped his mouth with the back of his hand and reached for the glass of bubbly which his valet offered him, swigging it back in one mouthful.

This however, was no delicate champagne flute, but a large half-litre glass which he always insisted on using. 'Bloody stupid little things,' he would say if offered a flute of champagne, 'can't taste the stuff in those things. You need a proper glass.'

It was the end of the day but the phone calls never ceased coming in from everywhere. His secretary and his valet would spend most of the day answering the calls, and when they were busy, anyone who was on hand would be told to answer the phone.

Maxwell would want to know who was on every line before making the decision to talk to them. Most of the time his insatiable need to know everything at all times made him want to speak to everyone who called. It didn't matter a jot to him how long they might be left holding on, waiting for the great man to complete another call before answering those patiently waiting. If he didn't want to talk to them he would either wave his hand dismissively or say brusquely, 'Tell them to fuck off.'

That night he wanted to chat. He collapsed on to the sofa, spilling some of the champagne as he did so, and patted the cushion next to him, a gesture of course that one took as an order, signalling me to sit down.

He raised his hand to the ever-attentive Simon, who knew the gesture meant that he wanted another spoonful of caviare. This wasn't the caviare the Ritz served to guests. Maxwell didn't like the caviare they provided; he complained that it was too salty for his palate. Maxwell always travelled with his own supply, in large dark blue tins, with those illustrious words 'Royal Beluga' written on the lid. They were provided by his private caviare supplier who called at Maxwell House in New Fetter Lane once every couple of weeks with fresh supplies. Price: £250 for a quarter-pound tin. And Maxwell usually took half a dozen tins a time.

'Do you know,' he began, 'what it was like for me when I was young? Have you any idea what my life was like back home in Czechoslovakia when I was growing up?'

'No,' I replied, 'tell me.'

Maxwell was a difficult man to talk to, a difficult man to get information out of. He would give his opinions, he gave you those all the time. He would hold the centre of any conversation, speaking in such a manner that those around him found it difficult to interrupt or get a word in edgeways. But Maxwell wasn't providing information, he was just issuing orders or stating his views.

Consequently, whenever the opportunity arose I always tried to get him to talk, to encourage him to speak out, speak his mind, so that I could understand this extraordinary man who ruled the lives of so many people, including most of my friends and colleagues. But it was difficult. It was as though he wanted to give nothing away, as though talking about

15

himself or his life exposed him in a way he didn't want. Now, with hindsight, one can understand why he was so secretive, why he compartmentalized his mind, his life, his business interests, his family, his underlings, so that no one ever knew the whole picture.

'I'll tell you,' he began. And then he went quiet, as though uncertain whether he did want to unburden himself. 'We lived like pigs; really like pigs. We ate anything we could get our hands on, and I mean anything. I can never remember eating meat as a child, except sometimes chicken. I can remember eating soup all winter, but there was never anything in it. It was gruel, slops. Sometimes it was potatoes or beans or maize, but it was never enough.'

He took another phone call, chatting away in French, and then he resumed, which surprised me. Maxwell didn't have a long concentration span; his mind was forever darting from one subject to another. It needed to.

'I was always hungry,' he went on. 'All I can ever remember about my childhood is the awful feeling of hunger in my stomach, going to sleep hungry, waking up in the night hungry, and scavenging for bread in the mornings, looking for anything to eat. We were like pigs.'

With effort he struggled to his feet, urging his twenty-stone frame from the sofa, and padded across the luxurious pale carpet to the table where the caviare was chilling to the perfect temperature. He grabbed two large Matzos biscuits and one after the other spooned them into the dish of caviare before pushing them greedily, hungrily, into his mouth; and I watched and recalled the words he had just spoken.

Maxwell was born in the small town of Solotvino which is surrounded by the wooded hills of Ruthenia in the Carpathians on the borders of Czechoslovakia and Russia. Those who live there describe it as the very centre of Europe and yet it has forever been one of the backwaters of the continent.

Maxwell was born Ludvik Hoch, the eldest son of a poor Jewish labourer and his wife, who had no money whatsoever. Their home was the front room of his grandfather's house and Maxwell shared a bed for most of his childhood with three or four other children of the family. He hardly had enough clothes to cover himself and went barefoot for half the year. During those days of the 1920s and 1930s, the Hochs shared desperate poverty with all the town's Jewish brethren. All suffered severe deprivation. It was surprising that so many of the Hoch family survived.

Maxwell's authorized biography recalls that the Hoch household did not even have an oven and that all the cooking was done on a wood-burning stove which belched smoke through a hole in the roof. The lavatory comprised a shack at the back of the house containing a pit with planks covering it.

Ludvik Hoch was born on June 10, 1923 to Mehel and Chanca Hoch, the third child and the first son of the family. The Hochs' first child, Gisl, was born in 1919 but died within two years. The next, Brana, born in 1920, was one of the three children to survive the war, even surviving the concentration camps of Mauthausen and Buchenwald. Their second son, Chamhersch, born in 1925, died two years later from diphtheria. Maxwell too caught the fatal illness, but somehow managed to fight it off. Next came Shenya, born in 1926, and three years later Sylvia, who also survived the holocaust. Two further daughters, Zissel, born in 1931, and Tzipporah, born in 1933, were killed by the Nazis, as was the youngest son, Itzak, born in 1940.

The young Ludvik had little general education though he did attend a religious elementary school for Jewish children, the Heder, for the teaching of Judaism from the age of seven. He was also sent to the local Czech government school. But his mother had high hopes and ambitions for her son Ludvik to become a rabbi, and when he was ten she sent him to a Yeshiva, a school devoted to the study of rabbinic literature, in nearby Sgiget. Five years later he was sent even further afield to a larger Yeshiva in Bratislava, three hundred miles from home. But the independent Maxwell had had enough of school by the age of sixteen.

It was while living in Bratislava that the teenage Maxwell started his business career. He was desperately embarrassed at being so poor, walking around in patched clothes and being sent to different houses each evening for a meal. So he decided to start earning some money for himself and went to the Bratislava market, buying and selling cheap jewellery and trinkets. And, to prove his independence further, he cut off his sidelocks and abandoned his skull cap, the visible signs of an Orthodox Jew.

At home the family spoke Yiddish, but because of the central position of the town in Europe many Jewish people in the area also spoke a smattering of Russian, Hungarian and Czech. That grounding in languages was the reason why Maxwell found it remarkably easy throughout his life to pick up languages with amazing speed. He boasted he could speak nine languages – Russian, English, German, Hungarian, Czech, Romanian, French, Yiddish and Hebrew – but he was a little rusty on some of them, though he would never admit it.

Maxwell's mastery of languages served him well as World War II approached and he had to survive on his wits. When war broke out he was sixteen. Six years later only Maxwell and two of his sisters had survived. Both his parents, his grandfather, three sisters and a brother, as well as aunts, uncles and other relatives, died at the hands of the Nazis. Some were shot, others died in the gas chambers, mostly at Auschwitz.

Maxwell's escape from Czechoslovakia to Britain during

1939 and '40 is still a mystery. It appears that since arriving in Britain, the young Hoch told different stories and was even changing and enlarging the drama of his escape to freedom after he published his own biography, written by Joe Haines, in 1988. None the less, perhaps the story which will be best remembered is the account Maxwell told on the BBC's *Desert Island Discs* in 1987, when he recalled that having been imprisoned by the Germans in Budapest and beaten every day for three months, he managed, while handcuffed, to overpower his one-armed guard on the way to court, and flee. He later added a rider – that the handcuffs were removed by a gipsy lady!

In 1966, in a Maxwell press release, it was stated: 'The sixteen-year-old Maxwell joined the Czech army, fought the Germans and the Russians in Eastern Europe, made a fighting retreat across Europe to the Black Sea with the Czech forces and back to France via Bulgaria and Greece, in time for another crack at the Germans, was wounded and captured by the Nazis in Orléans and then escaped.'

One way or another the teenage Hoch arrived in Marseille in 1940 and was evacuated with members of the Czech Legion in May that year, arriving in Liverpool by ship. The description of Maxwell at this time, given by a former Czech air force pilot, is revealing: 'A scarcely literate teenager, like a young man from the mountains . . . quite unruly, like a young bull'.

In October 1940 Maxwell, along with hundreds of other Czech soldiers, joined the Auxiliary Pioneer Corps, the only unit at that time open to foreigners. He hated it. Most of the time all he did was hard, backbreaking work, digging roads, breaking rocks or loading ammunition trucks and trains. And all for two shillings a day! This boring work lasted for three years. But he learned English, brushed up on other languages with the other foreigners in the Pioneer Corps and read books. He claimed he was

19

a voracious reader, picking up anything, anywhere, and reading.

When nineteen, Maxwell fell for a young widow who introduced him to Brigadier M. A. Carthew-Yorstoun, DSO, CBE, of the Black Watch, commander of the 176th Infantry Brigade, who took a liking to the brash young Czech. He arranged for Maxwell, who had by then changed his name to Ivan du Maurier – the surname he chose because they were the brand of cigarettes he smoked – to join the Somerset Light Infantry and then the 6th North Staffords, a battalion Carthew-Yorstoun commanded. Maxwell was on the move.

He was rapidly promoted to lance-corporal and by the time of the Normandy landings was a sergeant. He changed his name again, to a more British-sounding Leslie Jones, and seemed to revel in the fighting, determined to kill, maim or capture as many Germans as possible.

Shortly after the liberation of Paris, Maxwell arrived on leave in the city, and at the French Welcome Committee met a sophisticated, educated young woman, the daughter of a wealthy Huguenot owner of silk factories. Her name was Elisabeth Meynard. Once again, the impressionable Maxwell fell instantly in love and within months he proposed.

In January 1945 Maxwell received his commission and once again changed his name, becoming Second-Lieutenant Ian Robert Maxwell of the Queen's Royal Regiment (West Surrey). Nine weeks later he was married.

It was during the final months of the war that Maxwell showed outstanding bravery on a number of occasions, and in March was personally presented with the Military Cross by Field Marshal Montgomery. The day before, he had heard the news that his beloved mother and a sister had been executed by the Nazis. Haines recorded in his biography that Maxwell wrote to Betty on that day: 'As you can well imagine, I am not taking any prisoners, and whatever home my men occupy, before I leave I order it to be destroyed.'

Stationed in Berlin at the end of the war, Maxwell's priority was to determine if any of his family was alive. In a desperate search, Maxwell discovered his father had died in 1944; he found to his joy that two of his sisters, Sylvia and Brana, had survived. The three were reunited in November 1945, just days after Maxwell heard that Betty was pregnant with their first child.

Because of his knowledge of languages, Maxwell was employed by the British Army in Berlin as an Intelligence officer interviewing Germans and other nationals. He was promoted to captain, a title he was proud of and kept for many years in 'civvy street'. Back in Britain, Maxwell was to insist that those who worked for him addressed him as 'Captain', an order he maintained until the 1970s. Maxwell's introduction to newspapers began shortly afterwards when he was appointed to head the press section of the Public Relations and Information Services Control (PRISC). His job was to censor *Der Telegraph*, the first licensed paper in the British sector of Berlin. Later, Maxwell would boast to his Mirror Group editors: 'At twenty-one I was in charge of a newspaper in Berlin selling a million copies a day.' It became one of Maxwell's favourite comments, reminding his editors he had more experience than they had.

In fact *Der Telegraph* only achieved a circulation of 250,000 a day, but this was a remarkable feat in war-torn Berlin. One reason for its success was Maxwell's ability to find and provide, no matter how, the ink, paper and printing machinery necessary to keep the paper in production. The other was the editor, Arno Scholz, then forty-one, a former Socialist writer for a left-wing newspaper who had been prevented by the Nazis from writing during the war. Maxwell looked to Scholz as a father figure and it was he who, during long conversations, inspired Maxwell

21

to embrace Socialism and imbued him with the inspiration
to own a newspaper.

During those heady days of victory when Allied officers
enjoyed a life of whatever luxury could be found in Berlin, Maxwell, quite naturally, became friendly with many
Russian officers. He would spend nights and weekends in
the Russian sector of Berlin, eating, drinking and carousing
with them. They had much in common. Many were from
a similar background to Maxwell and he enjoyed their
company far more than that of those brother officers in
the stuffy British Army messes.

Tom Bower, in his painstakingly researched book, *Maxwell: the Outsider*, which Maxwell did all in his power to
suppress when it was first published in 1988, wrote:

> Apparently, at one stage during his posting in Berlin, either
> willingly or unwillingly, Maxwell compromised himself with
> the Russians. The KGB claim that the young officer signed
> a document which promised to assist the security agency if
> required. Since everyone involved in the incident is said to
> be dead, the circumstances are unclear but the existence of
> a document seems certain.

There was one other event of some moment during Maxwell's twenty-two-month stay in Berlin. The young Army
captain met the elderly Ferdinand Springer, who before the
war had been the world's leading publisher of scientific
books. The two men became friends and Maxwell, using
his position as an officer of the Control Commission, helped
the Springer family restart their publishing business in
Heidelberg. It was the catalyst that founded Maxwell's
fortune.

During his time in Berlin, Maxwell also reverted to his
first job, buying and selling, bartering and dealing, as
he had done as a teenager on the streets of Bratislava.

22

Inevitably, he made money which he would boast about in letters back home to Betty. He was still working for the Commission when he became a director of Low-Bell Ltd, a small import–export firm run by another Czech from offices in London's Trafalgar Square.

In October 1947 Maxwell was demobbed and in a hurry to start a business and make money. Within seven days he had formed his first company, EPPAC (European Periodicals, Publicity and Advertising Corporation), distributing German newspapers around Britain to German POWs. He would tour Britain in his large grey Dodge which he had somehow acquired in Berlin and transported back to Britain. But with the POWs returning home to Germany, that business had a limited future. Maxwell had not forgotten his elderly friend, Ferdinand Springer, and he returned to Berlin to offer his services. Due to Allied restrictions imposed on German firms, Springer could not at that time export his scientific books around the world, but if a way could be found to transport the books to Britain, then Maxwell's company could distribute them on Springer's behalf. A deal was struck and Maxwell was provided with Springer's unique list of customers worldwide. Maxwell easily persuaded the authorities it was vital for the Allies to gain access to German scientific information which they had been unable to since before the war. Indeed, German scientists and engineers had consistently outclassed the Allies throughout the war, not only in military hardware, but more importantly, for peacetime, in revolutionary new chemicals, metals and fuels which German scientists had discovered and refined. Removing this restriction ended the principal obstacle to worldwide distribution. Maxwell also obtained a remarkably good Deutschmark–Sterling exchange rate. He was on his way.

Within months, however, the mistake which Maxwell made time and again in his life, and never learned from

23

the experience, dogged this first major business effort: a failure to manage a business satisfactorily. It seemed he was incapable of managing a business, any business, properly; and yet he would not let the managers he appointed do their job either. He would interfere, never stop interfering, until he drove his managers to quit, or they gave up trying to manage his business the way they knew best. Maxwell was a brilliant wheeler-dealer, but a lousy manager. To his dying day, however, he never accepted this simple fact.

Once, and once only, I spoke to him about this when he was complaining to me about the people he employed. It was a Saturday morning in his offices in Maxwell House, next to the Mirror Group headquarters in Holborn. He often called me in on a Saturday, primarily I believe because he was bored, wanted someone to talk to and knew that I lived near by.

'Why won't people do as they are told?' he stormed as he gently replaced the phone on the console. 'I tell them exactly what to do and they do something entirely different. Then they begin arguing with me. They think they know more than me.' After a pause he added, 'He'll have to go.'

'Any way I can help?' I volunteered.

'No,' he paused, 'it's management.'

'Are you sure he's wrong?' I queried.

Maxwell looked up from the round mahogany table in his office where he conducted nearly all his interviews and business meetings, and looked me straight in the eye. He didn't like sitting behind his large imposing desk at the end of the room. I could tell he didn't like that. But he remained calm. 'Why do you say that?'

'Because if he's a manager and you had confidence in him, then maybe he knows what he's doing. After all, he has all the facts.'

He banged the table with his hand, pressed the button to call his ever faithful Portuguese butler, Joseph, and said:

24

'One large coffee for me and . . .' he looked across at me, 'a coffee?'

'Yes, please,' I replied. 'And a coffee for Mr Davies,' he added. It was his way of terminating a conversation he didn't want to continue.

After some months of patience, Springer began to realize that things weren't working out with Maxwell. The efficiency they had been promised, and had expected, was not forthcoming. Accounts were late, book-keeping was sloppy, records weren't kept and orders were not being promptly delivered. Springer complained; Maxwell responded by launching a new company, solely to distribute the journals. In a trice Maxwell had assumed even greater control of the Springer distribution, dividing, and thereby establishing a vicelike grip. He was learning fast.

In 1949 Maxwell also learned how to borrow money from a bank. He needed to establish his new distribution company firmly. But he didn't have any capital. He had already borrowed money from Betty's family to begin the Springer distribution business, but he needed to employ more people in the new set-up. He was introduced to Sir Charles Hambro, of the merchant banking firm. Sir Charles was impressed with the ebullient, confident young entrepreneur who could speak several languages and who seemed to be a man he should support. Maxwell left the meeting with a cheque for £25,000, equivalent in 1992 to over £250,000, an amazing coup in those dark days after the war.

As the money began to roll in, Maxwell led the life of a rich London spiv, being driven around by his chauffeur in flash American cars, wearing expensive suits, seemingly unaffected by the restrictions every other Briton suffered. And so he could. Maxwell had obtained healthy discounts on the Springer books of forty and fifty per cent and orders were coming in thick and fast from libraries and scientific establishments around the world, ordered by those who had

25

been starved of their life blood – scientific information – for nearly a decade.

It was in fact the British Government of 1946 that formed a top-level Scientific Advisory Committee to encourage the setting-up of an aggressive and effective British scientific publishing house, along the lines of the pre-war Springer firm. Supported by the Government Committee, the long-established and highly reputable publishing firm of Butterworths was encouraged to start scientific publishing houses. The second, established in 1949, was called Butterworth–Springer; and it was this company that led directly to the birth of Pergamon Press.

The scientific brain behind Butterworths was an Austrian, Dr Paul Rosabaud, the spy who during the war had tipped off the British Government that Germany was planning to build an atom bomb. It was his Intelligence reports that led to the successful bombing of the German heavy-water programme in Norway. In May 1951 Maxwell purchased the Butterworths interest in the joint company with £13,000 coming from the money advanced by Hambros, and the name was changed to Pergamon Press.

It was a wonderful coup for Maxwell. Springer had the worldwide reputation; Rosabaud, who took a twenty-five per cent interest in the new company, had the scientific brain; Butterworths represented the British Establishment, and the venture had the support and backing of the British Government. In Maxwell, the company had a man with drive, ambition and ruthlessness.

Buoyed up by his newfound importance, Maxwell was flattered further when, in 1951, he was invited by British publishing houses to rescue the loss-making Simkin Marshall, the unique organization which acted as a central distributor for all publishers. The twenty-eight-year-old Maxwell saw this as a wonderful chance to make fast money and establish himself among the publishing élite.

26

Maxwell agreed to pay far too high a price for the company –
£160,000. He put down £50,000 and agreed to pay off the rest
in nine annual instalments. Within a year Maxwell offered
to repay the debt immediately if the former owners would
accept £98,000. They agreed. What only Maxwell knew was
that he found the money by stripping the assets of Simkin
Marshall simply taking the money from the company bank
account. It was a trick he was to pull often down the years
– but it was perfectly legal. Now his confidence was flying
high and he recklessly agreed to buy the British Book Centre
in New York, another loss-making company.

Eventually, after much acrimony and the inevitable High
Court action brought about by a man whom Maxwell persuaded to invest a staggering £470,000 in Simpkin Marshall,
the company went into liquidation in 1955, owing £656,000.
The Official Receiver urged a close investigation into the
New York deal since Maxwell was aware of the financial
difficulties and debt was already mounting at the time of the
deal. British publishers were angry and vented their rage at
Maxwell. At the end of the sorry affair the creditors, mostly
publishers, only received nineteen pence in the pound; but
there was nothing they could do. They had handed Simpkin
Marshall over to Maxwell. The publishers' view was that
Maxwell's guilt lay in his rash and reckless interpretation
of the responsibilities of a company director. He was not
to change. What is surprising is that no one investigated –
or demanded an investigation into – Maxwell's handling of
the companies, as the Receiver had recommended.

Joe Haines quotes Maxwell, who refused to admit any
error on his part, as saying that the only lesson he had
learned from the affair was: 'If a gentleman of the Establishment offers you his word or his bond, always go for
the bond.' It was no wonder that the Establishment began
to eye Maxwell with suspicion.

*

27

The following fifteen years saw the irrepressible Maxwell go from strength to strength. He realized that Pergamon was a winner and he put all his undoubted energies and ability into making the company one of the foremost scientific publishing houses in the world. Perhaps because of ignorance in scientific matters, Maxwell did in fact give his scientific editors absolute freedom, only demanding that advisory editorial boards should be strong and independent. In the Festschrift, published to celebrate Maxwell's sixty-fifth birthday and forty years of Pergamon Press, all the academics, scientists and engineers noted with acclamation and respect the editorial freedom allowed to all Pergamon editors – so very, very different to Maxwell normal *modus operandi*. Perhaps that was the reason Pergamon was so successful over so many years.

Under the Pergamon imprint, and encouraged by Maxwell, an impressive and immense expansion in new scientific, medical and technical journals took place. Pergamon expanded from one cramped office in London to forty-eight overseas offices, from publishing three journals in 1951 to over four hundred in 1990; its booklist expanded from five books to some 3,500. A history of success of which Maxwell could rightly be proud.

It was his son Philip Maxwell who wrote in a short article contained within *Robert Maxwell & Pergamon Press*, which he also edited, in 1988:

> The creation of Pergamon Press is the achievement for which Bob Maxwell is least known, but will be best remembered. It is the cornerstone of the structure of the Maxwell group of companies . . . Though Pergamon's success would not have been possible without the devoted and untiring work of many scientists and educators as well as the many thousands who have worked for it and still do, he has been its dynamo. He built an idea into a publishing empire.

28

All so very true. And how sad.

Maxwell threw everything into Pergamon, travelling the world recruiting scientists as editors and advisers to the growing number of journals. He seemed inexhaustible, travelling non-stop, offering Pergamon's services to scientific conferences around the world and presenting scientists with the chance to establish editorial boards and publish new journals. There were, as ever with Maxwell, a couple of hiccups; Pergamon authors complained of being paid minute fees and being given poor contracts, and editorials appeared in the prestigious journals the *Lancet* and *Nature* complaining of Pergamon's high prices and monopoly.

But nothing deterred Maxwell. He was a millionaire, driving around in a chauffeur-driven Rolls, and had moved into Headington Hill Hall, renting it from Oxford council for £2,000 a year.

In the early 1960s Maxwell noticed that American publishers were making fortunes selling encyclopaedias and believed he could step in and make himself another fortune. He first purchased the subscription-book division of Newnes in 1965, which published Chambers and Pictorial Knowledge, and two years later bought Caxton Holdings. In 1967 Maxwell, ever the adventurer, set off in a round-the-world whirlwind tour including India, Thailand, Japan, Hong Kong, Indonesia, Malaysia, Australia, New Zealand, Mexico, the United States and Canada to sell his encyclopaedias. And despite the dreadfullly inefficient international phone systems at that time, Maxwell would call up his London headquarters daily, teasing whoever he talked to with his waspish wit: 'And where do you think I am?' It was a Maxwell joke that he loved to use – and did so for decades.

He returned home, called a press conference, and announced: 'In seven weeks I travelled 70,000 miles, was interviewed by journalists 140 times, sold 7,000 sets of encyclopaedias worth £1 million with another £3 million-worth to follow.' His staff were thunderstruck at the amazing sales – but it was not to last twenty-four hours. Later that day, Maxwell called in his executives and told them not to increase production because his claims were only for publicity; he had hardly sold any sets at all. It was typical Maxwell.

But that setback didn't perturb Cap'n Bob. In another press conference that year an ebullient Maxwell claimed there was a £200 million world market for encyclopaedias – and people believed his forecast. The sales never materialized though Maxwell issued statements claiming they did.

Seemingly, Pergamon continued its striking progress. The company claimed profits of £2 million, claimed assets had tripled in the previous four years. Given these 'facts' Pergamon became a glamour stock in the City, its share price doubled over two years. Then Saul Steinberg of Leasco Data Processing phoned.

Steinberg, then only twenty-nine, had made a fortune from leasing computers in America. Maxwell was looking to expand into computers in the States and Steinberg wanted Pergamon's books and journals to put on his computers. It seemed the perfect match. The two go-getting entrepreneurs believed a joint company would make millions. It was arranged that Leasco would take over Pergamon, but before doing so they wanted to check the books. After much argument, wrangling, claims, counter-claims and the inevitable writs and injunctions, Leasco did eventually take over Pergamon. But the department of Trade and Industry was called in to check claims and appointed investigators. Maxwell ended up with egg all over his face, accused of massively inflating Pergamon's profits. And in 1972 the DTI inspectors wrote the words that were to haunt Maxwell till his dying day: 'We regret having to conclude that notwithstanding Mr Maxwell's acknowledged abilities and energy, he is not in our opinion a person who can be relied on to exercise proper stewardship of a publicly quoted company.'

Maxwell was devastated. He fought on for three years to no avail. He protested his innocence, and continued to do so for the rest of his life. The DTI, the City and the bankers knew the truth, yet they failed to learn the lesson. In 1974, with the support of many Pergamon editors, Maxwell bought back Pergamon for £1.5 million but he never satisfactorily explained where he got that money from. Maxwell admitted to Haines, for inclusion in his official biography, that at the time he was all but bankrupt.

Maxwell told Haines that the money was borrowed from Microforms International Marketing Corporation, a newly formed American-based company owned by a French lawyer acting for Betty Maxwell's family and set up with the consent of Leasco. This, however, seems most odd. A new company, with no track record, Microforms had no asset-backing or capital at that time, and yet it was allegedly able to raise the money from banks without any problem.

How Maxwell raised the money is now academic. Maxwell was back and Pergamon was now his own private company, and there was no one to whom he had to explain the profits. With renewed enthusiasm, Maxwell was determined to build up Pergamon once again. He was fortunate that Pergamon's editors welcomed his return with open arms, for their four years under Leasco had not been very satisfactory; the share price, for example, had plummeted from 185p a share to just 12p.

Ever since he began his business career Maxwell loved having numerous totally different interests going at the same time and, convinced of his own political brilliance and acumen, he wanted to become involved in Party politics.

31

Typically, though, his political career was a crazy helter-skelter affair with which he became involved because he was convinced he would one day be prime minister. Anne Dove, Maxwell's trusted secretary during the 1950s, knows full well that the only reason Maxwell decided to seek election as an MP for Labour was because the Tories wouldn't have him. Maxwell first approached the Labour Party in 1959 and, surprisingly, within months was adopted as the Labour candidate for Buckingham. As expected, he lost, but undaunted he stood again in 1964 and won narrowly; improved his majority when Harold Wilson went to the country again in 1964; lost the seat in 1970 and failed to regain it in the two 1974 elections. By then, however, he didn't mind too much for he had just regained Pergamon; in any case he had lost his appetite for active politics, though that interest was to emerge later, but on a stage that Maxwell believed was right for him – the world stage.

Maxwell won the reputation of being a good constituency MP, but in reality nearly all the work in Buckingham was done by the indefatigable Betty who most of the time ran the constituency on his behalf. In the Commons he argued, interrupted and barracked, seemingly to draw attention to himself, and many Labour MPs found him more a liability than an asset to the Labour cause.

In 1980, looking to expand his empire once again, Maxwell turned his attention to the huge but loss-making British Printing Corporation, the biggest printing company in Europe, which was beset by union problems. He launched a dawn raid on the stock market, buying 29.9 per cent of the stock for around £3 million, and set about charming the unions and turning round the company.

But the prize that Maxwell had sought in BPC eluded him. Just ten days before Maxwell took control, BPC's chief executive, Peter Robinson, in a bid to reduce company debt, sold Jane's Publishing – the BPC imprint which produced authoritative annual reports on the world's fighting ships, fighting armies and fighting aircraft. *Jane's* was the Bible of every arms manufacturer, every defence department, every government, and every fighting arm of every nation through-out the cold war years. Its reputation was beyond reproach.

Robinson commented: 'Maxwell came on the phone to me in an absolute rage. He was spluttering with fury and anger that I had sold Jane's without telling him. But I told him it had been necessary to sell the company for the future of BPC. Maxwell was beside himself and never forgave me. But I know I did the right thing for the company.'

If Maxwell, who then had control of Brassey's, the other major defence-publishing house in Britain, had taken control of Jane's as well, he would have had absolute control of the nation's defence publishers. And the knowledge contained in those books – and the top secret sources they relied on for their accurate information – would have rested with Maxwell alone. One can only guess the alarm that that would have caused in security and defence circles in Britain and the West.

Maxwell could not have taken over BPC at a more oppor-tune time, for only days before, Robinson had secured a remarkable £125 million order to publish the revamped *TV Times* for the following seven years. Today, there are those who believe Maxwell was tipped off – and that was why he made his dawn raid when he did.

But Maxwell did succeed in turning round the com-pany. After months of wrangling and hard-fought battles, union leader Bill Keys commented: 'Maxwell is the greatest wheeler-dealer we've ever met . . . a man who can charm the birds off the trees and then shoot them.'

His new idea of becoming a printing and publishing giant grew apace. In 1983 he acquired Odhams from Reed International and a twenty per cent stake in Central TV. He bought other companies, many allegedly owned and controlled not by Maxwell, but by the Maxwell Trusts he had set up in Liechtenstein.

THREE

'It looked as though the good life would never end. But now it is about to.'

By the 1980s Robert Maxwell had virtually given up all hope of becoming a so-called press baron. His efforts to buy a national newspaper had all come to nought, thwarted at every turn, more often than not by that audacious Aussie Rupert Murdoch.

Maxwell's first attempt was way back in 1964, twenty years before he eventually powered his way to buying the Mirror Group, when he tried to take over the ailing Labour paper, the *Daily Herald*. The *Herald*, which staunchly supported the Labour Party, was haemorrhaging badly; forty-nine per cent was owned by the Trades Union Council and fifty-one per cent by the International Publishing Corporation, which also owned the Mirror Group. IPC's chairman, Cecil King, put the *Herald* up for sale, announcing that if not sold, he was to hand over the newspaper, lock, stock and barrel, to the TUC.

The Labour Party believed the *Herald* was essential to the future of the Party and sought a buyer. Maxwell stepped forward and produced one of his famous survival plans. He argued that while the presses were idle during the day, the new print plant should be used for general printing, including the £11 million the TUC spent each year on contract work. The TUC didn't want to know. And Maxwell's plan came to nothing.

Four years later, Rothschilds, the merchant bankers, were seeking a buyer for twenty-five per cent of the *News of the World*. They were acting for Professor Derek Jackson, a cousin of the incumbent chairman, Sir William Carr, then fifty-six; Jackson, who was into his sixth marriage, had little time for the Carr family and wanted out. Sir William Carr, who had been chairman for sixteen years, enjoyed the affluent lifestyle of a respected press baron, owning racehorses and playing golf on his own personal course. Maxwell's takeover offer spurred him into action.

The *News of the World*'s long-serving editor, Stafford Somerfield, replied to the takeover with a famous front page leader: 'Why do I think it would not be a good thing for Mr Maxwell, formerly Jan Ludwig Hoch, to gain control of this newspaper which, I know, has your respect, loyalty and affection – a newspaper which I know is as British as roast beef and Yorkshire pudding?' Somerfield maintained that the right-wing editorial policy would change under Maxwell, a Socialist. He ended his leader: 'This is a British paper, run by British people. Let's keep it that way.' It was a typical *News of the World* hard-hitting leader but it was anti-foreign and smacked of anti-Semitism. And against a man who had fought courageously for Britain during the war.

The *NoW* attack in fact helped Maxwell, for most of the national press, unhappy at the unfair attacks on Maxwell, decided to back him, including the authoritative newspapers of the time – *The Sunday Times* and *The Financial Times*. *The Times* stated that Maxwell had become a 'humbled parliamentarian' who admitted he had been 'a bit brash' in the House; despite the image of 'a boastful dictator and a megalomaniac' the profile suggested Maxwell was really 'surprisingly mild'.

Maxwell knew he had not only a battle on his hands, but a dirty one. What he didn't know was that twelve thousand miles away in Adelaide a brash young newspaper owner, the Oxford-educated Rupert Murdoch, then thirty-seven years old, had been phoned by William Carr and told of the Maxwell bid. Murdoch was the son of Sir Keith Murdoch, an old newspaper hand, who had bequeathed him South Australia's daily newspaper. Murdoch's mini publishing empire had already taken over the *Sydney Daily Mirror* and launched the ambitious *Australian*, the country's first national daily.

Murdoch jumped at the idea of a chance of breaking into the British newspaper scene; he had undergone his apprenticeship at the *London Daily Express*. He took the first plane to London and immediately bought three per cent of the shares, giving Carr and Murdoch fifty-one per cent. Maxwell complained to the Takeover Panel but to no avail. Simply to thwart Maxwell, Carr agreed to sell the paper to Murdoch for far less than Maxwell's offer of £34 million.

The Carrs attempted to dig any dirt possible on Maxwell and stories began emerging of unfair selling practices by Maxwell's encyclopaedia salesmen, of queries about Pergamon profits, hitting the Pergamon share price and thereby reducing Maxwell's offer to *NoW* shareholders. Maxwell issued writs galore in an effort to stop the smear campaign against him, but to no avail. And in a move which he was to repeat time and again, and which was to lead directly to his plundering MCC and Mirror Group pension schemes, Maxwell decided to support his own share price. He spent nearly £2 million buying shares, promising the bankers who purchased the shares on his behalf that he would buy them back at the price they paid. Maxwell even toyed with the idea of trying to buy Murdoch's own newspaper group in Australia, but that was impossible because the Murdoch family controlled a majority of the voting shares.

The shareholders' meeting in January 1969 was high drama. The *News of the World* had made the battle a very public affair and no previous City takeover battle had been fought in such an open and dirty way. The *News of the World* had urged shareholders to attend the meeting to support their fight against 'the Foreigner' and they packed the meeting. Maxwell's bid was still higher but the meeting didn't want to know. They jeered and catcalled Maxwell, would hardly let him speak, and the meeting ended in chaos. The vote was taken; Maxwell had lost. He was miserable, dejected and close to tears. He couldn't understand how the shareholders had refused his better offer.

Despite the success of Pergamon, which was once again making good profits, and his bid to break into the big time in British printing, Maxwell still hankered to own a newspaper. That was the reason he agreed in 1975 to back the former employees of the *Scottish Daily Express* and their workers' co-operative venture in establishing a new newspaper to be called the *Scottish Daily News*. Virtually without a thought he promised to contribute 50p for every pound invested by the workers, up to a limit of £100,000. Backed by money from Tony Benn's DTI Industrial Development Unit, which supported workers' co-operatives, and a loan from Beaverbrook newspapers, the workers bought the printworks from Beaverbrook and launched their paper. It was an immediate success, selling 330,000 by the end of the first week!

Within months, however, the *Scottish Daily News* was losing money, advertisers shied away, the paper was dull and the circulation dropped to around 100,000. Maxwell offered to step in and rescue the paper but only if he controlled the finance, editorial, advertising and circulation – in other words the entire outfit. To prove his enthusiasm

37

for the paper, and to influence the workers, Maxwell literally moved into the printworks, putting a bed in the office and eating his food in the kitchens. There was no other way of saving their beloved paper and the co-operative went along with his plan. On his demand the paper changed from a broadsheet to a tabloid and sales soared. Maxwell's price for his absolute involvement was the heads of those who had fought against him, and the workers backed Maxwell. Now more than ever, Maxwell was a publisher, in overall control, but those original leaders who had been kicked out by their fellow workers contacted newspapers in London and began to talk. *The Sunday Times* investigated the so-called workers' co-operative and concluded that the *Scottish Daily News* was doomed and Maxwell was to blame. Maxwell was forced to resign and within weeks the paper went into liquidation, five hundred workers losing their jobs. Maxwell was understandably livid – and so were the workers. He had tried in his inimitable way to run a newspaper but the Establishment had once again foiled his efforts. He was disappointed and bitter, so to console himself he once again put all his energies into the single jewel in his crown, Pergamon.

Maxwell knew that his takeover of Odhams Press in Watford from Reed International (in Chapter 2) had been a brilliant deal. For just £1.5 million he had obtained the loss-making Odhams printworks with twenty-three acres of land, the £125-million *TV Times* order, a £30 million print order for Reed magazines, plus a £7 million interest-free loan from Reed for two years. All Maxwell had to do was cut the workforce by 1,500. The unions, fearing he would shut down the entire place if they didn't agree, actually cheered him when he called for the 1,500 redundancies.

A year later Reed decided it wanted to sell the Mirror Group.

It was heartily fed up with the non-stop wrangling with the thirteen Fleet Street print unions who at that time were virtually running the place. The management was weak and the profits were a mere £800,000 a year on a turnover of £200 million! Worse still, Reed knew that within a year or so the Mirror Group would be in loss. They just wanted out – at any cost.

But there was a major problem. The *Mirror* was the only substantial newspaper group in the country that supported the Labour Party and Reed knew there would be a political uproar if the group was sold off to a Tory press baron. Selling to Murdoch was out of the question because he already owned the biggest newspaper group in Britain, including *The Times* and *The Sunday Times*, the *Sun* and the *News of the World*. Even under a Thatcher government, the Monopolies and Mergers Commission would simply not condone it.

The Mirror Group comprised the *Daily Mirror* (circulation 3,250,000), the *Sunday Mirror* (3,400,000), the *People* (3,300,000), the *Scottish Daily Record* (750,000), the *Scottish Sunday Mail* (800,000) and the loss-making racing bible, the *Sporting Life*. Even with the stranglehold the unions still had in Fleet Street at that time, Reed should have been capable of producing reasonable profits from the Mirror empire. But they hadn't the stomach to take on the unions. Reed decided to float off the group so that no one man would own it.

They installed the amiable Clive Thornton, the former chairman of the Abbey National Building Society, as chairman and he was appalled at what he discovered: Mirror Group executives taking each other out to expensive lunches every day in their chauffeur-driven cars and then claiming the bills on expenses; management and editors opening their private bars in their offices each night at six o'clock, popping champagne corks, all provided free by the Mirror; worse still, he discovered hundreds of union workers clocking on using one and sometimes two false names for a shift, going home after an hour or more, drinking in the pubs and calling into the Mirror cashiers for their pay on the way home. It was Paddy O'Gara, the *Mirror*'s sardonic design editor who commented on Thornton's arrival at Holborn Circus: 'In the land of the legless, the one-legged man is king' – for Clive Thornton had only one leg.

The Reed boss, Sir Alex Jarratt, put out feelers in the City to see how they could best dispose of the group, but there were no takers. So, after taking advice, it was decided to float off the Mirror Group on the Stock Exchange as a separate company, with a vital provision that no one individual would be able to win overall control. In the sale prospectus Sir Alex gave two conditions for the sale: one, that *Mirror* editors would have unfettered freedom; two, that support for the Labour Party would continue.

But relations between Reed bosses and Thornton became strained as the new chairman took a high profile, as he had done at the Abbey National. He talked of massive investments, of new newspapers, of tackling union power, of workers' participation, all of which horrified Reed, who had simply wanted him to steer the group quietly to a successful flotation and then retire. As Thornton warmed to his new job the float was repeatedly postponed until Reed decided enough was enough and set a final date for the float.

At the end of June, just three weeks before the float date, Reed's bankers warned that it might be lucky to get £60 million, nothing like the £100 to £120 million it had expected. Naturally, Reed was more anxious than ever to get shot of its problem child, before the price plummeted further. In hindsight such a valuation seems low when the entire Scottish operation of the *Daily Record* and *Sunday Mail*, with their new printworks, was probably worth £50 million alone. And, if the *Mirror* had been shut down, the site in Holborn Circus on which its aesthetically ghastly 1950s glass and concrete office block stood was then worth £50 million. It was ironic that Establishment bankers, who

40

Maxwell had repeatedly complained thwarted his every ambition, should now produce figures which were, in effect, to throw open the doors for him to take over one of the jewels of the British newspaper industry.

Enter Robert Maxwell.

Before his audacious takeover of the Mirror Group, Maxwell was seen by the people of Britain as a foreigner, a go-getter, a meddler and a person who took chances and sometimes achieved results. Indeed, many had a sneaking admiration for the man who was prepared to take on the Establishment, rescue ailing football clubs and ride roughshod through some of Britain's cherished institutions and archaic practices. It must not be forgotten that in a poll taken in the late 1980s Bob Maxwell was voted one of the most popular go-getters in Britain. As he would say often enough in boasting of his own success: 'Not bad, eh, for a boy born in absolute poverty in Central Europe?'

Even the threat of Maxwell's takeover of the *Mirror* had thrown the directors, managers and journalists into turmoil, though some journalists at that time thought a dose of someone like Maxwell might shake up the place and put some spark back into a paper which had grown dull and middle-aged. For some years it had certainly appeared so compared to the youthful, upstart *Sun* which had shown cheeky irreverence to the more mature tabloid.

Some *Mirror* journalists even talked naively of stopping the paper publishing to prevent Reed's reneging on its promise not to dispose of the *Mirror* to a single individual, but that would have achieved nothing. What worried the *Mirror* journalists was that their cushy lifestyle, good pay and generous expenses, along with their four-day working week, might be in jeopardy; some others who realized they had lived a charmed life on not much ability also feared a

41

new broom might brush them away; they believed, probably correctly, that floating the company on the market with no individual boss would allow the gravy train to continue.

Ironically, the muscular sections of the workforce, the printworkers, but certainly not the journalists, believed they didn't have much to fear whatever the outcome, for their control of management had gone on for so long that they wrongly believed their privileged lifestyle would continue no matter who owned the newspapers. It was truly surprising how the Mirror Group had made any profits in the 1980s, so powerful were the unions and so pathetic was the management.

Maxwell was riding high at the time the *Mirror* hove into view. The price of BPCC shares had risen dramatically from 12p to 160p since he had taken over the ailing printers, and Pergamon, as far as anyone knew, was reporting 'record' profits. Somehow, either from a mole in the *Mirror*, or from 'City' contacts, Maxwell heard the float was in danger, saw his chance and struck.

Within forty-eight hours Maxwell called a press conference, announced Pergamon had made a formal offer of £80 million for Mirror Group Newspapers, and if justified would pay up to £100 million. He shrewdly added assurances about the papers' future prosperity and political line.

His statement concluded: 'Some people may call me a predator but it is the proposed public flotation which will expose the group to the laws of the jungle. I regard myself as the saviour of the group against the heavy commercial advantages of its rivals. Mr Molloy, editor of the *Daily Mirror*, has said in a recent article in the *Guardian* that the Mirror Group has lacked the kind of autocratic player who can "take his seat in the Fleet Street poker game". If Pergamon succeeds, then, as Mr Molloy and all his colleagues must wish, power will once again truly return to the ninth floor at Holborn Circus.'

A week passed as Reed directors fought with their consciences and turned a deaf ear to Maxwell's pressure for a deal. He upped his bid to an unconditional £100 million with a further possible £20 million. And that was only days after Reed had been warned the float might only produce £50 million. Finally, they agreed to talk to Maxwell. It was now just a matter of time. Maxwell turned up the heat, moving into a suite in the Ritz in Piccadilly, directly opposite Reed headquarters, seeking the support of Labour politicians and making public statements daily, upping the price he was prepared to pay. It worked. On July 12 Maxwell and Reed's chief executive Leslie Carpenter shook hands on a deal; Maxwell had paid £90 million. He was to boast that the buildings and plant were worth that, the papers he had been given for nothing. Furthermore, Maxwell had taken pains to check the balance of the Mirror Group's pension fund, which he was delighted to see was very, very healthy. After twenty years of frustration and despair that he would never own a national newspaper, Maxwell had, in the end, been handed one on a plate. He had finally got his train set. But to most at Mirror Group Newspapers the important point was the date: it was Friday the 13th of July.

In a front page article the following day Maxwell wrote a signed statement. It read, in part:

> The Mirror Group Newspapers have changed ownership. Their policies will not change . . . I certainly hope to make the papers more efficient and thereby more profitable . . . We stand for a modern Britain, a country which truly needs modernizing, with industry and trade unions alike prepared to face the hard facts of survival in the Eighties . . .

Maxwell set about placating the journalists and print unions. *Mirror* journalists and union officials were invited to meet their new boss on his first day. He looked nervous in front of the 250 or so sceptical newspapermen who crowded into the Rotunda on the first floor. His speech was upbeat, calling for every effort to restore the *Daily Mirror* to the top spot in Fleet Street, which had been usurped some years before by Murdoch's *Sun*. He wanted the *Mirror* to return to the days of its former glory. He wanted an extra million on the circulation . . . and there would be no redundancies! There was an audible sigh of relief and the journalists and union officials winked and nodded to each other. Too soon.

But Maxwell added in a quiet voice: 'If you had stopped the paper last night, it would have stayed shut and if you don't believe me, ask the people at Park Royal.' Some present began murmuring and Maxwell told them to shut up and listen. He went on: 'I want you to know that I am the proprietor. I am the boss. And I want that to be understood clearly. There can be only one boss and that is me.' It seemed to some present that Maxwell's ambitions for the *Mirror* were to be used to put Rupert Murdoch in his place – second place, behind the *Mirror's* new publisher. On his way from the meeting, however, I heard him say to two of his sidekicks: 'I didn't give away too much, did I?'

He had also taken the opportunity to lull the journalists into a false sense of security, telling them: 'It will be my philosophy that the journalists will be on top and the management on tap.'

Maxwell's arrival put everyone on their toes but he played the journalists and the unions cleverly. On the day he arrived he warned the Scottish unions that if they did not bring out the papers, as they had threatened, then he would close down the whole Glasgow plant and sack everyone. They brought out the paper. That tactic worked brilliantly for at a stroke Maxwell had, to a great extent, tamed the print unions at a time when they believed they were invincible. Months went by without any trouble whatsoever from the unions and the paper came out on time with more editions than it had managed to produce for years.

The rest of Fleet Street, and especially the cartoonists,

thoroughly enjoyed the arrival of Maxwell at the *Mirror*, and it wasn't long before detractors began referring to the *Daily Maxwell*. It was Maxwell's own fault; he began writing a column in the paper, thinly disguised under the name Charles Wilberforce, and his picture appeared at least two or three times a week somewhere in the paper. No other Fleet Street proprietor had ever used his paper for such self-aggrandisement and pathetic self-publicity and it did Maxwell, and the paper, nothing but harm. But his arrogance was so great he would brook no opposition.

His handling of the *Mirror* campaign to fly food and clothing to the starving millions of Ethiopia was a perfect example of what happened when Maxwell took command of operations. There was no better example of his overweening pride when he grabbed the headlines and the initiative in funnelling funds and food to the starving children.

He believed his dramatic action in getting a plane and instantly flying to the wretched, starving Ethiopians would win him, and the *Daily Mirror*, great credit throughout Britain and boost circulation. He couldn't see that his style, his manner of arranging the event, made it seem almost like a circus, as if he was Santa Claus taking Christmas gifts to the needy. There was no hint of compassion for the dying. What *Mirror* readers saw on their front page was Bob Maxwell, beaming all over his face, waving goodbye as if he was seeking office in a Presidential election campaign.

Other newspapers sneered that Maxwell's visit was just an ego trip, which it was, and another referred to Maxwell 'distributing loaves and fishes to the starving'. But to his credit Maxwell did persuade Ethiopia's Marxist government to allow an RAF Hercules to transport relief supplies around the country; and the *Mirror* did raise £1 million for Ethiopian relief, which was more than the rest of the British press combined.

He had already shown himself to the people of Britain in a round-Britain train journey, the idea being for the people to meet Maxwell, the Publisher, realize how brilliant he was and start buying the paper. But it didn't quite work out like that. Along with *Mirror* executives and well-known *Mirror* personalities like the lovable agony aunt Marje Proops, Maxwell travelled from town to town for two weeks, answering *Mirror* readers' queries. Sales leapt when the train hit each town, then fell again the following day. What was worse, however, was that the readers didn't flock to see the great Maxwell, despite the efforts, encouragement and pleading of those executives detailed to make sure that wherever the *Mirror* train pulled into a station there should be hundreds waiting to greet him. Maxwell realized it wasn't going to be the breakthrough he had dreamed, lost faith in the idea and flew back to London, leaving the others to soldier on.

Editorially, the man who took most of Maxwell's initial blustering and pushy behaviour was Mike Molloy, the urbane *Mirror* editor who had held the chair for nearly ten years. Molloy believed the only way to play Maxwell was to ride out the storm and, to a great extent, give him his head. Perhaps his honest comment when asked how he dealt with Maxwell speaks volumes: 'Oh,' he would proclaim, 'that's easy. When Bob asks me what time it is I simply reply, "What time do you want it to be Bob?"'

Much has been suggested of the power the inimitable Joe Haines exercised as Maxwell's adviser, analyst and political ally. Haines, a small, thin, balding man, was born in Rotherhithe, south-east London, an only boy with four older sisters. He served as Harold Wilson's press secretary between 1969 and 1976, was highly intelligent and knew the Labour Party inside out. He was also a first-rate leader writer with a brilliant turn of phrase which epitomized tabloid comment-writing at the highest standard.

When the spectre of Maxwell appeared on the scene, Haines

had told his colleagues at a packed chapel (union) meeting: 'That man Maxwell is a liar and a crook and I can prove it.' Haines had apparently always advised Harold Wilson against Maxwell, saying: 'Don't touch that man with a bargepole.'

Haines said he was prepared to leave the *Mirror* when Maxwell arrived but senior MGN executives urged Bob Maxwell to keep him. Former *Sunday Mirror* editor Bob Edwards told him: 'Haines loathes you, told the chapel you were a crook and said that if you walked in the front door he would go out of the back. But he's the one to keep.' Maxwell took the advice and using his redoubtable charm persuaded Haines to stay on. He immediately promoted him to assistant editor and soon after he became the paper's political editor.

During the next few months Haines was to become Maxwell's leader writer, speech-writer and most favoured journalist, surpassing the editors with his access to Maxwell. He became his principal adviser over editorial matters, editorial appointments and, more importantly, editorial sackings.

Haines seemed to take a dislike to former *News of the World* journalist Wendy Henry who was appointed editor of the *People* primarily because she wanted to have more control than she did over the leaders that went into the paper she had been appointed to edit. After a short time Haines declared that because of her attitude he was going to have nothing more to do with the *People*.

I was sitting in Maxwell's office one Monday when Haines came through on the phone. Maxwell put the call on the loudspeaker so that I could listen as well.

'You will have to do something about the *People*, Bob,' were the first words I heard on the loudspeaker. 'We cannot allow the *People* to print such leaders when they appear to be following a different line to the one we establish in the *Mirror*,' he went on, as Maxwell downed a cup of coffee.

Haines continued for a few minutes pointing out other

47

matters in the paper, of a political nature, that he thought should not be tolerated. To everything Maxwell replied: 'Right,' but seemingly taking very little notice of anything Haines was saying. As Haines reached the end of one sentence Maxwell leant forward, and in a gentle voice said, 'Thank you, Joe,' and put his finger on the button, cutting off Haines.

'You know that Haines and Wendy don't get on, don't you?' I said.

'Yes,' he replied, 'I've known that for some time.'

'But she seems to be doing a good job, circulation is going up,' I volunteered.

In a non-committal way Maxwell replied, 'Yes, a little.'

'So why do you let Joe undermine her? It can't be good for Wendy or the paper,' I queried.

'I don't,' Maxwell retorted, 'that's just Joe being Joe.'

I let the matter drop; I had made the point I wanted. I thought Wendy Henry should be given a chance to make a go of the *People* though I disagreed with some of her more adventurous editorial ideas.

Within a matter of months, however, Ms Henry was fired over a photograph she printed showing Prince William having a pee in public.

To his credit, Maxwell always regretted firing her. On a personal level Maxwell had liked Wendy Henry and he didn't mind too much what she did with the *People* because Maxwell never cared about the paper in the same way as he cared for the *Daily* and the *Sunday Mirror*. Maxwell always seemed slightly embarrassed to have the *People* in his stable of papers and was happy for the paper to battle it out with the major opposition, Murdoch's *News of the World*. The fact that Wendy Henry had been a senior executive there was one of the reasons he appointed her in the first place.

There was always a close rapport between Maxwell and Haines and Maxwell rewarded him handsomely for his diligence and hard work, eventually making him a director of some of the companies and giving him special interest in the Scottish newspapers, which Haines took most seriously.

And yet, as with everyone who worked for him, Maxwell never seemed to trust his favourite leader writer completely.

One day, after Haines had written the official biography of Maxwell, I was talking to Maxwell during one of our Saturday morning chats. I asked why he appointed Joe to write the book when he was surely better employed writing for the *Mirror* at that time.

Maxwell replied: 'Two reasons: one, because I could rely on him to do a good job; two, because after he had written one biography of me he could never write another.' Maxwell had pulled the teeth of the political insider who, after leaving 10 Downing Street, had written a devastating indictment of the Wilson years and the antics of the Prime Minister's notorious kitchen cabinet.

Maxwell arrived at the *Mirror* wanting to be the greatest newspaper publisher the world had ever known and determined to prove he was that man. He would show Murdoch and the rest of them how to run a paper, put on sales, increase advertising and make profits the like of which Fleet Street proprietors had only dreamed of. Ironically, Maxwell had understood how a good publisher should behave; and most of the time, had taken care of administration, management, printing and the financial aspects of Pergamon, leaving editors to edit. And yet Maxwell couldn't even do that well, for the history of Pergamon is that of a company whose books and journals sold well but whose management was poor.

The one quality he bestowed on Mirror Group Newspapers was the best colour printing the national tabloids had ever seen. And that was totally down to Maxwell's insistence that he would only accept the very highest quality. He borrowed heavily to fund a huge £350 million investment programme in new technology, bringing high-grade colour printing to Fleet Street and forcing other newspaper owners to follow suit. The *Daily Mirror* had full colour printing eighteen months before its main rival, Murdoch's *Sun*, and some years before its other rivals, the *Express, Mail* and *Star*. Maxwell anticipated this would lift circulation by approximately twenty per cent – 600,000. With the introduction of colour he managed to boost circulation by only 100,000. Maxwell was not impressed.

It was nine months after taking over that Maxwell decided the time had come for action – announcing it would be necessary to cut staff drastically in order to produce profits, to invest in new technology and achieve the necessary increase in advertising – and circulation. He was absolutely right. But he continued to play cat and mouse with the unions.

Maxwell decided to strike at the weakest link in the union chain – the heavily loss-making *Sporting Life*. The *Life* was losing £1 a week for every reader and its circulation was 75,000 copies a day. Maxwell decided to typeset the *Life* outside London to cut his losses – a move he knew would strike at the core of the print unions' agreements with the employers – that no paper could be typeset outside Fleet Street. The NGA (the National Graphic Association) stopped the *Mirror* presses in protest, losing 750,000 copies. In response to their action Maxwell suspended production of all *Mirror* papers for eleven days. A tentative agreement was reached but five days later SOGAT members at the *People* stopped its publication. Maxwell replied by sacking all those involved.

Crisis loomed but Maxwell knew that, at the very worst, he could close all the titles and sell the whole company, lock, stock and barrel for perhaps £200 million, giving him a profit of about £90 million in just eighteen months. But Maxwell wasn't to give up his train set without a fight. He ordered his managers to bring out a few copies of the *Mirror* and they did so with the famous leader written by Haines.

The headline read: 'Fleet Street. The party is over,' and continued:

> For years, the newspapers of Fleet Street have told the rest of Britain how to run its business. How to be efficient. Competitive. Modern. And all the time Fleet Street has been the most inefficient, uncompetitive and old-fashioned industry in the country. Fleet Street has lectured everyone else about cutting their costs. And indulged in a spending spree itself. It looked as though the good life would never end. But now it is about to. THE GRAVY TRAIN HAS HIT THE BUFFERS . . . Its wild and wasteful party is over.

The following day the SOGAT secretary, Brenda Dean, complained her members had been treated like 'downtrodden eighteenth-century workers' but the strike was called off in twenty-four hours. Days before Christmas 1985 Maxwell announced his survival plan for the group had been agreed and the papers would be produced with 1,600 fewer employees. Maxwell had won a historic victory which was celebrated with glee and relief in every newspaper boardroom throughout Fleet Street. The employers knew that Maxwell had paved the way; what he had achieved in eighteen months could therefore be done in every newspaper office.

Now, Maxwell began to reap the benefits. Having installed new technology, halved the staff and slashed overheads, he could make big profits for himself. And his papers began doing just that. In the late 1980s Maxwell would boast repeatedly: 'When I took over this group it was making £800,000 profit a year, now I am making £800,000 profit a

51

week.' It was a remarkable turnaround and one which he could be justly proud of.

But his journalists weren't happy. Maxwell had promised that after the success of the survival plan he would ensure that *Mirror* journalists would be the best-paid journalists in Fleet Street. He not only reneged on that promise, he did much worse. By the time Maxwell died, *Mirror* journalists were among the lowest paid in Fleet Street. Ironically, this was another reason certain *Mirror* men didn't like Haines, because, in the end, Haines was negotiating on Maxwell's behalf, for the management, over the pay of *Mirror* journalists. To the union negotiators Haines claimed he was doing the very best possible on behalf of the journalists, securing for them payrises higher than anyone else negotiating on behalf of Maxwell would have achieved. But in spite of Maxwell's rhetoric *Mirror* journalists never did become the best-paid men in Fleet Street.

Maxwell had problems with most of his editors throughout his seven-year reign as boss of the *Mirror* empire. Roy Greenslade, editor of the *Mirror* for fourteen months (December 1989 to March 1991), in his book *Maxwell's Fall* puts Maxwell's relationships with his editors perfectly:

> To my mind I was editor of the *Daily Mirror*. In his mind, I was merely another employee and, as such, a servant. He was fond of saying: 'I treat my editors like field marshals.' Few people stopped to think what that meant: as a man in a position to hire and fire field marshals he saw himself as head of state.

Mike Molloy had already been editor of the *Daily Mirror* for eight years when Maxwell swept into Holborn Circus.

Maxwell liked Molloy, possibly because Molloy didn't argue too much with him but believed that Maxwell had to be humoured otherwise he would make life too unpleasant for everyone. Molloy was very good at gauging Maxwell's moods and knowing when to speak or when to keep quiet; and he happily let Maxwell do most of the talking, nodding in agreement much of the time. Molloy also had a wonderful way of making tongue-in-cheek remarks which Maxwell didn't fully understand, but the audience usually did. Molloy was criticized for allowing Maxwell too much editorial interference in those first few months, but it would have been impossible to contain the ebullient Maxwell at that time.

The publisher did have considerable trouble with Richard Stott who was editing the *People* when Maxwell took over in 1984. A year later he was promoted to the *Daily Mirror* and remained there for nearly five years. Their relationship was occasionally turbulent but Stott never pushed Maxwell too far. He knew when Maxwell meant business and would give in to his demands. Maxwell often showed annoyance that Stott had an antipathy to putting foreign news in the paper despite the fact he knew Maxwell had a deep and profound interest in foreign affairs, especially Europe's. Stott's attitude was that most foreign news was of little or no interest to the readers.

It did therefore make my job as foreign editor rather difficult and Stott and I had innumerable arguments when I would try and persuade him to put into the *Mirror* what I believed were foreign stories that readers would expect to find in their paper. Most of the time he didn't want to know. It also meant that Maxwell and I had something in common – real interest in foreign politics.

My first direct contact with Maxwell was an argument over a matter of fact. In May 1985, Maxwell had the brainwave of writing a front page article, in the style of a letter, to Mikhail Gorbachov, saluting the 'workers, peasants and intellectuals' of the USSR, commemorating the fortieth anniversary of 'our joint victory' over Hitler's Germany. Molloy was then still editor and I was called in to look at the letter which had been written. It was addressed to President Mikhail Gorbachov.

I said: 'Well, the first thing is that Gorbachov isn't the president.'

Maxwell turned round slowly and looked at me. In his deep, sonorous voice he asked coldly: 'What do you mean? Of course he is.'

Molloy and three other senior executives were in the room. 'Yes he is,' came a chorus of support for Maxwell.

'No he's not,' I replied quietly. The room fell silent, waiting for Maxwell.

'Well, what is he, then?' asked Maxwell.

'He is the General Secretary of the Central Committee of the Communist Party, not the president,' I replied, desperately trying to think of the name of the Soviet President. For a second or so there was silence as two of those in the room shook their heads at me, signalling that I should shut up and stop arguing with the great man.

Maxwell took the letter from me, looked at it and gave it back. 'What else is wrong?' he asked, his voice softening.

I pointed out two minor points that were incorrect and Maxwell turned to Molloy: 'He's right. Do as he says.'

That was the start of our relationship which continued till the day he died. Maxwell took me on his many journeys to meet world leaders, on business trips, on buying sprees in former Eastern bloc countries. It also started six years of phone calls from Maxwell, calls which would start at seven in the morning and occasionally go on till late at night. Not every day and sometimes not every week. They would usually go in spasms, with hourly calls for a few days, then silence for some days.

He also appointed himself my immediate boss, the *Mirror*'s foreign editor-in-chief. Some months after appointing Stott as editor he called me up for a chat. 'What do you think of your new editor?' he asked mischievously.

I told him I thought Stott was more news orientated than Molloy and the paper had more zip, more drive than before, which was good.

'Why don't you put more foreign news in the paper?' he asked accusingly. I had forgotten that Maxwell had no idea how a tabloid newspaper operated with so many stories every night competing for a show in the paper. Maxwell had already fired one news editor, P.J. Wilson, for not putting what Maxwell believed were the right stories in the paper. As news editor Wilson's job was solely to bring in the news and put it forward to the night editor and the editor to decide what should be used, and what left out. Wilson had tried, in vain, to explain this to Maxwell who stubbornly refused to comprehend how the system worked.

'I try,' was my answer, 'but as you know it's not up to me what goes in the paper.'

Maxwell was in one of his stubborn moods: 'You are the foreign editor, you are responsible for what foreign news goes in the paper.'

I tried to explain: 'Yes, and no.'

He continued: 'Explain yourself.'

So I did, half smiling to myself that I was giving my boss, the owner and publisher of the *Mirror*, the plain man's guide to how newspapers worked. I explained how various sections of the newspaper, the political desk, the news desk, the foreign desk and all the specialists brought in news, wrote their stories and put them forward to the night editor and the editor, who would take the decision to use or not use the stories.

Maxwell was nothing if not a brilliant lateral thinker. Peter Jay, his 'chief-of-staff', was always surprised, and sometimes amazed, at Maxwell's thought process. 'He is the most incredible lateral thinker I have ever met,' he would say, 'God, it's annoying sometimes.'

'So, why don't you have part of the paper just for foreign news?' he suggested. It had been tried before under various *Mirror* editors but I knew Stott was against the idea, believing foreign news, like all home news, had to rely on its merits to make the paper.

'You will have to persuade Stott of that argument. But, naturally, I would be very keen for such an arrangement.'

'We shall see,' said Maxwell, 'I'll be in touch.'

He was. At a subsequent meeting Maxwell told me: 'I think the way round this is for you to report to me anything of any importance in the world. I will then tell the editor what to do with the story. I will be the *Mirror*'s foreign editor-in-chief.'

My heart sank. The last thing I wanted was Maxwell as one boss, with Stott as my editor who would take umbrage, at the very least, every time Maxwell phoned ordering him to put some foreign story in the paper. It was a recipe for a total breakdown of my relationship with Stott, which had not exactly been friendly for the previous fifteen years!

I went immediately to Stott and told him of Maxwell's new plan for foreign news. 'Oh Christ,' he said, 'that's all we need.'

'Leave it to me,' I said. 'I'll deal with it. When there is a foreign story of major importance, that I believe the *Mirror* should use, I will let you know and then I will tell Maxwell, so you're prepared. Otherwise I'll play it by ear.' Stott, who of course had many other problems on his hands, agreed. I had acquired a new boss.

From that day on, Maxwell would phone out of the blue with a simple question: 'Anything happening?' And I would give him the main items of foreign news which I judged he would see later either on BBC news or CNN. Because of his insatiable interest in overseas news, Maxwell grew to love CNN and would sometimes phone me late at night to see whether I had seen whatever the news item was on CNN at that precise moment. I didn't have CNN at home because I lived in a Grade II listed Georgian house in inner London and Southwark Council would not allow the large one-metre-diameter disc to damage the roofline. Maxwell ordered executives to make sure I had CNN installed at once, but to no avail. It never was, which infuriated him every time he wanted to discuss what he had just seen. He hated having to explain the news item and then discuss it.

Maxwell's relationship with Stott grew steadily worse; he was annoyed at the way Stott would try to take the mickey out of Maxwell whenever speeches were made. He appeared to be trying to show everyone else present that he could do and say what he liked because Maxwell needed him to edit the paper. But Stott forgot one important factor: Maxwell would rid himself of anyone, at any time. No one was indispensable.

Another trivial way Stott teased Maxwell was to walk out with cut-glass whisky goblets from his suite in Maxwell House whenever he was invited for a drink. Many times, Stott would be seen leaving Maxwell's room, having had a few drinks, with glasses which he would proudly display in his own cupboard in his office. Time and again Maxwell's valet or butler would be sent to Stott's office, when he was not about, to collect the glasses and return them upstairs.

Stott often clashed with Maxwell over the foreign content in the paper. For example Stott didn't send any *Mirror* reporter to Berlin in November 1989, to cover one of the great postwar stories – the tearing down of the Berlin Wall. I had advised Stott to send on the story as the Communist dictators in Eastern Europe crumbled one by one, and Erich Honecker of East Germany would be next in line for the chop. I had informed him that the Berlin Wall, the symbol of the great divide between Communism and Western democracy, was about to be smashed down.

Every other Fleet Street national newspaper sent to Berlin and covered it with massive amounts of space dedicated to what was without doubt one of the great foreign stories since the cold war began.

The phone rang. 'Why aren't you in Berlin?' boomed Maxwell.

'We're covering it from here,' I replied.

Maxwell snapped in rage: 'You can't cover this fucking great story from Holborn,' he shouted. 'Get out there immediately.'

I told him: 'There's a problem, the editor doesn't want to send.'

All I heard then was a great roaring noise emanating from the phone, like a football crowd in full throat when a goal has been scored: 'Whaaaaat', I think was the word. And the phone went dead. I went in to Stott to warn him.

Within weeks Stott had been promoted, being given the privilege of organizing the management buyout of the *People*. Many on the paper were blaming me for his departure. Stott told his *Mirror* colleagues that he had requested the move to the *People* for months; that he had been actively discussing with Maxwell that he should lead the MBO.

The departure of Mike Molloy, after some years as editor-in-chief of Mirror Group Newspapers, however, caused Maxwell many sleepless nights. He genuinely liked Molloy, that was why he had made him editor-in-chief rather than axing him with a pay-off. Maxwell positively encouraged Molloy to spend most days in the office writing his novels in longhand with his loyal secretary typing up the manuscript for him. In any case, to all intents and purposes, Maxwell was his own editor-in-chief. That was the reason Maxwell had cancelled the appointment of an editorial director when he bought the group. It was an appointment that Joe Haines coveted but was never given.

Maxwell discussed Molloy's departure with me: 'What do you think of Mike Molloy?' he asked one day.

'A delightful chap,' I replied.

'No, no, no, as an editor, as editor-in-chief,' he tutted in annoyance at my dimwit answer.

'I don't think he's got a job, really,' I replied, 'because you are your own editor-in-chief. Mike's wasted.'

He replied: 'What do you mean?'

I told him that Molloy was a brilliant newspaper designer, and a first-rate lay-out man, whose talents should be used on the three titles. Molloy was put back into harness and Maxwell made use of his remarkable talents for more than two years designing Maxwell's most cherished baby, the *European*.

Later, after Maxwell fired Molloy, with a pay-off, Maxwell told me that he had wanted to axe him many months before but couldn't bring himself to do so. He said: 'In a way he was like a son to me. I don't know why but I felt he wasn't a shit; I felt he liked me too. But it was time for him to go, to move on.'

But that didn't stop Maxwell telling Molloy, when he did fire him, that he wouldn't give him the usual two year pay-off for a long-serving *Mirror* editor but only one year because he had spent so much of Maxwell's time writing novels.

The man who succeeded Stott, Roy Greenslade, author of the entertaining, first-rate account of what working for Maxwell was like, *Maxwell's Fall*, admits he came from the Murdoch group, where he was Number Three on *The Sunday Times*, believing that he could cope with Maxwell, despite what he had heard on the Fleet Street grapevine and all he had read in *Private Eye*. He brought to the *Daily Mirror* a freshness of mind and a new spirit along with some good professional newspapermen from Wapping. For the fourteen months Greenslade lasted, the *Mirror* returned to its good old days of the 1970s trying to interest and, dare I say it, educate its readers rather than just serving them a diet of Princess Diana, violent Britain, Bingo and sport. Almost from the outset, however, Greenslade made an enemy, Haines.

Greenslade brought in a columnist, John Diamond, with the full permission of Maxwell, a columnist whom Haines believed was a challenge to his own column. In fact there was no reason why the *Mirror* couldn't have accommodated both, for at that time Haines seemed to be concentrating on politics while Diamond was meant to be more amusing and avant-garde.

Frequently, I discussed Greenslade with Maxwell, as I learned later, but for totally different reasons, Maxwell had discussed me with Greenslade. Maxwell could not understand the antipathy between Haines and Greenslade.

He asked me one Saturday morning over an orange juice and coffee: 'What is the trouble between them?'

It was a difficult question. I rated Greenslade. I believed he had achieved an important breakthrough among the jaundiced journalists at the *Mirror*; there was a camaraderie, a confidence, a feeling that everyone was involved in the task of producing a better newspaper, not just taking Maxwell's money.

'What am I to do?' he asked. There had been rumours that Haines was to retire; he had indeed announced his retirement and had named the approximate date some time before; he wanted to tend his beloved garden and watch cricket.

'You could stop them meeting by letting Joe retire to his home in Kent and write his column from there,' I volunteered.

'But that wouldn't stop Joe phoning every day complaining about the paper and how it was being run,' he replied.

Tongue in cheek, I answered: 'You could always be busy, you usually are.'

But that was not what Maxwell wanted. He wanted them to be friends, to work together for the good of the paper.

Disingenuously, amazingly, Maxwell replied: 'I work with everyone, even those I don't like very much. I'm friends with everyone I work with, why can't they be the same?'

I said: 'There is a major difference, Bob, you're the boss.'

The phone rang and the conversation ended.

On several other occasions Maxwell asked me what I felt about Greenslade and this at a time after we had broken off everything but basic diplomatic relations. I told him straight: 'He's a good editor, the paper is once again respected and there is a feeling of pride and optimism on the editorial floor. That must be good for the *Mirror* and must be good for you.'

Totally ignoring my remarks, he said: 'He speaks highly of you too.'

I decided to push him. 'Why, what's on your mind?'

He said: 'It's not working.'

I knew what he meant but chose to ignore it. 'But, Bob,' I protested, 'it is working and working very well and you know it is.'

I knew from Greenslade that he was having problems with Maxwell and I sensed trouble. Maxwell was in one of those moods when he didn't want to hear the truth; he wanted me to say Greenslade was a disaster and the quicker he left the better.

I made one last effort, guessing that Maxwell was being fed information that was putting Greenslade in a bad light. I said: 'Listen, Bob, I don't know what you're hearing from other people who have access to you, but if it's different from what I'm saying, then they have it wrong. They're up to no good. I'm telling you what people on the editorial floor think. I have no axe to grind on this matter, some other people do.'

He sat there, nodding. Then he looked up, banged the table with the palm of his hand, the signal that the interview was over. He showed me to the door. 'Keep this between us, won't you?'

Greenslade's demise came during the Gulf War in February 1991. In his book he tells of the final conversation:

> Maxwell began with a splendid understatement: 'You and I are not getting on . . . our relationship isn't working . . .' Then came the list of differences once more . . . the stories, pet projects, interviews we had fallen out over before he referred to my always 'shooting from the hip'.
>
> I was not going to fight, simply saying: 'You want to be editor.'
>
> 'There you go,' he replied. 'The trouble with you, mister, is that you have a short fuse.'
>
> Maxwell asked: 'What is it about me, about coming here, that you didn't expect?'
>
> 'Interference,' I said without a pause. 'You interfered more than I thought possible, and not just with me, but by ringing so many staff, dealing with so many people. Murdoch doesn't do that and it took me by surprise.'
>
> He beamed: 'That's me, a man of detail. I must be involved. Anything else?'

It was great the way *Mirror* journalists reacted to the news of Greenslade's departure. Though Greenslade had been sworn to silence in return for a £100,000 pay-off, everyone knew he had been fired. In an unprecedented show of support the journalists called a meeting and voted 139–0 for a resolution recording their 'regret and anger' at Greenslade's going. It was some time later that I was very happy to let Maxwell know how the journalists had reacted. When I told him, Maxwell just grunted and gave me a cold look.

It was the end of Greenslade but with the *Mirror* flotation on the Stock Exchange only weeks away he had made no decision as to who should succeed him. As a stop-gap he asked Charles Wilson, the former editor of *The Times*, to take over. Wilson had joined Maxwell the previous year as chief executive and editor-in-chief of the *Sporting Life*, a job which would have suited a keen racing man as he approached retirement. But Wilson, the man who was accused of taking *The Times* downmarket to such an extent it read like a broadsheet *Daily Mail*, was seen by the *Mirror* journalists as a Maxwell man, and to he watched. He didn't endear himself to many, by calling certain people 'dickheads'.

Maxwell had sought advice from various people when selecting editors and one person he trusted to give straightforward honest answers was Ernie Burrington. When Maxwell arrived, Burrington, a quietly spoken North Countryman, had been deputy editor of the *People* under Stott and when Stott moved to the *Mirror*, Burrington took over. He was a first-class editor, respected by his staff, a shrewd judge of stories and a man who many had always believed would have made a first-class editor of the *Mirror*, where he had spent many years in senior positions.

He never confronted Maxwell but managed to get his own way by gentle persuasion, using sound northern common sense. As a result Maxwell had often sought advice from Burrington when selecting editors.

Maxwell enjoyed having women editors. He felt they were less trouble, more amenable to his wishes and his demands, but he only wanted them to edit his Sunday papers, not the flagship *Daily Mirror* which was his consuming passion and interest. He had not only felt close to the unfortunate

Wendy Henry during her brief sojourn at the *People* but he liked having the glamorous, bubbly, friendly Eve Pollard as editor of the *Sunday Mirror* for five years. She was in fact the only editor to leave his employment without being eased out or fired when she went to edit the *Sunday Express* six months before Maxwell's death. I believe that Eve Pollard quit the Maxwell empire because he did not want her as editor of the *Daily Mirror* despite the stalwart work she had put in to keep the sales of the *Sunday Mirror* constantly on a high. She felt slighted that he wouldn't promote her after Greenslade's departure for she felt she had earned it. Pollard knew how to handle Maxwell and they had a good working relationship.

After Greenslade's dismissal Maxwell called me up for a chat and asked my opinion about the next editor of the *Daily Mirror*. He informed me that Haines wanted Stott back again and, if that wasn't possible, he had suggested putting Greenslade's deputy Bill Hagerty into the job. I reminded Maxwell that in Stott's second tour of duty as editor, the *People* had lost 500,000 copies in the last six months from September 1990 to March 1991, driving the circulation down from 2,770,000 to 2,270,000, despite having had millions spent on promotion. I believed that after five years editing the *Mirror* he had given of his best.

'Rubbish,' Maxwell replied, 'it's not that bad,' as he picked up the phone and asked his secretary to call the circulation boss. As he waited for the call he said, 'And what about Bill?' (meaning Hagerty). I told him I didn't think Hagerty would make as good an editor as the man he had just fired, Greenslade. When the circulation man phoned, Maxwell simply grunted, a sign he had heard something he preferred not to know.

Within weeks Maxwell had reappointed Stott as editor and I watched as Stott, followed by Haines, walked into the editor's office together and closed the door.

FOUR

'Leave me alone, will you, woman!'

Throughout his life Robert Maxwell stressed how important his large family was to him; he spoke in public of what a stalwart and faithful wife Betty had been to him during their many years together. They had nine children, a large family even by the standards of post-war Britain when many young couples were determined to build large families after the horrors of six years of war.

In his unofficial biography, published in 1988 when Maxwell was at the height of his career and in sight of achieving his ambition of heading one of the world's biggest publishing empires, Haines wrote in a chapter entitled 'The Family' that the greatest wealth Robert Maxwell possessed was the love his family showed him: 'They display their affection openly in a way most English families do not. Each and every one of them is his defender and advocate . . .'

Those people who knew Maxwell well, however – and who watched him on Michael Aspel's TV show *This Is Your Life* in 1989 – know that his appearance that night showed a man ill at ease with his family, nervous, diffident, even a touch embarrassed by the events going on around him in the studio. And so he should have been.

Maxwell behaved towards his family, all of them it so seemed, as though he didn't care a damn for them or their feelings. I found particularly painful his treatment of the stoic, patient Betty who seemed to have the patience of a saint. I would sometimes find myself in the most embarrassing situations as I witnessed Maxwell monstering members of his own family, particularly his long-suffering wife.

Employees through the decades complained of the bullying tactics Maxwell would sometimes apply to make a point, get his own way, bluster through a difficult interview, or how he would sometimes simply bully someone because he knew the person would crumble before him. He liked that. And somehow more awful was the fact that he knew full well that he could always bully his wife and his children.

I remember being in Paris on one occasion in the spring of 1988 with Maxwell and his wife. We were in his tiny, cramped apartment in rue des Écoles which he had owned for forty years. It was darkly but tastefully furnished although only a double bed and a large mahogany-panelled bath would fit in the small bedroom. Maxwell seemed to fill the entire room with his bulk.

It was cold outside and Mrs Maxwell was concerned. We were leaving the apartment and she was trying to help him on with his coat. 'I can do it myself, thank you,' Maxwell told her in an irritated voice.

'You know you will get a cold if you don't put on your coat,' replied Mrs Maxwell in her very French English accent, chiding him like a mother.

'Leave me alone, will you, woman!' he said, as his coat fell off his shoulders.

Mrs Maxwell bent down and picked it up off the floor, struggling to put it back over his shoulders. Maxwell exploded: 'I have told you to fuck off, now fuck off,' and he grabbed the coat and stormed out of the flat.

I looked at the floor in embarrassment and Mrs Maxwell, to her credit, barely reacted, just pulling a face, shrugging her shoulders and then following him.

There was another occasion in Paris when I witnessed

Maxwell's appalling treatment of his wife. It was during the summer of 1989, at the time of the bicentenary of the French Revolution, when Maxwell spent at least one day a week in Paris trying to edge ever closer to President François Mitterrand.

Maxwell liked Paris. He could speak the language fluently and he was treated with respect. Every time he flew into Le Bourget airport he would be met at the aircraft steps by his chauffeur, Pierre Lemaine, and as Maxwell flopped into the front seat of the large Renault 25 he would say to Lemaine, *'Mettez le feu.'* That was his instruction to Lemaine to take out the blue flashing lamp and put it on top of the car in true Head of State style. Lemaine hated having to produce the blue light because it was, of course, illegal.

Then Maxwell would urge Lemaine to drive like fury, overtaking every other vehicle, driving at speed down the centre of the road, blasting his horn and with the blue light flashing on the roof. Once, he was stopped by police and Maxwell sat, head down, as he let the police demand from Lemaine by what authority he was speeding, driving down the centre of the road and using the blue lamp. Lemaine was told the matter would be reported to higher police authority. And Maxwell had to use his French lawyer, Dr Samuel Pisar, to get him off with a caution. It didn't of course make the slightest difference to him; the next time we flew into Paris he gave the same instructions to the wretched Lemaine and off we set again with the light flashing. It was typical Maxwell at his most incorrigible.

It was around eight o'clock in the evening and Maxwell had just asked me if I would like some champagne and caviare. He was in a good humour, padding around his sumptuous suite in the Ritz which cost around £1,000 a night. He usually gave me a small suite which cost £500 a night. We had drunk a couple of glasses of chilled Dom Perignon, at about £75 a bottle, and we were chatting about the *Mirror*.

There was a knock at the door and Simon, the valet, went and opened it. It was Mrs Maxwell. The phone rang at that moment and Maxwell took it, so I asked her in, gave her a flute of champagne and offered her some caviare.

Chatting idly as Maxwell boomed away on the phone, I asked her if she was staying for dinner, or the night. She told me: 'Yes, I am staying here,' and her eyes looked upwards. She went on: 'Not here, of course, I have a room at the very top of the building; that's where I have to stay.'

Trying to make light of the embarrassment, I said: 'There's plenty of room here, stay here, I'm sure there's a spare room in the suite.' She pulled a wonderful French face of doubt and said: 'You must be joking; he would never allow it.'

The phone call ended and Maxwell looked at his wife. 'What do you want?' he asked challengingly.

'Nothing,' she replied, defensively, 'I just came in to see you.'

Picking up his tumbler of champagne Maxwell replied: 'Well, I'm busy, good night.'

Sheepishly, Mrs Maxwell put down her glass and walked out of the room. She had been summarily dismissed, as though she was a servant.

Poor Betty Maxwell had, however, become used to such treatment for it appears Maxwell had behaved like this to her over many years, if not decades. On most of the occasions I saw Betty Maxwell with her husband she appeared to be someone prepared to accept his decisions and his orders no matter what they were. She sometimes appeared almost humble, in deference to his every whim, but on other occasions she would argue with him for a moment or so and then accept his ruling.

And yet when acting on her own, as an individual, Betty Maxwell knew what she wanted and would be forthright in her approach and her arguments in any discussion. On her own she certainly gave no hint that she would ever accept the role of a down-trodden wife but seemed to give the impression that she had the resolve, the same intellectual strength as her husband. And whenever I heard her talking to someone about her husband she always spoke of him with devotion and respect.

And she steadfastly upheld the myth throughout his life that Maxwell was the person who would want to attend every meeting, every dinner, every gathering in support of Israel, Jewish charities and social affairs. The truth was something different however. He did not. He would accept, and he would attend, those where he believed he might meet important people; or those that Maxwell deemed important. And he would accept invitations to many with no intention that he would go himself. That was why at so many functions Betty or Ian or Kevin would be deputed, usually at the last minute, to attend.

On many occasions he would say a matter of hours and sometimes days before such a Jewish gathering: 'I'm not going to that boring meeting, a total waste of time.' And the excuse would invariably be the same – pressure of work.

Mrs Maxwell, a Christian, was remarkable in her support and work for the Jewish cause – all on Maxwell's behalf. It was as if Betty Maxwell, embarrassed at her husband's attitude, wanted to make amends for his indifference.

Betty Maxwell has many other remarkable qualities; she is intelligent, bright and amusing. She has none of her husband's arrogance, but rather portrays an unpretentious attitude to life, almost a humility which was the more so in contrast to the boorish Maxwell. At dinner parties she would happily hold forth when Maxwell wasn't present, but when he was in attendance she would usually remain far more subdued, allowing him to hold court – as he usually did at every dinner table.

What constantly amazed me, and many other people, was that Betty Maxwell remained so loyal to Maxwell throughout his life. Many other women would have walked away from such a marriage.

Maxwell had never been particularly close to his children either, even when they were growing up. His life was his work, it always had been, it always was, and his work was to consume his life until the day he died.

Maxwell himself confessed to this, saying in the *Sunday Express* in July, 1983: 'I wish that I had known the importance of parenthood. We have had nine children, two of whom died, and I wish I had been able to spend more time with my children in the early years. I thought then that I did; but I can see now that I missed a great deal of the pleasure involved in being a parent.' It was a sentiment which I am afraid Maxwell probably expressed at the time because he thought it was the right thing to say. That was one of Maxwell's traits, and he didn't seem to care, or even notice, that he might contradict himself some time later with a different story about the same event. Many were the stories Maxwell would tell that one would know were sheer invention. (Perhaps the perfect example of his storytelling was the number of stories put forward by Maxwell himself concerning his escape from Czechoslovakia as a teenager and his final arrival in Britain. The stories changed every few years, and the older Maxwell became, the more dramatic and daring were the exploits of the teenaged Maxwell as he fought Germans, was jailed, beaten and tortured, sentenced to death, escaped dramatically and ended up in Britain spending the first few years of the war in the Pioneer Corps of the British Army digging ditches.)

Maxwell indeed spent very little time with his family for he was far more intent on making money, doing deals, determined to be a success and a millionaire. And living the part. And when he was with them he adopted the same bullying ways that he did with those who worked for him. But it is also true that Maxwell was devoted to his children and he wanted them all to be ambitious, brilliant and successful – just like him!

All nine children were born with dual British–French citizenship and Maxwell encouraged them to work hard and study hard at school. But there was strict discipline in the Maxwell home. He referred to it as 'the three Cs – consideration, concentration and conciseness'. In effect, Maxwell expected his children to act in exactly the opposite way that he led his own life. He wanted them to be polite at all times, to be well behaved and only to speak when spoken to. He believed they should show respect for their elders, especially their parents and in particular their father. Above all he demanded they be concise when speaking. He hated anyone, adults or children, who didn't come straight to the point, say what they meant and then kept quiet. He laid down the rules in the house and demanded they be obeyed, despite the fact that he never obeyed rules and took a delight in disobeying them, going his own way and not caring whom he upset, ignored or trod on in the process.

Sunday lunch was always the big occasion of the week in the Maxwell household, particularly when Maxwell was at home. Headington Hill Hall was often the venue of lunches for politicians, businessmen and celebrities, and the Maxwell children would always sit down with the guests. They were expected to speak up to those sitting next to them and join in the adult conversation. Mrs Maxwell recalled in an interview with the *Tatler* in 1987:

> Sometimes the children told their father that they did not want to sit next to these people at lunch, that it was boring, that they were bored. But Bob would tell them that if it was boring it was because they weren't making enough effort themselves. Sometimes I would feel sorry for the children but they knew what was expected of them.

71

Some of Maxwell's children had a tough time at school. Betty Maxwell recalled in an article in *Woman* magazine in 1982 that the younger children were taunted at school by those who said their father, known derisively as 'the bouncing Czech', was a crook. She commented: 'It was a terribly stressful time for us with court cases, lawyers and bad news most days.'

Maxwell was rightly very proud of the academic achievements of his children: Philip, the eldest, Ian and Kevin all won scholarships to Balliol, Oxford, and gained good degrees; and Ghislaine, the youngest child, also went to Balliol when the college became co-educational. Showing her independence, Mrs Maxwell also studied for a degree as a mature student at St Hugh's, Oxford, taking a BA honours degree in French.

One of the reasons that Maxwell wanted his own children to try hard at school, do well, go to university and obtain good degrees was because he had had no proper education. He always resented that, and even suggested that one of the driving forces of his life was that he had to constantly prove to himself, as well as show others that, despite having no education, he was brighter, more intelligent, more quick-witted, more intellectual than many of those whom he met and dealt with, who had been fortunate in having a first-class education. He boasted that he would have made a first-class scientist and that was one of the reasons for the success of Pergamon; and he loved receiving honorary doctorates from any university, anywhere in the world. He loved attending the ceremonies, dressing in mortar board and gown and addressing hundreds of academics and students; it seemed to make up for what he had missed out on during his youth.

Maxwell was also tough on his children; he did indeed bully them, not physically, but certainly mentally. And yet his 1988 authorized biography stated that the children did not stand in fear of him and were allowed to express their own opinions. It also mentioned that all but one had at some time worked for Maxwell, but that this was their own choice.

All I can say to those high-sounding words is 'humbug'. They do not bear out the scenes I witnessed time and again between Maxwell and his two youngest sons, Ian and Kevin, and daughter, Ghislaine, who worked in the business with him.

Despite his frequent travels Maxwell did see more of the younger children, for he moved his home and Pergamon, lock, stock and barrel, from London to Headington Hill Hall in Oxford in 1960, though he still kept offices in Fitzroy Square, London. The following year the Maxwells' firstborn, Michael, the son whom Maxwell had adored more than the others, was involved in a horrifying car crash. Michael was just fourteen, studying at Marlborough. Maxwell was truly devastated. Michael never recovered consciousness but was kept alive for seven years on a life-support system until dying in 1968. That was the family's second tragedy; the first was in 1957 when their daughter Karine, then three, was diagnosed as having acute leukaemia and there was no saving her. Nothing could be done and she died just three weeks later.

It had been only a few years earlier, in August 1950, when their twin daughters Christine and Isabel were born prematurely, contracted toxaemia and nearly died a few weeks after their birth. After three devastating weeks, when doctors believed they would die, the girls finally pulled through.

Though Headington Hill Hall was both home and office, nearly all the employees worked in offices Maxwell put up, as a temporary arrangement, in the grounds. Though officially temporary, they were still there when he died thirty-two years after moving to Oxford. Of course, Maxwell had his office in the Hall itself but that caused continual strife between Maxwell and Betty particularly when vital staff such as Jean Baddeley, his long-standing secretary, were required to stay overnight – sometimes for weeks at a time.

Maxwell decided it would be better for the sake of everyone if Jean Baddeley moved out, and a home was found for her in Oxford. From those days at Headington Mrs Maxwell always referred to Jean Baddeley as 'the B' but with her French accent it sounded like 'zee Bee'. Their children used the same nickname and for ever Jean Baddeley was referred to as 'the B'.

It was decided that Maxwell would have a Birthday Book, the so-called Festschrift, to celebrate his sixty-fifth birthday which everyone inscribed, including all the children, who wrote whatever they wished in the book, to be presented to him as a souvenir of their memories of him during their childhood. The book also had notes written by many people who had known Maxwell throughout his life.

Ian, who had been sacked by his father when he was twenty-five for 'gross dereliction of duty', meeting a girl rather than meeting his father at Orly airport, wrote in the book:

> You are not a man to hold grudges or to belabour a point. I often think you unnecessarily use a howitzer to shoot a chicken, but when the smoke has cleared the chicken often discovers you were only firing blanks . . .
>
> You know of course that you are an impossible act to follow, but you're a marvellous example to try to emulate in so many ways . . . I do wish, however, that you would apply your oft-quoted principle of 'a pat on the head being worth fifty kicks in the b— ' more frequently – not just for myself

as much as the rest of the family and the many people that work with you directly every day.

It was perhaps the most public smack in the eye Maxwell ever received from one of his children – but it didn't do one ounce of good, for Maxwell never changed. Ian Maxwell's relationship with his father did sometimes seem warm and they would occasionally share a joke together, but not often. What was more normal was for Ian to be explaining something to his father who would cut him off in mid-sentence shouting: 'How many times have I got to tell you, get to the point or shut up!' That would put poor Ian into more of a dither and his father would monster him again. It was painful to witness. That, however, meant nothing to Maxwell, who never cared a damn whom he was putting down, insulting or embarrassing.

I did see at first hand the way Maxwell treated his children and it was not a dignified sight. I remember sometimes being in Ian Maxwell's prestigious office, just a stone's throw from his father's. His job changed regularly; it was almost impossible to follow his high-flying titles. I believe Ian lived in dread of his father. But Ian and I worked together some of the time prior to the launch of the *European*, Maxwell's pet project, which deserved to succeed. I remember chatting to him when his phone rang, showing on the large thirty-line system that it was a call from his father: 'I can't talk to him now, I can't talk to him,' he said. 'Nick, will you take it? I'm not here, tell him I'm not here.' So I picked up the phone, told him Ian wasn't around and tried to find out what the call was about. Maxwell wouldn't say, so I just took a message he had phoned.

Ian always had a good relationship with Bob Cole, a man a few years younger than Maxwell who began working for him way back in the 1960s. Cole was a general factotum who had done stalwart work for Maxwell, usually working seven days a week, as well as helping all members of the family whenever they asked. To the children he became a sort of uncle and certainly a family friend. Maxwell treated Cole appallingly despite the fact he was perhaps one of the most loyal and trustworthy men Maxwell ever employed. Finally, having employed so many press officers, and fired most of them, he gave the job to Cole. And, disgracefully, when he got that job in 1989, Maxwell was paying Cole a salary of little more than a secretary.

Cole was always happy to run errands for the family and give help whenever he was asked. One day when Maxwell was in New York, Ian asked Cole if he would collect some suits that had been altered for him from his tailor, Lord & Stewart in Conduit Street, London. As luck would have it, Maxwell phoned asking to speak to Cole, and Ian, in a panic, told his father Cole had gone out on a mission of mercy. When Cole returned Ian told him Maxwell had called and said: 'I had to tell him you were out on a mission of mercy. If I had told him you had gone out to collect some suits for me he would have gone mad. If he asks you, tell him you were out getting my glasses repaired because I had broken them.' Cole stood looking at Ian, perplexed: 'But Ian, I can't say that; you don't wear glasses, you wear contact lenses.' It was yet another example of the fear that Maxwell instilled in his children.

Incredibly, Maxwell issued Cole with a formal employer's warning just months before he died. Cole tells the story: 'It was part of my duties to collect Government reports relative to the newspaper industry or any of Maxwell's companies. Usually I had to collect them within the hour of publication, an order given me by Peter Jay on instructions from Maxwell. When the Calcutt Report on Press Freedom was issued I immediately went to collect a copy and when I returned Maxwell called for me. He demanded to know why I had left the office without permission.

'He began shouting at me, asking, "Who told you to get it? Did I instruct you? No, I didn't." Maxwell then turned to Robert Gregory, the director of human resources, who was in the room at the time, and told him to issue me with an official warning about my behaviour and to put it on my file. Three days later Gregory handed me the letter but I refused to read it. I just tore it up and threw it away. I felt so insulted, so offended. I had given my life for Maxwell and his family and that was the way he repaid me.'

There was the famous Maxwell line that his children were never going to receive any of the money that he had amassed during his lifetime; and he told everyone that his children accepted and welcomed that decision of his. Maxwell made this statement apparently so that his children would have to make their own way in life without looking for support from their parents. Time and again Maxwell used that line and the children were always instructed to agree whenever the matter was raised.

Ian always seemed to want to please his father and win his praise, a normal psychological trait in many children, especially those who have been repeatedly put down by their fathers. Maxwell liked Ian because of his character and personality. Perhaps if he had given him more pats on the head he would have been more successful.

One day in Ian's office I can remember one of Maxwell's finance directors walking in with some papers for Ian to sign. Ian ran his eyes over them and said to him: 'Has my father authorized this?' The reply was 'yes' and Ian signed the papers and handed them over. The finance director walked out.

When Ian became involved with Laura, his lovely American wife, there would be the most wonderful charade played at night whenever Ian was called to the *Lady Ghislaine*. Ian had no idea how long he might have to stay with his father and if he believed it would be some days then he would

77

phone Laura who would fly down to wherever the boat was moored. But she would never come on board because Ian did not know what his father's reaction would be. All day Ian would be working on the boat with his father, answering phones, calling other people, being his general dogsbody while Laura lay on a beach, getting a suntan and swimming. Ian would be expected to stay for the sumptuous dinner with his father, entertaining him, chatting or, more often, sitting and listening to what the great man had to say. Shortly after that Ian would yawn a few times, say he was tired and retire for the night. In reality, having seen his father go to his cabin, Ian would be off to Laura, stay the night with her in her hotel and then return by seven o'clock the next morning, for another day.

Maxwell's relationship with Kevin, his youngest son who was born in 1959, was totally different from that with Ian. Both sons would kiss their father on both cheeks when he returned from a trip, but there seemed little affection in the brush of the cheeks, particularly with Kevin; it always seemed to me the boys were performing a duty they had been taught to carry out and seemed so until the last.

Kevin is a tougher, stronger character than Ian and very bright. He played his father as though playing a game of chess, giving nothing away. I noticed that their eyes hardly ever met, as though they were deliberately avoiding looking directly at each other. But Kevin was the son whom Maxwell decreed would be the heir apparent. Maxwell would, however, still give Kevin short shrift whenever he felt like it.

Yet Kevin and his father fell out when Kevin was in his early twenties. It was in 1982 and Kevin had fallen in love with Pandora Warnford-Davis when they were both at Oxford. Maxwell didn't like that. The real problem was that Pandora was a strong-willed girl who, despite her youth, had the courage to stand up to the bullying Maxwell. Kevin had just started working for his father in New York and Maxwell was angry when he discovered Pandora was with him. So he gave Kevin an ultimatum – give up Pandora or give up the family firm. Kevin had the guts to stick with Pandora and walked out of Pergamon. For the next eighteen months he worked for CBS Publishing, selling college text books. But Maxwell needed Kevin back to help run his growing empire; Maxwell needed his family around him because he knew he could trust them to keep secrets, to work hard and to do what he told them. So Kevin returned to the fold – and he married Pandora.

By 1989, Maxwell believed Kevin had what it took to run Macmillan's in New York but called him back after a few months. Maxwell, who never wanted to live in New York on a permanent basis, decided Kevin should be in command in New York and he sent him over there to run the business, buying him and Pandora a large, expensive house. On his return to London, Maxwell decided Kevin needed more tuition and moved him out of his large office and made him sit in a rather ordinary, plain, smaller one immediately behind his, which had interconnecting doors into Maxwell's palatial office.

I remember being with Maxwell on one of our overseas trips in Eastern Europe in 1989 when he was involved in trying to buy a company. He had sent Kevin to hold discussions on his behalf with strict orders not to take any decisions at all without consulting him. Maxwell said to me: 'He thinks he knows everything but I know he doesn't.'

On another occasion, in 1989 when Maxwell was trying to buy Elsevier, Kevin was sent to the Netherlands to carry out preliminary discussions with the company, which eventually bought Pergamon from Maxwell in 1991. Kevin was ordered to bring back the chairman in his private Gulfstream 111 but not to commit himself in any way during the air trip. Indeed, the story goes that Maxwell told Kevin not to answer any questions about the deal whatsoever, but to go to the lavatory on the aircraft every time he was asked a question, and phone Maxwell on the mobile to relay the question. Maxwell would then give him the answer he was to pass on.

During the last few years of Maxwell's life, Kevin was given more and more work by his father so that he would often work from 7.30 a.m. till after 9 p.m. at night. It was a punishing, if not impossible, workload for anyone, especially a young man with a wife and children at home. Understandably, the strong-minded Pandora was appalled at the way Maxwell drove Kevin so hard. After all, they had three daughters and a son. Kevin tried desperately to keep the peace between his wife and his father. Pandora would send faxes to Maxwell complaining that he was responsible for wrecking their family life, demanding he stop driving Kevin so hard, complaining that Kevin was thirty years old, but going on fifty! She stood up to Maxwell magnificently and he, in turn, ignored her, hardly ever going to visit their London home.

Both sons and, to a lesser extent, Ghislaine, and certainly Mrs Maxwell, were expected to drop everything if Maxwell phoned or if he wanted them to do something for him, no matter what appointments they had made, no matter what jobs they were doing, no matter to whom they were speaking. Their diaries and their appointments always had to play second fiddle to any of his demands, and these would be made at any time of the day or night.

Maxwell never overpaid his sons. Of course they had BMW cars, expense accounts and American Express cards, which Maxwell would check to determine whether his sons were spending too much of 'his' money. Maxwell would allow his sons to have the car they wanted, but he would have to give permission on every occasion. A year before Maxwell's death, Kevin was allowed a car he had wanted for years – a Mercedes soft top costing about £80,000. During the last few years, however, after Maxwell had decided that Kevin should succeed him, he showed his heir more generosity: he arranged for Kevin to be bought a £2 million Chelsea house and Kevin had enough money to buy a lovely, good-sized cottage in the country.

Ghislaine Maxwell, the youngest child, was born in 1961, within days of the Maxwells' first son Michael dying while still in a coma from the road accident years before. Undoubtedly she was spoilt as a child and she was always the apple of her father's eye. He was proud that she also went to Balliol for her degree and more proud still that, like him, she could speak several languages including French, Spanish and Italian. Maxwell, always the sexist, was proud that she was a good-looking young woman too. Ghislaine's photograph was the only one he kept on his desk.

There were problems, however, between Maxwell and Ghislaine. He was always choosy over her boyfriends and would tell her so, often saying that she should 'forget' whoever her current beau was and find someone more suitable. He was very keen that his favourite daughter should marry well into a wealthy family. Like Kevin and Ian, Ghislaine always wanted to please her father.

She joined Pergamon for a while but wanted to make her own way in the world and found a job in the fashion industry. But in 1988 she returned to Pergamon. Now she was back in the fold, Maxwell decided it was time to put her under pressure to see how she could cope. She would be seen leaving his office in floods of tears after being given another berating, probably totally uncalled for, from her father.

It was while she was working as managing director of a new Maxwell enterprise, corporate gifts, that Ghislaine came to her father for help. She was going to New York and was thinking of dropping in on Donald Trump to sell him her corporate gifts. She asked Maxwell if he would phone Trump, as they were friends, to get her an appointment. She naïvely believed her father would praise her for showing initiative and help her; after all it was only one phone call. Maxwell rounded on her angrily: 'Have you got your bum in your head?' he exploded. 'Why the fuck would Donald Trump want to waste his time seeing you with your crappy gifts when he has a multi-million-dollar business to run?' And he slammed down the phone. Even Ghislaine couldn't win.

When Maxwell decreed that she should stop selling her gifts, he found another job for her. A year or so later she was given the rather grand task of flying around Europe writing about the great and the beautiful as a budding columnist for his brainchild the *European*.

I witnessed Maxwell together with Ghislaine on a number of occasions, usually in his office. She would be affectionate, going up to him and kissing him on his forehead while he was sitting at his desk, calling him 'Daddy', and he seemed, momentarily, to be genuinely pleased to see her. But if she stayed in the room for more than a few minutes Maxwell would grow impatient and want her out, suggesting she should go and leave him alone. But all the time she was in his presence Ghislaine would never be able to relax.

Maxwell would blow hot and cold towards his favourite child. Sometimes he liked having her around, to show off to important visitors, demonstrating that his progeny were slim and beautiful. He would often ask her to attend lunches or dinners to entertain important guests. He bought her a lovely little house in London's Stanhope Mews; he gave her a black VW Golf GTi cabriolet to flash around London, which she wanted; and yet on other occasions he showed remarkable meanness towards her.

Ghislaine, who only seemed to eat enough to keep a mouse alive, would occasionally pop into her father's kitchen in the suite and nibble at some smoked salmon or cheese or take some fruit. For some reason that made Maxwell furious and he would ban her from the kitchen, ordering his chef Martin not to give her food at any time without his express permission and, on one occasion, Maxwell ordered the locks of the kitchen to be changed just to stop Ghislaine helping herself to a tiny amount of the vast hoards of food that were kept there at all times. To me it was yet another example of Maxwell's pathological need to demonstrate his power over people. He exercised it over everyone who worked for him and more so over his own family. For some extraordinary reason Maxwell had to know that he was in control over everyone at all times.

Philip Maxwell was the second son, who felt, after the death of Michael, Maxwell's favourite son, that he had an impossible task ahead of him: to live up to his father's ambitions for him and to fill the shoes of his elder brother. Philip was blessed with a remarkable intellect, winning a scholarship in natural sciences to Balliol at the age of sixteen! He was to gain other degrees and achieve his doctorate at Sussex University.

Maxwell's overbearing attitude to his children is illustrated most graphically in a remarkable letter he sent to Philip after rewarding his entry into Balliol by sending him, at the age of sixteen, on an extended tour of North America. In his letter, which was businesslike and formal, Maxwell advised his son in five single-spaced, closely typed pages to pay heed to his advice, which made certain that Philip would have his father's guidance wherever he went.

Maxwell's letter was constructed under headlines ranging from 'Gaining Experience and Having a Good Time' to 'Observing the USA' and others such as 'How To Make Friends Amongst Young and Old' and the final heading was perhaps the most important, 'How to be of Use to Pergamon Press'.

So detailed were Maxwell's instructions to Philip about pushing Pergamon Press and meeting all Pergamon's editors, advisers and authors that his vacation seemed more like a busman's holiday for a travelling Pergamon salesman. Philip was instructed by his father: 'At each major centre that you visit be sure to telephone and arrange to call upon the university librarian, university bookseller and leading technical bookseller, bring him greetings from me and ask him whether he is satisfied with the services given by Pergamon. If not, what complaints does he or she have and what suggestions about improvements . . .'

Maxwell was never to use Philip to carry out any business deals, however, or give him responsibility within his empire, as he liked to with his other children and yet he always seemed to feel guilty towards his second eldest son and feel uneasy about the distance between them.

But it was Philip who put together *Robert Maxwell & Pergamon Press*, the prestigious 900-page history of the firm to celebrate Pergamon's forty years' service to science, technology and education, that was published in 1988.

Maxwell did not seem to have much contact at all with his three other daughters – Anne, the eldest, or the twins Christine and Isabel – but he did say once that he was unhappy about the way all his daughters had turned out, as though he had expected far, far too much of them all and somehow could not understand why they were not all brilliantly successful and famous.

*

84

Of course, it was Betty Maxwell who bore the brunt of Maxwell's abusive behaviour towards his family. I only witnessed scenes between them after 1986 when I began spending more time with Maxwell and travelling overseas with him. But it seemed to be of a pattern that had gone on for many years.

To all intents and purposes Maxwell often treated his wife as just another employee. He would ask her to attend such-and-such a dinner on his behalf; he would ask her to come to a lunch or a dinner at his suite in Holborn if he felt he should have his wife at his side for some occasion; he would request her to do this or do that, with hardly a please or a thankyou. Amazingly, Betty usually went along with what he wanted.

In New York, David Adler, Macmillan's communication director, remembers Mrs Maxwell asking him what bus she should take from the Helmsley Palace to go up town. 'Why take the bus, Mrs Maxwell?' Adler said to her. 'There are two cars out there with drivers standing idle.' Mrs Maxwell scrupulously replied, 'Oh, I couldn't do that, Mr Maxwell hasn't given me permission to take a car.' And she took the bus.

Sometimes Maxwell would play for sympathy, as though he were a child seeking favours from his mother; he often called her 'Mummy' and would sometimes seek her comfort, complaining he was tired, unwell and needed her support. She always heeded these rather pathetic cries for help and found herself again in a position in which she had to help him. He often used those tactics on his wife, particularly when he needed her assistance for whatever, even attending a dinner he couldn't be bothered to go to.

Infuriated at never seeing him for weeks at a time, Mrs Maxwell would send her husband memos informing him of her schedule. Other times she would fax him messages complaining that it was the only way she could contact him. On the occasions she arranged to get through on the phone, Maxwell would do all the talking – and she had phoned him!

On some occasions Mrs Maxwell would arrange to have dinner with Maxwell in his suite in London. Beforehand, she would arrange the menu with Maxwell's chef, Martin Cheesman, and be driven down from Oxford in her Bentley, always well dressed for an evening meal alone with her husband. She would ask his secretary or his butler, Joseph, to inform Maxwell that she had arrived. Sometimes Maxwell would tell her he could not have dinner with her, as he had important business. She would have to eat alone in the kitchen.

In front of guests, Maxwell often fawned over Betty, singing her praises in every speech, telling the world what a wonderful wife and mother she was and how fortunate he had been to find such a wonderful person to be his wife. I quite often sat and listened to this eulogy, watching Betty sit looking down at the table, thinking I know not what, seemingly embarrassed by this praise. She was forever faithful to him, never telling the world the downside of their marriage, totally supportive of him.

From remarks Betty Maxwell has made in interviews throughout her life, it does seem that she had happy times in her marriage. In 1982 she commented: 'I feel my life has been much richer with Bob than with anyone else I could have expected to marry . . . A girl should definitely not marry an ambitious man if she is not prepared to work with him, to take the rough with the smooth, to entertain thirty people to dinner without notice . . . And if you are lucky enough to live next to an exceptional man, you would be extremely stupid to think that a cushy life would have been better. I am very happy with my lot, although I must admit that sometimes it is hell.'

Betty did live a comfortable life. She had her own Bentley and a fulltime chauffeur; she had as many staff as she needed at Headington Hill Hall and she had an expense account for clothes. Usually, she liked to wear clothes she was comfortable in, that she had owned for some years, and would spend most of the money on designer ballgowns for the occasions when she had to substitute for Maxwell, attending social dinners and charity functions he couldn't make.

Maxwell was mean in other ways towards the wife who did so much for him. In 1989 Betty Maxwell had decided to buy a larger apartment in Tignes, France, where many of her children and others would go skiing in the winter and where Mrs Maxwell herself loved to go to enjoy the lovely alpine air. But she needed some more furniture for the larger apartment and asked Maxwell for money. He refused, telling her she had to find the money herself. So Mrs Maxwell went about raising the money and in the end took her jewellery to be valued to see if she could raise enough cash for the furniture. She then wrote to Maxwell, saying that if she sold most of her jewellery, and if he helped her with just a little extra money, she could afford to buy the furniture she wanted. To that Maxwell agreed.

Conflict would occur over the yacht, the magnificent 155-metre-long *Lady Ghislaine* of which he was most proud. Mrs Maxwell liked to visit the yacht for a week or so at a time and loved to be there, if possible, when Maxwell was aboard, which was usually during the holiday month of August. Maxwell sometimes, however, had other ideas for he complained that his wife fussed over him. One August, both Maxwell and his wife went to the yacht together to spend two weeks cruising around the Mediterranean. But after one week he ordered Kevin and his PA, Andrea Martin, to fly down, and invited some businessmen along as well.

Only hours after they arrived Maxwell announced at lunch that he had arranged for Betty to stay with her sister in

France for the following week and that she could use his plane to fly there. The plane, he added, was leaving in two hours so she had better pack immediately; and if she didn't take the flight in two hours then she could go later that day by a commercial flight.

Perhaps the best example of Maxwell's attitude towards his wife in his later years was at the wonderful dinner party laid on by her children to celebrate her seventieth birthday in 1991. Maxwell made a speech, a long speech. He never mentioned his wife – once!

And yet, at the end, when he knew his empire was about to crash like a pack of cards, he turned to his saintly wife for help. As he desperately tried to raise more funds from the banks, he phoned Oxford. 'I need you here,' was his way of inviting her. When she arrived she spent the next couple of days answering phones, handing him faxes. To the last, Mrs Maxwell was prepared to help her husband in any way he wanted, even down to doing the mundane office work that any number of secretaries employed by him could have done.

FIVE

◼︎◼︎◼︎

'Something must be done. I can't go on like this.'

Maxwell's mother appears to have been the principal influence on his life, far more so than his father, to whom he never showed the same respect, perhaps because Maxwell believed him to be a failure, unable to support his family properly on his wages as a humble labourer. On the very few occasions I spoke to Maxwell about his early life, his background, his parents or the holocaust, he always referred to his mother, and whenever he did so there were nearly always tears, genuine tears, in his eyes. He never forgot that the Nazis killed his mother and never forgave them, for, at a stroke, the person whom he respected and loved above all others had been torn from him.

Women were to play an important role, a vital part, in Maxwell's entire life because he felt he could depend on them in a way he never felt with men. In his unique way he depended on his ever-faithful wife Betty, whom he married during the war when he was a young man and whom he was to treat disgracefully. Yet he relied on her to bring up their large family and run the home so that he could get on with his life's work of making money and seeking power and influence.

He also came to rely on women as his trusted confidantes throughout his extraordinary business career. He seemed unable to cope unless he had by his side, at his beck and call, a woman whom he respected, who was super-efficient, helpful, competent, good company and good at her job. Maxwell wanted and needed personal assistants not just to help him work, and organize his life, but as a support to his ego, as an essential part of his idiosyncratic fibre.

Apart from his mother and his wife Betty, the first woman Maxwell put his faith in was Anne Dove, a woman in her thirties from an impeccable background, who had worked as a secretary for SOE, the prestigious and rather exclusive wartime British secret overseas executive, set up by Winston Churchill. She had worked first in London and later in Cairo and Italy. Though still young she was described at that time as extremely bright and highly efficient.

Anne Dove joined Maxwell in 1950 after answering an advertisement in the *Daily Telegraph* because she liked the idea of travelling the world, and was fascinated by his boundless energy and ambition.

Dove recalls that those times in the 1950s were breathless and exciting, as Maxwell charmed or, more frequently, harangued people into profitable deals. She recalls that Maxwell's staff were either amused or frightened by their boss's frequent and lightning changes of mood; from being generous, fun and amusing to venting his rage and anger at the slightest sign of insecurity by any member of staff – the sign of a bully. He was never to change.

Tom Bower in *Maxwell: the Outsider* states that many Jewish refugees believed Dove was instrumental to Maxwell's success in British society by introducing him to her impressive list of contacts gleaned while working for SOE. One of her more important contacts was Charles Hambro, of the London banking family, who had also worked for SOE.

Anne Dove remained Maxwell's loyal personal assistant for eight years before having to leave because she had a lung problem which doctors said would only improve if she lived at altitude. It was an amicable ending to a relationship which had seen Maxwell prosper amazingly, and much credit should have been given by Maxwell to his trusted colleague and secretary who had gone out of her way to introduce him to the powerful élite in Britain and make him a successful businessman.

Jean Baddeley was the next young woman on whom Maxwell was to depend a great deal for nigh on twenty years. Jean was an attractive, vivacious individual who caught Maxwell's eye and who was to devote her life to working for him and helping him in every way possible to be successful. Baddeley saw Maxwell through the deep depression of the Leasco fiasco when he was pilloried by DTI inspectors and nearly ended up bankrupt; and the high points when he took over a whole succession of British printing firms to become the number-one printer in Europe. She was still with him in 1984 when he finally caught the fish that had eluded him for twenty years – the ownership of a national newspaper.

Ms Baddeley gave up her life for Maxwell and ended up with very little; a Porsche 924 car, a directorship of some of his companies and a job, at a reasonable salary, in charge of promotions for the *Daily Mirror*. Maxwell was also to leave her £100,000 in his will, not much for a life's dedication and loyal service.

Jean Baddeley did everything for Maxwell. He would frequently take her on his journeys across the world and she would work night and day on his behalf. Not only did she toil as his personal assistant and secretary, typing all the important letters and messages, answering the phones and keeping in contact with London, she was also his hostess on these occasions, serving drinks, chatting to people and keeping them happy while Maxwell, as ever, kept them waiting. She also took care of his clothing, oversaw his packing, and checked that he looked immaculate for guests and briefed him on his next visitor.

At Pergamon headquarters Ms Baddeley ran his office for him with efficiency but, because she undertook so much of the detail work herself she was very demanding of the secretaries who worked under her. She was a hard but fair boss who only wanted super-efficient young women around her; she had no time for slow learners.

Quoted in the *Evening Standard* after Maxwell's death, Jean Baddeley still remained loyal to the boss she had loved and worked with for twenty years:

> What I felt for Robert Maxwell was love, but for all the right reasons. We were not lovers despite whatever people might think. My love for him was based on huge respect and deep affection for someone who was very important to me.
>
> What started as a kind of hero-worship – he was a kind of father figure at first – became love and admiration. He taught me a lot and I find it hard to believe he's gone. I miss him so much . . . I miss the phone calls . . . I miss not being able to talk to him, not having him there. He was incredibly kind. He was my best friend.

Still ferociously loyal, Ms Baddeley went on:

> I don't care if I am a lone voice in the wilderness. Nobody knows him better than me and although I know his faults – and like everyone, he's got them – I know the man he is at heart . . . I don't believe he ever intended to do anything criminal. I refuse to believe he meant to steal that money from the pension funds. It was just a desperate gamble to hold everything together. He would have paid it back. He always had.

Legend held that Maxwell had affairs with many women but Jean Baddeley refuted that. She commented:

> He had always been a very attractive man. I remember when I first met him he was very good looking and he's always had this magnetism. I used to fend off predatory females. When this woman claimed after his death that she'd had a seven-year affair with him, I laughed. I'd like to know when it took place. I was with him during all that time and, believe me, there was no room in his schedule. He was completely immersed in the business. But he did like pretty girls.

It was true. Throughout the seven years at *Mirror* headquarters Maxwell always had numbers of attractive young secretaries and receptionists but they seemed to be there to please the eye rather than for any other reason. After Maxwell took over the Mirror Group, their relationship seemed to change. I witnessed the most dreadful shouting matches in Tokyo in September 1987 when I accompanied Maxwell on one of his visits there. I was in Maxwell's suite reading a newspaper when I heard him shouting at Jean Baddeley, telling her: 'Stop flapping around me like a mother hen, will you, and leave me alone . . . I don't need your help . . . go away and leave me alone.'

I couldn't discern what Ms Baddeley said in reply, but then Maxwell replied in a rage, shouting: 'Just go, woman, get out, go,' and a disconsolate, red-faced Jean Baddeley emerged from the room looking understandably perturbed and annoyed. But she dealt with Maxwell and his moods in a remarkable way and when he monstered her, usually for no good reason, she simply withdrew until the rage had subsided and she could return to her duties, smoothing out whatever had gone wrong. Her reign as Maxwell's personal assistant had been remarkable, because she had been all things to him, and more, doing the work of two or three people.

For a short while, the effervescent Debbie Dines, a New Zealander with a risqué sense of humour, became Maxwell's chief assistant after Jean Baddeley's promotion. Maxwell liked having her around because she was light-hearted, jokey and, on occasion, treated Maxwell with a remarkable lack of respect. She loved to tease the new young secretaries who came to work for Maxwell, warning them to be prepared whenever they were alone with RM because he would 'jump on them', causing consternation in some of the girls, and interest in others. The secretaries would talk amongst themselves of how best to cope with Maxwell if he did indeed 'jump on them' when alone in a hotel suite in a far-off land. They also discussed, giggled and laughed at what it would be like having a six-foot-tall, twenty-stone man 'jumping' on them. Maxwell was casually chauvinistic towards some of them and disrespectful, occasionally smacking his secretaries on their backsides as they passed, whether he knew their names or not. Some smiled and giggled, others turned and glared, a few took no notice and said nothing and some decided they didn't like the treatment – and quit.

Ms Dines' temperament did not suit Maxwell and Ms Baddeley had been pushing forward a bright, young girl by the name of Andrea Martin, whom she had brought into her office as a member of her back-up staff.

Maxwell didn't like having Ms Martin around to start with; he never liked having new faces about him, preferring always to surround himself with those he felt at home with, not strangers whom he had to get to know. Ms Baddeley persisted, supporting Ms Martin and telling Maxwell that she was bright and competent. He didn't want to know.

One day in the autumn of 1987 Maxwell had to go to Paris for a day trip and Ms Baddeley had to stay in London. She suggested Ms Martin should accompany him. Maxwell was irritated, he didn't want to take a stranger with him, who didn't know him and his foibles.

Truculently, he asked Martin: 'Do you speak French?' trying to make her feel inadequate.

'Yes,' she replied.

'Fluently?' he demanded.

'Yes,' she replied again.

And in a gauche attempt to suggest he didn't believe her, he began speaking fast in French to her.

She replied perfectly to every question. Maxwell stood up straight and looked at her: 'You do,' he said, 'come along.'

During that day trip to Paris, Maxwell put Andrea to the test, asking her questions in French, making her phone people, pushing her with his demands. She passed the Maxwell examination, apparently with honours. After their return from Paris, Maxwell began phoning through to his outer office asking that Andrea should be sent in to do whatever was required. Within weeks she was acting as his personal assistant and when Maxwell moved his headquarters from the Mirror building in the spring of 1988 to the one next door, Maxwell decided the time had come to sever relations with the faithful Ms Baddeley and Debbie Dines. They were provided with other jobs and Andrea Martin stepped into the hot seat.

Andrea Martin was then twenty-four, a graduate from Bristol University, where she had gained a 2:2 in modern languages, who spoke French and German fluently. She had also attended a secretarial college and was efficient in shorthand and typing, the ideal qualifications for a personal assistant to someone like Maxwell. As Roy Greenslade recalls: 'It is difficult to avoid clichés in describing her: she was a good-looking blonde, well-dressed, cool, efficient and apparently unflappable. As the daughter of television comedian Bill Martin she had a well-developed but understated sense of humour which probably helped her cope with Maxwell's temper and his sudden changes of mind.'

Given the chance of being the PA to someone as ambitious and self-important as Maxwell, who appeared to be on speaking terms with every president and prime minister, Andrea Martin was determined to succeed. She virtually gave up her social life to work for Maxwell. Within weeks of taking the job she was expected to be at her desk by eight o'clock every morning and would usually still be there at eight o'clock at night. Lunch was a sandwich at her desk, or whatever she wanted from Maxwell's kitchen which was located in his private suite of rooms on the floor above his new offices next to the Mirror building which he purchased in 1986.

And she travelled the world with him. By 1987 Maxwell was playing the big billionaire for all it was worth; Pergamon was making money, Mirror Group was making money and Maxwell was being described as one of Britain's wealthiest men, at least a billionaire. He revelled in the limelight and was determined to live life to the full. It was at this time that he bought British Airways' helicopter division, not because he had any interest in running a helicopter firm but because he wanted a helicopter for himself to fly around Britain.

One of the main reasons why Maxwell had bought the building next door to the Mirror Group headquarters in Holborn Circus was because the Mirror building was not structurally sound enough to have a helipad on the roof, but the building next door was. It had been the headquarters of W. H. Smith, the newsagents.

He was also heartily fed up with airports and air travel.

He had been the first person to clock up a million miles' travel with BOAC back in the 1950s and, with his natural impatience for instant attention, he was a dreadful passenger for the hard-pressed ground and air staff to cope with. They were probably more relieved than anyone when Maxwell decided the time had come for Mirror Group to own its own aircraft. So, using Mirror profits, which of course all went to him as he owned the company totally, Maxwell purchased a Gulfstream 11 and its call sign was 'GO-VIP'. Maxwell loved that. Ostensibly of course the helicopter was owned by Mirror Group Newspapers and many were the times when the helicopter was needed to fly a photographer over the scene of a live news story, but when Maxwell was asked, as he had to be on every occasion, the picture desk was often told it was impossible, as Maxwell needed it for some other reason.

Maxwell was confident he had really staked his claim as one of the high rollers on the world scene when he purchased what became his pride and joy – his yacht, his floating palace, his favourite toy. Once again, presumably for tax reasons, the *Lady Ghislaine*, named after his youngest daughter, was officially owned by Mirror Group Newspapers but I cannot remember any occasion when the majestic, 155-metre yacht, which had been built for Adnan Khashoggi's brother, was ever used for any reason by the newspaper.

During those years at the end of the 1980s I accompanied Maxwell on many of his overseas excursions and he took with him his personal retinue, the team he had built up to accompany him. Occasionally, Peter Jay, his chief-of-staff, the title Maxwell borrowed from the White House chief-of-staff, would come too, but Peter preferred to stay at head office in Holborn and man the ship while Maxwell was overseas. Sometimes Joe Haines would be brought along, but he was happier on *terra firma*.

Wherever he went Maxwell wanted Andrea Martin to accompany him. To add prestige and distinction he employed Sir John Morgan as Head of International Affairs. Sir John, a highly respected career diplomat, had been British Ambassador to Poland, South Korea and Mexico before retiring and joining Maxwell. He and Peter Jay became good friends with a mutual respect for each other. I was there more, I believed, as a sort of equerry, to take the notes at Maxwell's meetings and converse with the officials and politicians we were meeting, while Maxwell was engaged in other matters. A most important member of the team from Maxwell's viewpoint was his favourite *Mirror* photographer, Mike Maloney. Whenever Maxwell met anyone, anywhere, any time, any place that he considered important, he had to have a photograph to record the event. Many was the time that the hard-pressed *Mirror* picture desk was ordered to send a photographer immediately to Maxwell's suite to photograph some dignatory or other. All these pictures were for posterity, to record the events of his life and the people he had met. It was a task which Mrs Maxwell was given by her husband, because Maxwell wanted to preserve, just like American presidents, a true and comprehensive record of his life amongst the leaders of the world.

And he often took with him on his travels his faithful, and very competent, personal valet, Simon Grigg, a charming young man who always kept calm, with a smile on his face, whatever mood Maxwell was in. Occasionally, he would even bring his personal chef, Martin Cheesman.

Maxwell was becoming more and more attentive to Andrea and giving her more authority. She had overall charge of his office, where Maxwell employed six or seven secretaries and receptionists; she controlled his daily schedule, ordered his business life, arranged his meetings, as well as taking the important letters and memos that Maxwell wanted only those he had complete trust in to see. Maxwell's suite of offices was a hive of activity twelve hours a day; there were never less than three receptionists at any time on the tenth floor answering phones and welcoming the people who came to see the great man.

And most of those Maxwell employed were good-looking young women. Maxwell was an appalling chauvinist, sacking newly appointed girls on the spot because he didn't like their looks. If they weren't easy on Maxwell's eye they were out, told to go that instant with only a week's pay in lieu of notice.

Time permitting, Maxwell himself liked to give potential recruits the once-over to see whether they appealed to him, but for most of the time Ms Baddeley and later Andrea Martin would make the selections because they knew what type of person Maxwell wanted around his office suite – and those he didn't.

On one occasion Maxwell fired a girl on reception, named Judy Welsh, because he said she was useless. But Judy was in fact a very good secretary and a job was found for her in the press office. A year later Maxwell, dealing directly with the press office, came across Judy Welsh. Immediately impressed with her excellent work he ordered her back into his inner office, blithely unaware that he had fired her the year before.

There were some budding secretaries and receptionists who wanted to work closer to Maxwell, their ultimate boss, to get to know this character, this alleged ogre about whom gossip never ceased. Others were attracted by his power, his position and, of course, his wealth.

One young, good-looking secretary Maxwell took a shine to was Lynn. He liked having her around his office, liked watching her as she walked around. He asked her to work late and stay behind for a drink and a chat; he put on the style, produced the champagne, played the tycoon billionaire with smiles and flattery, not a hint of aggression, rudeness, coarseness or violent temper. This was Maxwell the seducer at work.

But mere attraction wasn't enough for Maxwell. He only respected those girls who were good at their work and competent. They needed to be able to cope with Maxwell, his moods, his tantrums, his chaotic way of working; he actually liked his PAs to take control of his day, organize his schedule and, in a way, organize his entire life. Lynn wasn't in that league and his fancy ideas for her promotion soon withered.

And if Maxwell turned against a secretary, or anyone for that matter, there was no way they could win. And Maxwell turned against Lynn. If his secretary didn't show him all the invitations that had arrived that day, even the piffling little ones that not in a million years would he think of accepting, he would upbraid them. On the other hand, if Maxwell was shown an invitation he didn't want to know about, the poor girl would receive some withering remark. A secretary without Maxwell's confidence just could not win.

Lynn walked in one morning and handed him the invitations for the day; one was to a northern English town and Lynn asked him if she should put it in his diary. Maxwell exploded: 'Why the fuck would I want to go there? That place is the pimple on the arsehole of the country.' Lynn didn't last much longer.

Maxwell liked pretty girls with slim hips and he also liked those receptionists who played up to him, showed off to him, tried to attract his attention – but only if he liked their looks. One was called Mary-Jane, an attractive, slim-hipped girl with a large bust. Occasionally, Maxwell would invite her into his office for a drink after work, and one day she suggested to Maxwell that all the receptionists should wear smart, sexy uniforms. Maxwell went along with this idea and sent her out to find a suitable outfit.

It was a perfect uniform for Mary-Jane, showing off

her excellent young figure to perfection, but it would not have suited any other girls unless they were slim hipped and well endowed. Maxwell was enjoying the idea of this fashion parade. So, while about seven of his senior executives waited patiently outside his office for their important meetings with the chairman, he was waiting outside the ladies' loo for Mary-Jane to change into her sexy outfit. When she emerged, showing a lot of leg in her mini-skirt outfit, Maxwell loved it. He and Mary-Jane spent some time discussing the uniform, while she stood in front of him twisting and turning and walking up and down as on a cat-walk. He then decided he liked the outfit and gave her a load of cash to buy four uniforms for the receptionists. Days later Maxwell decided the girls also needed new white blouses to complete the effect. Again, he asked the lovely Mary-Jane to go and change and show off the new uniform, this time complete with the white blouse. Everything came to a halt while he stood watching her 'model' the outfit. He was enjoying himself immensely. In the end Maxwell purchased four complete outfits for his receptionists, but not many of the girls were happy with his selection.

Another attractive blonde girl who caught Maxwell's eye was a French girl, Marie. He liked having her around, one reason being that she often walked about his suite wearing short mini-skirts, see-through blouses and a big smile, but there was one problem; her English wasn't exactly perfect. That didn't seem to worry Maxwell too much, so, because she couldn't really work as a secretary with her poor English, Maxwell came up with the solution of making her a junior executive instead!

There were many rumours and stories of Maxwell's alleged sexual peccadillos while he was still alive, as there were about alleged goings-on at Maxwell House involving him and some of the lovely girls who worked there. The reality, however, was far more mundane in the years he lived in his suite high above Holborn Circus.

One of his secretaries did allege she was seduced by Maxwell in 1987. Dark-haired Vincenza Astone, just twenty at the time, was working in a secretarial pool when she caught Maxwell's eye. In one of Maxwell's own papers, the *Sunday Mirror*, Vincenza claimed, just a month after Maxwell's death, that she was seduced, bedded and fired by the tycoon.

She said:

> I was twenty at the time and very naïve; Maxwell was a very intimidating man. You couldn't say 'no' to him – or you would be fired. All his staff lived in fear of him.
>
> Sometimes he could be fun to be around, but sometimes he would come in to work in a terrible mood. He was always very affectionate in the office, putting his arm around me and saying how beautiful I was. I don't know why I slept with him – it just happened. He started fooling around and we ended up in bed. Immediately afterwards I regretted it. I went home and didn't tell anyone. He promised to give me a car and a flat but after seducing me he made me go home to Oxford on the bus. Days later he sacked me.

Asked if Maxwell was a gentle lover, Vincenza said: 'Only as gentle as a twenty-two-stone man can be. And he made me call him "Mr Maxwell" even when we were in bed.'

But for Maxwell this sort of fling seems the exception, although it is obvious he derived a vicarious pleasure from pretty, young staff surrounding him. The cool, efficient Andrea Martin was to become his most trusted and privileged personal assistant. She was the only person allowed to wander at will into his office no matter who was present and no matter what discussions were going on. She had the run of the place and in Maxwell's eyes could do no wrong. He came to rely on her to run his diary, his business life, his meetings, his office and his office staff. And he in turn became attentive to her needs. He would make sure she had what she wanted from the kitchen and the butlers were asked to provide her with whatever she wanted to eat; Joseph Pereira, his ever-faithful Portuguese butler, was instructed to serve Andrea with coffee, tea, wine, champagne or anything she required. Maxwell gave her her own American Express card to use 'when she saw fit' and all the bills went back to Pergamon. Maxwell provided her with an office car and was later to give her her very own black BMW 325i as a personal birthday present from him on her twenty-sixth birthday. Yet, as always with Maxwell, he didn't want to give too much – he paid Andrea peanuts for the job she was doing.

I first noticed Andrea when she was working for Ms Baddeley in Maxwell's outer office in the Mirror building and we met occasionally when I was called to see Maxwell after she had become his permanent PA. It was during a flying visit to Paris in 1987 that I saw her being pushed hard by Maxwell, demanding this and that, asking her to do two or three things at once. We were flying back to London in the helicopter, Maxwell, as always, sitting up front in the passenger seat next to the pilot and Andrea and I in the back. I saw tears streaming down her face, and instinctively put my hand on her knee and asked her, mouthing my words over the noise of the helicopter engine, 'Are you OK?' She nodded, and dried her eyes. I automatically knew Maxwell was the cause.

When we landed, Maxwell walked off and I asked her: 'Are you sure you're OK? Is there anything I can do?'

She just shook her head but was obviously still upset and miserable.

I said: 'Listen, if there is any problem just call me and I'm sure I'll be able to help. Don't let him get you down, don't let him push you too hard.'

She nodded and replied: 'Thanks, but I'll be all right.'

From that day on, there was an unspoken bond between us. She didn't call me about the helicopter incident and the next time I saw her in Maxwell's office she smiled and was cheerful and she looked in control of the situation. We began to see more of each other as we travelled frequently together to various European capitals with Maxwell. We would always have a chat, a drink in the evenings, but she complained to me that Maxwell would never let her out of his sight. I suggested to her that she should come out at night for dinner but Maxwell wouldn't let her. It became a challenge.

In Paris one evening in 1987, rather than stay and have a rather boring dinner in the Plaza Athenee Hotel, I preferred to go out to a small Parisian bistro to enjoy the real flavour of France. I suggested to Andrea that she should come.

'I can't, you know I can't; he won't let me.'

I asked her: 'Do you want to come?' and she replied that she would. So I tackled Maxwell.

'We're going out to a bistro and I thought it would be a good idea to take Andrea as well.'

'No, I need her here,' he replied.

'Come on, Bob,' I said, 'don't be a stick in the mud. She needs some fresh air; she has been confined to the suite all day; she should get out a little.'

Maxwell thought for a few seconds and then turned to Andrea: 'I hear you want some fresh air?' he queried.

'Well, it would be nice to get out,' she replied.

'All right then,' he had the audacity to reply, 'this once.'

It was during a visit to Tokyo that I really noticed the way Maxwell treated her. In the office in London he was quite correct with her, asking her to do this or that and treating her as though she was simply his personal secretary. But alone in his suite he behaved like a young swain towards her. I watched one day when Maxwell thought he was alone with her, as he often was. It was around eight in the evening and I walked in to have a glass of bubbly before dinner. Andrea was sitting on the sofa in his huge presidential suite in the Imperial Hotel and Maxwell was walking towards her with two glasses of champagne. He was smiling, looking attentively towards her, as though he were wooing her. I had never seen him act like this before, and I stood in the doorway and watched, feeling almost guilty at being there, like a voyeur. Maxwell behaved with such sweetness and charm. He seemed like a young man in love, trying to win the affection of a girl, smiling, laughing, joking, gesticulating, sitting on the sofa next to her, revealing in his body language that he was interested in her. For her part, Andrea sat stiffly on the edge of the sofa with her knees together, holding the champagne glass with both hands and hardly looking at Maxwell as he did all in his power to win her attention.

Somehow I couldn't barge in, so I left, quietly shutting the door, then walked back in five minutes later with a cheery 'Good evening, Bob, evening, Andrea, anyone for a glass?' I took no notice of Maxwell's frown, picked up the bottle from the ice and poured us all a drink.

Maxwell had always tried to be all things to Andrea: friend, father-figure, supporter, mentor, adviser and provider of all the best things in life. He had told her that he only wanted the very best for her, that he was happy to teach her everything he knew, introduce her to rich friends and the important people of the world. He had lent her a company apartment for some months while looking for a place near Holborn Circus where she could live with her boyfriend of long standing. She had found a place in Docklands and Maxwell said he would act as guarantor for the mortgage, which was too high for Andrea and her boyfriend to afford comfortably. He gave her a payrise of £3,000 a year which was still very low for the job she was doing, but he liked to keep her short of funds to show how wealthy he was.

For some time, Andrea and her boyfriend had been drifting apart, primarily because of the incredibly long hours Andrea worked and the time she spent abroad with Maxwell. They decided to split and Andrea told Maxwell, hinting that she would need another payrise to cope with the mortgage on her own.

Maxwell became a new man. He was more attentive than ever. In the evenings he insisted on opening Dom Perignon pink champagne, suggesting she stay for a bite of supper, suggesting they fly to the yacht for a few days in the sun to relax, inviting her to casinos to gamble. A few days later he suggested she should sell her apartment to save paying the high mortgage and she could stay instead in the spare suite in his apartment upstairs. Andrea related all this to me and I warned her to be careful.

He would phone her at her apartment at night, just to say goodnight, and he would ring again in the morning, allegedly to see whether she was up and on her way to work. His operation was a classic of its kind, but utterly transparent. At the office he was all sweetness and light, repeatedly asking if everything was all right, whether she needed more help in the outer office and making sure she was happy.

I began to sense a cooling in my relationship with Maxwell though he continued to phone often at night and first thing in the morning. When he couldn't contact me instantly he phoned the *Mirror* newsdesk and told them to contact me and ask me to phone him urgently. He would phone them every few minutes, demanding to know why they hadn't yet found me and castigating them for being inefficient.

How he discovered our affair I shall never know. But I

strongly suspect it was by his usual method of acquiring information inside the office – arranging to have people's phones tapped. It was a practice that to my knowledge began shortly after he moved in to the *Mirror* in 1984 and continued till his death.

It was always rumoured, and had always been suspected, that Maxwell bugged people's phones, but it was very difficult to prove. Maxwell kept a tape machine in his office specifically to listen to the tapes which had been recording his employees' conversations, along with a large box full of the 'bugged' ninety-minute tapes. He would listen to them either late at night when everyone had gone or early in the morning before seven o'clock, when he was alone. Over one period of several months every Monday morning when Peter Jay arrived at his office he had to ask the telephone engineers to come and unscramble his phones because they weren't working!

As his empire expanded and he took on more senior staff, particularly the accountants involved with the business side of the operation, Maxwell decided he needed a top security man to take care of everything. So Maxwell hired a former Scotland Yard chief superintendent of some repute, John Pole, a man who always called Maxwell 'Sir' and who suited his mania for security as well as his near-paranoid belief that everyone he employed was ripping him off.

I had always told Maxwell that the one overseas trip I did want to accompany him on was to Moscow to interview Mikhail Gorbachov, and Maxwell had promised that I would. So I found it slightly strange when Maxwell told me, in Jaunuary 1990, that he was going to Moscow and then on to Jerusalem but that I would not be going with him. 'I don't think I shall be seeing Gorbachov this time,' he proclaimed. But there was in fact a different, and very personal reason he did not want me in Moscow at that time.

Twenty-four hours after he flew out to Moscow I received

a phone call from Andrea who had, as usual, gone with him. She sounded concerned.

'He knows, he knows everything about us,' she said.

She then went on to tell me that from the moment they had left Heathrow, Maxwell had repeatedly asked her the same question, over and over again: 'Have you anything to tell me?' with no clue as to what he might be hinting at. Of course she replied that she hadn't, because she had no idea to what he was referring; but he persisted.

Eventually, she told me, Maxwell could contain himself no longer and blurted out that he knew she was having an affair with me. Then he began a long, obviously well-rehearsed speech, which amounted to a tirade against me; informing her that he knew what had been going on and telling her that he was only bringing up the matter for her own good because I was no good for her, a twice-married, twice-divorced man with teenage children who was old enough to be her father. Andrea told me he had quietened down but she was concerned at his total change of mood towards her.

Forty-eight hours later I received another call from Andrea from the King David Hotel in Jerusalem. She was in tears, obviously distraught, and sounded frightened. She could hardly talk through her tears. She told me that Maxwell had walked into her room that morning while she was only in her dressing-gown and had tried to force himself on her, trying to kiss her as she fought him off, shouting at him to stop, hitting out at him as she struggled to escape his bear-like arms.

She told me that Maxwell had suddenly come to his senses, realized what he was doing, as she refused his pleas to let him kiss her, let him hold her, as she shouted at him, 'No, no, no.' She told him to get out of the room and he had gone, saying that he only wanted to talk to her. She had locked the door and phoned me. I advised her that if she really feared he would attack her again then she should tell him she was flying back to London immediately on a scheduled flight and that if there was a problem I would book her flight from London. She hoped that he would have cooled down, realized how appallingly he had behaved towards her and that the matter would be ended.

'I can handle him,' she said before ringing off, 'I'm sure I can, but if I need you I'll phone again.'

Andrea phoned again the next day to report that all was well and that Maxwell had apologized, explaining that he had only wanted to talk to her, to persuade her that she was throwing her life away going out with someone like me. He had also told her that she should concentrate on her career, that he had given her a wonderful opportunity to make for herself a successful career in the business world, with his support, his help, his contacts and his money behind her. He kept telling her everything he had done for her during the past three years and how grateful she should be to him.

Later he put another proposition to her, suggesting that it was necessary for him to move to New York for six months to oversee the recently acquired Macmillan business. He offered her a salary of £50,000 a year, but she told him she didn't want to move to the States; he then told her that she wouldn't have to work at all but would still be paid £50,000 a year, would be given all the credit cards she wanted and would just have to be his companion in an apartment he planned to buy. But Maxwell refused to understand she didn't want to know.

Back in London the pressure continued. Every night before leaving the office Maxwell would warn her about me and my intentions; not wanting to use my name he would describe me as 'that dreadful man'. He offered to show her photographs of me with other women, but Andrea said she didn't want to know. He threatened to fire her, then told her he would fire me. His obsession to have Andrea for himself,

109

whatever the cost, reached a head one evening when he proposed to her, asking her to marry him and be his wife – without saying a word about Betty Maxwell, the woman to whom he had been married for nearly fifty years. Andrea was dumbstruck, just shaking her head and saying, 'No,' hoping he would understand that she wanted no personal relationship whatsoever with her boss.

Andrea needed her job and didn't want me to risk losing mine so it was decided we should separate for a while to see what happened, to let Maxwell calm down, to take the heat out of the situation.

It was in January 1990 that I had been tipped off by one of the *Mirror* security officers that I was a 'marked man', that Maxwell was out to get me. I will not give the guard's name for that would be unfair, he is still employed in the same job but at a different company. We met for a drink together, a mile from the office.

He told me that Maxwell had ordered a private detective agency to follow me round the clock, and another team had been assigned to follow Andrea. Every detail of our movements and any possible meetings had to be reported back to Maxwell every twenty-four hours. Maxwell told his security man that this was a high-security alert because Andrea and I were getting information from his office and passing it to Maxwell's rivals, which, of course, was bunkum. The security guard told me my company phone was bugged and advised me to lie low. I had suspected it for some time. He also reported that an investigation had been ordered to see whether Maxwell could purchase the apartment immediately adjacent to Andrea's in Docklands; and if that was possible the security staff were ordered to purchase it immediately, drill holes in the wall and install cameras to spy on her, all allegedly to protect the security of MCC and the Mirror Group!

I told Andrea what was happening and suggested she

110

check her office for bugs. She found what looked like a microphone, attached to a tiny camera, hidden in the high ceiling above her desk – and she immediately went in to Maxwell and asked him for an explanation. Feigning all knowledge and seemingly consumed with interest at this amazing discovery, Maxwell immediately hurried into her office to see the alleged evidence.

Shaking his head, unable to understand what on earth the object could be, Maxwell reassured Andrea that it was 'nothing to concern' her, and said that 'to make absolutely sure' he would immediately call John Pole to investigate. Pole came straight away, looked at the ceiling and said he would carry out a further investigation that night after everyone had gone home. Surprisingly, the next day the offending 'object' had disappeared and Maxwell informed Andrea, and the rest of the outer office, that the mystery object had been part of the air-conditioning system. Engineers had been called and the system repaired.

I knew I was being followed by private detectives and presumed my phone was constantly bugged. I was also fed up with Maxwell's continued tirades about me that he was giving almost daily to Andrea, and decided to go and see him.

'What do you want to see me about?' was his first question.

I wasn't going to be put off by Maxwell's sham surprise: 'You know perfectly well why I want to see you. I want you to stop bugging my phone and having me followed.'

An actor to the end, he opened his eyes wide as though in utter disbelief. 'I don't know what you're talking about,' he said, spreading out his hands.

I replied curtly: 'Come off it, Bob, you know damn well what I'm talking about.'

'Wait a minute,' he said politely as he picked up the phone. 'Get me John Pole and ask him to come and see me immediately,' he said. While waiting we talked about work.

As Pole entered, Maxwell told him that I had just made some very serious accusations against him, that my phone was being tapped; that I was being trailed. And then in a charade that must have been rehearsed a dozen times Maxwell said to Pole: 'Tell Mr Davies, is it possible to bug his phone?' Pole replied: 'Absolutely impossible, sir; couldn't do such a thing on this phone system.'

Maxwell turned to me with a hurt expression on his face: 'There you have it, your accusations are without foundation.'

I said: 'Bob, not for one minute do I believe my phone can't be bugged. You know full well that with the right equipment any phone can be bugged.'

'You're right,' he said, 'I will have John Pole and the telephone engineers go to your phone immediately to examine it and see what we can find.' He turned to Pole: 'You must do that right away as a matter of priority and report back to me,' and dismissed Pole with a flick of his hand.

I knew there was no point in continuing the discussion. He knew that I knew I was being bugged, whatever he said, and he knew that I knew he was lying through his teeth. But we both knew the conversation had come to a point where there was no point in continuing. I left wondering if I had done enough to stop him snooping. I doubted it.

Then Maxwell began his plan to have the new *Mirror* editor, Roy Greenslade, who had only taken over the editor's chair weeks before, fire me. It was a gauche plan by Maxwell's standards. Greenslade described in his book the time when Maxwell tried to make him fire me for lying.

One example was when Maxwell asked me to fly to Berlin to check on the progress of the East German elections. I discussed the matter with Greenslade and set off. On arrival, as usual, I phoned the *Mirror* newsdesk in London and gave them my hotel, room and phone number. In the early hours of the morning Maxwell phoned me directly and told me I had to take the dawn flight to Bonn to cover another story. In the morning, while I was in transit, Maxwell phoned Greenslade, allegedly looking for me. He raised hell that no one knew where I was, that I had insulted the editor in moving without his permission and that Greenslade should treat it as a most serious offence. Of course no one knew where I was, but, as always, I called the *Mirror* desk as soon as I had checked into my Bonn hotel. They were most relieved to hear me: Maxwell had been giving them a rough time as they had been unable to locate me. Then I spoke to Greenslade.

'What the hell's going on?' he asked, totally perplexed.

I explained.

Greenslade was stunned. He spluttered: 'Maxwell sent you. But he's been raising hell that you had disappeared.'

I told Greenslade that when I returned to London I would see him and I would explain everything. What I didn't know was that Maxwell used this alleged 'offence' of mine to push Greenslade very hard into firing me. It was as a result of this fracas that Greenslade realized that Maxwell was probably bugging his phone calls, for Maxwell began commenting on matters only Greenslade and I had discussed over the phone.

As a recently appointed editor Greenslade showed considerable strength in refusing Maxwell's repeated demands that I should be fired.

In an effort to make sure Andrea and myself saw as little of each other as possible, Maxwell contrived to keep us as far apart as possible. He would send me on foreign trips as often as he could, whenever a story arose. He sent me all over Europe on one pretext or another, telling everyone that I was his most important journalist, that I was carrying out the most important work on behalf of the

Mirror and the *European*. I realized of course that it was all a charade.

Maxwell arranged for me to spend most of the day working at the *European* and then going to the *Mirror* at 4 p.m. and working as foreign editor there. I had no deputy at that time and was, in effect, doing two jobs. Then most Saturday mornings he would phone and call me in to work on the *Sunday Mirror*, making sure I was working six or seven days a week.

Andrea meantime was having a tough time with Maxwell because he would not let matters rest, but kept nagging her to go and work in New York with him as well as keeping up an incessant tirade against me. On one occasion she phoned from home at lunchtime telling me that Maxwell had reduced her to tears and she had broken down in the office and walked out.

After seeing her I persuaded her to return to work and said I would see Maxwell. I went immediately to his office to confront him. In no uncertain terms I told him that I thought his behaviour was disgraceful, that he was treating Andrea in a despicable and grossly unfair way and that he should apologize to her. I warned him that she would quit unless he changed his attitude to her, that he should show her the respect she warranted for the work she did for him and that he should also apologize to her for reducing her to tears. I was quietly furious and was not going to let him behave in this way to her. I told him I thought it was appalling that he should employ her at such a low salary when she was the most vital person on his staff, working twelve hours a day and more.

Later that day he did apologize to Andrea, promising he would treat her better in future and increasing her salary by £10,000 a year.

But that was not the end of the matter. The crunch came on the day the *European* was launched in the spring of 1990. He discovered that we were once again seeing each other and summoned me to his office.

He shut all the doors and told the secretaries to put no calls through, a rare occurrence. He sat, slumped on a chair, looking across the table at me. 'We must talk,' he began and I nodded. I wondered what his ploy would be. 'I have to talk to you about Andrea.' I nodded again. But Maxwell couldn't talk, he was physically unable to talk, emotion was running so high through his body, constricting his throat.

He managed to say 'water' and as I thought he was about to faint I rushed out and asked a secretary to get a large glass of water immediately. That helped, and after drinking the water slowly he began to talk.

'We can't go on like this, you know,' he said. 'We must have an agreement.'

I asked him what he proposed. 'I don't know, but something must be done. I can't go on like this.' I had never seen Maxwell so exposed, so open, so vulnerable and as I sat there I began to feel sorry for him. It crossed my mind that the old bugger might be acting, but I didn't think he was.

I told him that I realized he was obsessed by Andrea, that she was a first-class PA, but that he had no rights over her; that she must be allowed to lead her own life. I told him that he had been kind to her, that he had given her an amazing opportunity at such a young age but shouldn't try to control her life. He nodded and looked downcast and defeated. But he wasn't finished yet.

He asked me to get him an orange juice and I did so, ordering a cup of tea for myself. He told me that I should stop seeing Andrea for her sake, that I was far too old for her and that she should be allowed to find someone else so she could settle down and marry someone more her age. I told him that I knew I was far too old for her, had told her so frequently, and that had to be a decision for her to take.

Then he said that if we continued seeing each other he

would have to fire Andrea because the editors would not want a senior editor having an affair with his PA, since I would then know more than they did. It would be bad for business. I nodded.

'That being the case, I shall resign,' I told him. 'Andrea is far more vital to you as your PA than ever I am as foreign editor; you're always describing her as your right arm; you can easily go and find someone else to do my job.'

He drank his juice and patted the table with his hand, the signal the chat was over. 'I'll be in touch,' he said, and he added conspiratorily: 'This is strictly between you and me. No one must know of this conversation. You are my friend.' I left not knowing whether I had a job or not; but I knew I had an enemy.

He changed tack. Maxwell began a 'phone bombardment' campaign, calling me wherever I was, morning, noon or night, accusing me of lying, of not informing Greenslade of my whereabouts, of not informing Maxwell of the stories I was covering every day. I told him most forcefully that he was wrong, and that I would not let him accuse me of lying when he knew his allegations were 'absolute bullshit'. I was determined not to let him bully me. After a couple of weeks he stopped.

We had three or four further chats about Andrea. He would call me up to discuss a story or office politics, and would become nervous and agitated and start to shake. I knew what was coming, and it always did. 'How are you getting on with our friend?' he would ask, meaning of course Andrea. 'Fine, thank you,' I would reply. Then he would go through the same routine, saying things couldn't continue the way they were and that he didn't want to lose me, nor his 'right arm'. Every time, I told him that if anyone had to leave, it should be me.

For a few weeks Maxwell managed to be kind and straightforward with Andrea but two or three times a week he would lose control and have a go at her, telling her she must stop seeing 'that dreadful man'. Then he would realize he had lost control of himself again and apologize to her, tell her he was only advising her for her own sake, for her future.

One day in May 1990, Maxwell could take the situation no more. For no apparent reason he exploded, yelling at Andrea to get out of the office that instant, that she was fired, that he wasn't going to allow her to stay a minute longer in the building. He ordered her to hand over all the keys, her cards, her security pass and to get out. She phoned and told me. I advised her to leave.

Within days he was on the phone to her begging her to return to the office, apologizing for his actions, and promising all would be fine; that the office could not operate without her and that he needed her at this most crucial time. She returned, but the same was to happen again and Andrea decided she could take no more. She told him she was leaving and he told her to get out, but that she wouldn't get a penny. He berated her until she broke down and cried. Every time she tried to talk sensibly to him Maxwell would go wild, tearing into her, shouting at her until she was reduced to tears.

I decided to go and see him again. Our relationship by now had changed dramatically. I told him most forcefully that I was amazed that he could treat Andrea in the way he had, when he said he cared so much for her. I told him he was behaving like a bully to a defenceless girl who was just trying to do her job under the most difficult circumstances. I said his behaviour was disgraceful and that he should be ashamed.

He didn't say a word but sat there and took it. Then he raised his hand for me to stop talking. 'What are we going to do?' he asked.

'Well, you've blown it with Andrea,' I told him, 'she can't take any more, she won't come back.'

117

He looked hurt. 'Are you sure?'

I nodded.

Later I was to return to thrash out Andrea's leaving package with him. He did agree that he had given her the black BMW as a birthday present in August 1989 and it was hers. After she had left, Maxwell never let up. Daily, usually two or three times a day, he would phone her at home, sometimes begging her to return, promising the world. On other occasions he would begin a conversation in a pleasant, chatty way and end up berating her till she could take no more and she would just put down the phone.

Until a couple of days before his death Maxwell continued to phone Andrea, usually a few times a week. Most of the time he would be pleasant because he had finally realized he couldn't bully her into going back to work for him. He kept telling her that he needed her expertise, her company, her professionalism. He told her the number of PAs he had employed but with whom he could not work. He told her he could not get her out of his mind and sometimes he begged her to return. He tried to be sweet but on occasions he couldn't control himself and would start haranguing her.

There was one other woman whom Maxwell had a crush on in the last few years – Mrs Ulrika Pohl, the wife of Dr Karl Pohl, President of the Deutsches Bundesbank. He told me that he thought she was 'the perfect woman'; beautiful, intelligent and stylish. He persuaded her to manage the public relations side of the *European* launch in Germany, which gave him the excuse for frequently phoning her and inviting her to London for business meetings. I saw the two of them together on several occasions and Maxwell seemed to have a mild crush on her, oozing charm towards her, smiling and joking and being over-attentive. At the first anniversary party of the *European*, held at the Waldorf in

London, Maxwell asked me to look after her, see that she wanted for nothing, as he expected to arrive late. 'Take care of her, she is a very important woman,' he instructed. At the party, Mrs Pohl reflected, when we got round to the topic of Maxwell, that she thought he was a 'sweet, charming man who still had a twinkle in his eye'. Later, I told Maxwell Mrs Pohl's view of him and he beamed, pleased with her description.

SIX

'I've decided to appoint myself Editor-in-Chief.'

The trouble with Maxwell and his passionate love affair with newspapers was that Maxwell was primarily a printer of newspapers, never a publisher and never an editor. It was probably one of the reasons why he demanded from the moment he took over Mirror Group Newspapers in July 1984 that he insisted he be called 'The Publisher'. He loved the title he awarded himself and many of his staff did indeed call him 'Publisher' when addressing him.

It was such a pity that Maxwell could not confine himself to the printing side of the business and leave the editorial decisions to those with more experience and more capability, but that was the furthest thought from Maxwell's mind. Though he had a thousand other concerns to occupy him his major interest was always the newspapers.

In fact Maxwell never liked journalists, nearly always referring to them as 'reptiles'. He was always very wary of them, believing their main object in life was to catch him out, prove him wrong and reveal anything that could be damaging to him or his business empire. He would tell his secretaries: 'Get me the reptile from such and such a newspaper,' and he would be equally dismissive of journalists who worked on the broadsheets as those on the tabloids.

Using his customary intuitive charm, however, Maxwell started surprisingly well at the *Mirror* in the days following his dramatic takeover, when the journalists and the printers believed having Maxwell as the proprietor was akin to putting a mad general in charge of nuclear missiles. Yet his early promises sounded like a breath of fresh air. He announced that he hadn't got the time to make changes in the papers and, more importantly, that the *Mirror* papers were staffed with such talent that it would be foolish to tell people how to do their jobs: 'I have given a genuine guarantee of editorial integrity,' he said, 'and, furthermore, the editors are not just a bunch of lackeys and zombies who will do what I bid them.' He decreed that there was to be no chequebook journalism and no Page Three nipples, high-mindedly saying his *Mirror* would leave that type of journalism to the *Sun*. Unfortunately, his high-sounding promises counted for absolutely nothing. During the seven years Maxwell owned the *Daily Mirror* hardly an editorial comment ever went into the paper without it first being approved by Maxwell personally.

And he could not keep his hands off his new toy. Within days he was demanding to see the leaders, and then rewriting them, demanding to see the front page, making suggestions – which sounded more like orders – that had to be carried out. Surprisingly, in those first few weeks and months circulation of the *Daily Mirror*, his flagship paper, increased. Maxwell believed it was down to his intervention, to his changes, to his picture appearing so frequently in the paper. Then sales turned down and Maxwell was convinced that more of his presence in the paper would send them up again. Everyone else realized that the public, at first inquisitive to see Maxwell's *Mirror*, now realized the *Mirror* spark had gone and it was becoming a *Daily Maxwell*. The readers stayed away in increasing numbers.

A year after Maxwell took control, the *Mirror*'s circulation fell by 350,000 to around three million, upsetting Maxwell's pledge to boost sales to four million in his first year at the helm. The combined daily loss of the group was a staggering one million sales. As *Marketing Week* said: 'It takes something close to genius to lose so much circulation so quickly.'

Naïvely Maxwell commented: 'I don't think my interference has any effect on the sales of the paper except to improve the adrenalin throughout the building . . . whether I appear in the paper or not, that's a matter for the editors to decide, not for me . . . It's the editors who interfere in the publisher's prerogative, not the other way round.'

As Maxwell took stock at the end of his first year as a newspaper tycoon he realized making profits in Fleet Street was going to be no easy task, nothing like the ease with which he turned round burned-out printworks and made them churn out profits. Not only were circulations falling around him like confetti at a wedding, but his Mirror Group was making less profit than the miserable £800,000 it had made in the last year under Reed's ownership. Something had to be done.

He challenged the unions to reach an amicable agreement with him, won over their help for his 'survival plan' which would result in the loss of more than 2,000 highly paid jobs, so that the *Mirror* would survive. Of course, Maxwell had to make generous redundancy terms but the Fleet Street unions realized by then that the days of plenty were rapidly coming to an end. To give him credit, Maxwell managed to achieve the much-needed cuts in the army of printworkers without the appalling scenes Murdoch experienced at Wapping.

Months later, with the staff slashed by two thirds, work began on training the staff to run the newly installed computer-controlled production technology. For once, having made the decision, Maxwell left the qualified staff to get on with their jobs, and the result was hugely successful.

It enabled the *Mirror* to lead the British tabloid press in full-colour printing but the editorial content lacked the flair required to take advantage of the opportunity.

Throughout his seven years at the *Daily Mirror*, Maxwell never lost his enthusiasm or his interest for the newspaper, or for that matter any of his newspapers. He wanted to edit them, run them, control them – and everyone who worked in them. That meant he clashed repeatedly with all his editors. Quite naturally, the editors wanted to be left in peace, left alone to do the jobs to which he had appointed them. The last thing they wanted was the management, let alone a megalomaniac publisher, issuing decrees from on high every day. And, with Maxwell's legendary short span of interest and low boredom level, his interests were either all-consuming or nothing.

He tried to settle the miners' strike of the 1980s by holding a secret meeting in Sheffield with Arthur Scargill and Peter Heathfield, the union's general secretary, but it came to nothing. He tried again at the 1984 TUC annual conference but once again nothing happened. What this meant to the *Mirror* was that the miners' strike was frontpage news – and Maxwell loved being involved in any front page.

Other campaigns followed. Maxwell was determined to do all he could to warn of the menace of drugs, heroin, cocaine and marijuana, that had started to be used among schoolchildren. He pushed stories warning of AIDS.

Naturally, Maxwell's main interests were overseas. One of his earliest briefings to me was his vision of foreign news: 'I don't want any of this African crap, that's finished. I want you to concentrate on Europe, that's the future. Understand?' I nodded. 'Good, get on with it, then.' And he dismissed me with a flick of his hand.

Shortly after taking over the *Mirror*, Maxwell issued a decree informing Molloy to close down every foreign bureau immediately. In the early 1980s the *Mirror* had staffers in

New York, Washington and Los Angeles, Paris, Rome and Brussels, a very creditable representation in the news centres of the world for a Fleet Street tabloid.

Furthermore, Maxwell had also banned all retainers (regular monthly payments made to freelance journalists working overseas for one particular paper, to keep their loyalty and make sure the paper has instant access to good journalists when necessary). Now, for a newspaper to work without staffers overseas is difficult enough but to work without freelances is virtually impossible.

I was called in by Molloy and given this devastating news.

'Absolute ban?' I asked him.

'Yes,' he said, 'I tried, but you know what he's like. On this one he's adamant.'

I nodded, and said I would try and find a solution. I had to find one, otherwise being foreign editor of the *Mirror* would be an impossible task.

Two days later I went back to Molloy and told him that he could tell the publisher with his hand on his heart that not only were all staffers being withdrawn as soon as practicable, but that no retainers would be paid; just as he said.

'What are you going to do?' Molloy asked.

'Don't ask me,' I said. 'But don't fear, you can tell him that no retainers will be paid.'

No retainers were ever paid. However, I did ask every freelance to submit his office expenses each month and before submitting them I would discuss what those expenses would be. From that day on I told each and every editor that when Maxwell asked them they could tell him quite honestly that no retainers were ever paid. He never found out.

In his book, Roy Greenslade recalled a typical example of Maxwell's interference, when Soviet tanks moved into

Vilnius, the capital of Lithuania, in a bid to subdue the independence movement. Greenslade asked leader-writer David Thompson to put together a comment piece either describing Gorbachov as a liar for sending troops into Lithuania, or saying he had lost control of his army commanders. When Maxwell, who was in New York at the time, read the faxed leader he exploded, ordering Thompson to change the leader totally, explaining the Lithuanians had brought the ordeal on their own heads for directly threatening Soviet authority.

Greenslade tried in vain to argue with his boss, who would brook no challenge on this point. Maxwell shouted: 'We must not abandon Gorbachov. I will decide.' Greenslade pressed his point, to no avail.

Finally, an icy Maxwell said: 'Look, mister, you are talking nonsense. Don't you realize Gorbachov wouldn't do anything without ringing me first?'

I was standing by Greenslade while all this was going on. Greenslade was understandably angry and frustrated. I suggested that I would go and write the story as hard as I thought fit – because Maxwell could not argue with the facts. Greenslade put a big picture on page one showing a baton-wielding Soviet paratrooper lashing out at a cameraman under a headline, 'Back to the bad old days'. And a sub-head reading, 'Gorby soldiers massacre thirteen in night of blood'.

Throughout the year Greenslade and I pulled many such manoeuvres over Maxwell when we felt justified in so doing. Sometimes, Maxwell would call me up and tell me what he wanted in the leader, particularly leaders about foreign affairs. I would then be told to pass on the 'golden words' to Greenslade and Thompson.

Sometimes he would call me upstairs and tell me what to write for the paper. But, from those times I had spent travelling with Maxwell, I knew two important facts; one, that he never bothered to read the *Mirror* in detail the next day, and two, that he could never remember what he had said. Quite often I would return from meetings upstairs and deliberately alter what Maxwell had written so that it made more sense and to stop the paper looking silly. After doing so I would then inform Greenslade, explaining why, and tell him to let Maxwell talk to me if there were any problems. There never, never were.

Maxwell's interference knew no bounds. He even decided to make himself in charge of wastepaper bins on the *Mirror* editorial floor. One day, after new technology terminals had been installed and the editorial floor spruced up to look as modern as any newsroom in the world, Maxwell came wandering down. He was very proud of his flashy newsroom. He stopped and looked at the large red wastepaper bins which had black plastic bags inside.

He turned to me: 'Who is in charge of these?'

I replied: 'I've no idea.'

So he turned to the newsdesk: 'Get me the man in charge of these bins.'

Maxwell quietly strolled around the hundred-metre-long room and waited. Within a few minutes two or three management men came up, out of breath. 'Why are there binliners in these?' he asked.

Naïvely, they replied: 'Because there are, there always have been.' But that was like a red rag to a bull.

'Then go away immediately and inform me in one hour,' he said, 'how much this is costing me. I want to know how many we use every year and how much I can save.' And he walked off.

The following day I was approached by those in charge of bins. They told me they had worked out that the binliners cost about £50,000 a year, and informed Maxwell, who had exploded and told them to take out all the black plastic bags and never use them again. They came to me for advice.

I asked them if the binliners were necessary.

'Of course,' they all chorused, 'no one will take away the rubbish if it isn't in binliners, no one.'

I asked them if anyone had told Maxwell and they shook their collective heads. 'Well, just go back up there, together, and tell him,' I advised.

Within hours they were back, their staff putting back the binliners. One said to me: 'He was great. He just said, "Do it"! You could have knocked me down with a feather.' But those victories were the exceptions.

In 1987 Maxwell suddenly decided that the editorial floor of the *Mirror* should be guarded. And he wanted to appoint a big, strong black man to fill the post. He called his advertisement boss and told him to put an ad in the paper for a 'big, strong black man' to act as a security guard. Aghast at such an ad, the man said: 'You can't put that in an advertisement, it's against the race relations law.' Immediately Maxwell came up with a solution: 'Put in any advertisement you like but I want to see a big black bastard there in a week.' And in a week a most delightful, shy, black Ghanaian who had been a shotputter in the Ghana Olympic team was standing there on duty.

As well as his consuming interest in the *Mirror*, Maxwell's brain was wrestling with other ideas he had always wanted to put into operation. He was always contemplating a new toy. For some extraordinary reason Maxwell had always dreamed of publishing a twenty-four-hour newspaper, though those papers in the United States that boasted they were twenty-four-hour journals were living under a misapprehension; in America they were just papers with more than one edition. Most of Britain's major newspapers have three main editions each night. As usual, Maxwell could not be persuaded of the case and he was determined to fulfil his dream of bringing out a twenty-four-hour London paper, to be called the *London Daily News*.

In some ways, one of Maxwell's strengths was that he was a man of action; he made a decision and expected it to be carried out immediately, come what may. Naturally, it was also one of his greatest weaknesses because he never believed it was necessary to plan anything. He believed everything worked as if he were talking to his stockbroker; all he had to do was say 'Buy' or 'Sell' and it would be done. Planning an entirely new newspaper from scratch takes time and trouble, planning and schedules, team building and a host of other vital ingredients to make sure the paper gets off on a sound footing. All that was anathema to Maxwell who, in reality, wanted an instant newspaper.

The birth, life and death of the *London Daily News* was classic Maxwell. He believed it was only necessary to hire some journalists, organize the printing, get in some staff to sell advertising, organize street vendors and, hey presto, a newspaper was born! It doesn't work like that except in Maxwell's mind.

The *LDN*, as it was always called, began with a week-end talk-in for the paper's twelve senior editors, to which Maxwell took immediate exception. It was held at beautiful Ettington Park and on the third day Maxwell arrived with Mrs Maxwell from Oxford by helicopter. He was bull-ish and confident, telling his editors: 'You are the staff I have hired, and I am going to stick with you through thick and thin. There will be no blood-letting. I am not the kind of proprietor who will close you down. You have my guarantee that you have two to three years to prove yourselves.' His speech ended on a churlish note: 'I see from all this,' gesturing with his arm to the excellent lunch they had just enjoyed and the lovely surroundings, 'that you have already learned how to spend my money.' The editors applauded his confidence in the paper and faith in their work, but the cheers were soon to turn to tears.

Stephen Clackson, a journalist with flair who had been seasoned by hard work on the *Evening Standard*, was appointed managing editor of the *LDN*. He recalls the haphazard way the paper came together with no one in full control of any department because Maxwell demanded that he be in command of everything.

One of the main problems was to be persuading the street vendors to sell the *LDN*, because Lord Rothermere had decided he was going to see off Maxwell's newspaper as quickly as possible; he didn't want any other proprietor nibbling away at the profits his *Evening Standard* brought in from its virtual monopoly of London's daily classified ads.

One day Clackson's wife had a chat with a newsvendor in Oxford Street who said that with all the aggravation he had decided to call it a day and hand over his pitch. This information was in stark contrast to reports that the vendors were falling over themselves to sell the *LDN*, hoping to double their income. Clackson told this to Jack Ferguson, the managing director, who ordered him to phone Maxwell immediately with the news. He told Maxwell the facts, who replied, 'This is very valuable information. Tell your wife I deeply appreciate this.'

'At the crack of dawn the next day,' Clackson recalls, 'something like six o'clock, there was a phone call from the porter telling us a bunch of roses had just been delivered to my wife. Remarkable.'

Clackson went on: 'Now, that's the odd side of Maxwell. In the midst of doom and gloom before the launch, chaos and energy, he performs a little gesture like that out of an innocent conversation. I was thinking how kind it was of him until I heard later that, as a result, the entire circulation staff had been sacked. It also made me think, because I worked for him, that to go to the trouble of delivering a bunch of roses at six o'clock in the morning some poor bugger had been told to get up at the crack of dawn, go to Covent Garden flower market at Nine Elms, buy some roses and deliver them to the Barbican. So my wife gets the roses and says, "Ooh, what a nice man Mr Maxwell must be", some poor bugger's home life has been ruined, and a number of people are fired on the spot. That was Maxwell.'

As launch date approached, chaos turned to frenzy at the *LDN*. Maxwell's appointed managing director, Bill Gillespie, a former Murdoch employee who knew the newspaper business well, had quit, unable to cope with Maxwell's turns and twists. So Maxwell took over as managing director.

Thames Television were waiting to interview Maxwell, and his public relations officer, a former Downing Street press officer in the Wilson era, Janet Hewlett-Davies, was scurrying around trying to put everything in order for the interview. Maxwell was shouting at her, asking her in his deep voice: 'What the fuck are you doing?'

Maxwell wanted a poster of the *LDN* pinned on the wall behind him so that it would be in the shot throughout the interview. Maxwell told Hewlett-Davies: 'All you had to do was pin a poster on the wall and you can't even do that. You are fucking useless.' Within a year she had quit.

Then he turned to Stephen Clackson and asked him how many free copies of the *LDN* had been given away as pre-launch dummies of the paper. Clackson told him: 'About 250,000.'

Maxwell turned to him: 'You're sure of that, you're positive of that figure?'

'Yes,' replied Clackson, 'I'm positive.'

Within seconds Thames TV's cameras were whirring and the interview began: 'Today,' Maxwell boomed, 'we have given away 500,000 copies of the *London Daily News!*' Totally oblivious to facts, as he was throughout his business life, the super-optimist Maxwell had exaggerated out of all recognition.

Sometimes, however, Maxwell was caught out in the web of lies and deceit he constantly wove. On one occasion the *LDN*'s editor, Magnus Linklater, who did a remarkably good job in a short space of time under the most enormous difficulties, was having a beer with Maxwell one evening when, by accident, a young boy came through on the phone. Maxwell loved picking up wrong numbers and having conversations with whoever was on the other end. It tickled his sense of humour. After debriefing this boy, who had just led a walk-out at his school, Maxwell decreed that it was a wonderful story for the *LDN*.

He put down the phone and said to Linklater: 'I recognize a good story, you know; it's training. I used to be a cub reporter.'

Linklater was convinced Maxwell had never been any-thing of the sort, so he replied: 'No, you weren't, Bob, you've never been a reporter.'

Maxwell looked at Linklater and the other people in the room, not sure how to play this lie. Finally, he replied: 'It was a previous incarnation,' and roared with laughter.

Clackson recalls walking through the advertising depart-ment a week before the paper folded. The classified depart-ment should have been buzzing with ten or so telephonists taking calls from advertisers, but all he saw were two girls, one having a cigarette and the other chatting to her boyfriend on the phone. So he moved on to display advertising, which should have been empty with the sales force out meeting would-be advertisers, but that was full, with everyone sitting around drinking coffee. He knew then the game was up, though Maxwell had not pulled the plug.

When Maxwell did close the paper in July 1987 after just five months, Clackson volunteered to become the 'under-taker', determined to get the staff, all 186 employees, the money due to them. He knew he had a hard task ahead. He recalls: 'Nothing had been computerized, so everyone's file, everyone's contract was just in old-fashioned, manual files and Maxwell refused to sign off anything until all the bits of relevant paper had been clipped together, checked, double-checked and then presented to him.

'But Maxwell being Maxwell he wouldn't just sign the top piece of paper with everyone's name on it. Oh no, he demanded to sign everyone's file personally. So each day I would go upstairs with a fresh bundle for signature, sometimes being made to sit and wait outside his office for hours at a time. Some days I sat outside his office for eight hours only to be sent away without him signing one. When he did call me in it would depend on his mood that day how many he signed; sometimes he would sign only two, on other occasions ten. Every day after signing a few he would refuse to sign any more saying: "That's enough, I've given enough of my money away today," and dismiss me. It took a month of waiting outside his office but in the end I managed to get all 186 files signed.'

Those who worked on the *LDN* believe it folded for various reasons, not just because Rothermere restarted his *Evening News*, putting it on the streets at just 10p a copy and forcing Maxwell to follow suit. They believe the editorial side was doing well but the paper never operated like the well-oiled machine it should have been. Maxwell had tried to do everything on the cheap, and consequently departments never worked properly or efficiently, from advertising to circulation, from printing to distribution. It was a shame, for many people put great effort into the paper to make it a success.

His next hugely ambitious project was the *European*. It was in October 1987, when guest speaker at a lunch organized by the Anglo-American Press Association in Paris, that

Maxwell announced his intention to launch a daily paper which would serve both Europe and the United States. What surprised some of those present was that Maxwell's plan sounded very much like that proposed some time earlier by former West German Chancellor Helmut Schmidt, publisher of *Die Zeit*. Asked about the similarity, Maxwell replied: 'Of course the ideas are not the same; mine is a daily paper, the other one a weekly.' Of course Maxwell had stolen the idea but he was never man enough to give credit to someone else's ideas; he had to be the man with the brilliant brain who had initiated them.

The problem Maxwell faced was financing his latest project. His plan was sound but he could find no takers to support him. He contacted many newspaper publishers throughout Europe and tried to reach an agreement with them; he wanted them to print copies of the *European*, which he would fax to them daily, on their presses and sell them in their country, thereby cutting down on costs. Advertisers would be recruited locally to give a national as well as international appeal; distribution would be carried out by each publisher alongside their other daily newspapers in their respective countries and profits shared. At first, many publishers showed an interest but he was unable to convince one of them that the project would ever make sufficient profits.

I travelled with Maxwell on a number of visits to see publishers and try to persuade them to support his grand project. All listened intently, all thought the idea a worthwhile concept which was good for Europe, all wished him well, but none would go along with his plan. So he had to think again.

He decided to fall back on the Schmidt plan and produce a weekly. Back in London, editor-in-chief Mike Molloy was put in charge of producing a dummy with the help of a French journalist, a former Hachette high-flyer, Jean Schalit, to create an Anglo-French *entente cordiale*. As weeks became months tempers often became heated as the British and French editorial teams disputed many editorial points.

Maxwell would hold editorial conferences prior to the launch, at which about ten people, including myself, would discuss progress of the project. Molloy and Schalit would contest each point, with Maxwell acting as referee. And after each meeting the two principal protagonists would stay behind in an effort to put their point independently. It was a recipe for disaster. For one thing it meant that Maxwell was being put in the position of making decisions about editorial matters of which he knew very little.

I am afraid that I may have been directly responsible for Maxwell coming to the decision to appoint himself editor-in-chief of the *European*. We were in Finland in 1988, drawing up longterm contracts to purchase news print, and one evening Maxwell asked me to go for a walk with him. To his credit, he really did want to get the *European* right. He was convinced it was a good concept for Europe, and Maxwell was always a good European, believing the political and monetary integration of Europe was essential for the future well-being of every European nation, particularly Britain. Frequently he talked about it.

On this occasion he wanted to talk about the editor. I believed that Maxwell was going to have severe problems pulling together journalists of real calibre to join and run the paper; and without good journalists from the broadsheets, I believed the project would fail. So I said: 'What you need is the right editor, someone who would have the respect of other journalists, someone who journalists have faith in, someone who journalists want to work with.'

'Like who?' he asked.

I replied: 'Like Harry Evans when he took over *The Sunday Times* in the '60s. The only way for the *European* to be successful is to have an editor capable of pulling together a good team like Whittam-Smith did when launching the

Independent. Without the right journalists, Bob, forget it, it won't work.' And I added: 'You might as well not bother.'

It was some weeks later that he called me to his suite: 'I have the answer,' he began.

'You have the answer to what, Bob?'

He loved playing these games. 'I have solved the problem that has been confronting us.'

Still having no idea to what he was referring, I said: 'What problem?'

He still wouldn't be drawn. 'The problem you and I discussed.'

Suddenly the penny dropped. 'An editor for the *European*?' I guessed.

'Exactly.'

This could have gone on, so I tried to find out: 'So, who's it going to be?' I asked.

'Me,' he said.

To say that my heart sank is an understatement. I searched my brain, trying to think, in an instant, of the way to stop him making what I knew was the greatest blunder imaginable in the selection of the editor. Maxwell would be a disaster and I knew Fleet Street would simply laugh at him – and the project, with Maxwell as editor.

'You can't, Bob,' I challenged, realizing the only thing was to stop him appointing himself.

'Why not?'

'Well,' I chanced as my reply, 'you haven't the time, and a project like the *European* needs a fulltime editor who can give it his whole attention twenty-four hours round the clock. You're far too busy.' And trying to con him, I added: 'You have the whole empire to care for, you can't just devote yourself to one paper.'

For a few seconds he thought. Then he said: 'I'll be the editor-in-chief, then.'

It wasn't as bad as having him as editor but I knew it

spelt disaster; I still feared that the journalists a paper like the *European* would need simply would not come and work for Maxwell. There was still the chance that he might appoint the right editor, but I was having grave doubts.

The *European's* first launch, but not the launch of the actual newspaper, took place on the island of Rhodes where the Common Market heads of government were holding their biannual meeting in 1989. At the last minute Maxwell decided that this would be a great venue to hold a press conference to launch the project, to capture the imagination of the journalists and heads of government, because, he believed, the journalists would be a captive audience.

Usually, such launches are organized weeks if not months in advance. Not with Maxwell. I think we were given seven days from Maxwell taking the decision to presentation day on Rhodes. I was sent out to head a team of about seven people to prepare everything for the launch – including making sure the journalists would turn up at the appointed time and place to report on Maxwell's new baby.

Everything on Rhodes had been booked months before, so the venue for the launch had to be five miles out of town in the only hotel we could find. Maxwell hired a yacht, at enormous expense, as his headquarters, which he moored in the harbour for his three-day visit. Everyone worked flat out, almost night and day, preparing press packs, preparing the venue, preparing quality food and drink, laying on coaches, as well as persuading the Common Market Secretariat to allow Maxwell to hijack the conference.

I met Maxwell at dawn at the airport and took him by car to his new rented toy, his luxurious ocean-going yacht. He had brought with him Andrea Martin, his chef, his valet and he was flying in other guests. His first task was to walk round the yacht with the captain, asking questions and having breakfast.

The next day he arrived by car at the hotel for the press conference he was to give for the launch. He came

136

immediately to rooms that we had turned into offices. But he looked fidgety, strangely unnerved. He demanded I take him through the procedure. He was not a happy man. He was in poor humour because he was convinced the launch would flop and he was preparing the target for the ritual slaughter to follow; on this occasion, me. He demanded a success, to show the world and the politicians on Rhodes that he was the Man of Europe.

I knew from his opening question that he was going to be difficult: 'What have you done?' he asked.

'Everything has been arranged,' I replied, hoping I had forgotten nothing.

'How are the journalists getting here?' he asked.

'By coach,' I replied.

'How many coaches?' he asked, looking worried. I told him I had hired four coaches which would leave every fifteen minutes from the conference press centre.

'That won't be enough, order some more,' he retorted. I knew the time had come to stop him riding me.

'It is more than enough,' I replied. 'The coaches will return until all the journalists, including the stragglers, have been brought here.'

He took the reply and changed tack. 'How do you know the journalists will come?'

'I don't, but I'm confident they will,' I said.

'What have you done to ensure they will turn up?'

I told him notices had been put up in the conference press centre; every journalist had been given a brief outline in their personal postboxes; journalists had been personally briefed by me and others; other arrangements that had been made included sending a reporter to the press centre to make announcements over the loudspeaker system telling everyone the coaches were ready for the *European* launch. Still not convinced, he was worried it would be a catastrophe. Maxwell often told me, and many others, his own law: that

137

Murphy's law, which decreed that everything that can go wrong, will go wrong, was correct. But Maxwell added the words: 'Murphy was an optimist.'

As the minutes ticked by Maxwell became more nervous and irate, pacing up and down and telling me that I couldn't organize a tea party, that I couldn't organize a 'piss-up in a brewery', that he would have to rethink my job, and that if the launch was a failure he would hold me personally responsible. He then decided to call off the whole launch, and told me to prepare a speech saying that he was indisposed, and apologizing for the fuck-up.

'Wait,' I replied, 'just wait. Give it ten minutes, till we've heard from the press centre.'

As the minutes ticked away I began to lose confidence. After what seemed an age the phone rang – the coaches, full of journalists, were on the way. The change that came over Maxwell was instant. As we sallied forth, with his entourage following in his wake, he was beaming all over his face. His praise could not have been more fulsome; from the lowest of life I had instantly become the saviour, embarrassingly so. I breathed a sigh of relief and thought what an incorrigible old bugger Maxwell really was.

He enjoyed the day, realized the conference had been most successful and decided to hold an instant editorial conference on his yacht that evening. He sat on the floor of the yacht's main lounge, leaning against a sofa, wearing an open-necked, short-sleeved shirt and trousers but no socks and shoes. It was faintly embarrassing as he ordered various people to take notes while he pontificated in true Maxwell style what the contents of the dummy paper would be, reporting the launch in Rhodes.

But Maxwell still hadn't decided who should edit the paper. He wanted someone whom he could trust – trust to do his bidding, that is. He had always admired Ian Watson, former City editor of the *Sunday Telegraph* and a

138

good financial journalist, and Maxwell had never forgotten that Ian Watson had, back in 1984, written a flattering article about him under the headline 'Fortune favours the bold Bob Maxwell'. It was the sort of headline Maxwell luxuriated in.

He called Watson in for a chat and discussed his latest pet project with him. Watson, the most honest of City journalists, didn't really want to know. As Watson says: 'I knew nothing about Europe; I was a City journalist and I told him that I was not the man to edit the *European.'* Undaunted, Maxwell continued to court Watson until finally Watson was made an offer he couldn't refuse.

The launch of the *European* was chaotic. As Watson confessed: 'Despite all Maxwell's grand words, there had been no research, no marketing, no target audience and we had no resources either. We were left on our own to muddle along while he made pronouncements from on high.'

Watson had very few staff to get the show on the road. As launch date approached, Watson had perhaps a third of the necessary staff and some *Daily Mirror* journalists were co-opted, including Tom Hendry, the *Mirror's* gentlemanly news editor, to organize the news gathering, and myself. At one stage I was the foreign editor, the City editor and the sports editor – jobs Maxwell gave me because he wouldn't appoint people until the paper was actually rolling. Those who had been taken on board worked amazing hours to get out the paper on time. Life was somewhat hectic. To create a feeling of camaraderie, and to stop people going to the pub, Maxwell opened up an eighteen-hour food bar, serving alcohol from 6 p.m.

He also appointed Robin MacKichan, the experienced and able managing director of the *International Herald Tribune,* as MD and deputy publisher at a very handsome salary; then he refused to let him do the job. Maxwell wanted to do everything. One morning, days before the launch, Maxwell phoned him at 6.30 a.m. in a furious mood ordering him to get into the office immediately. MacKichan arrived to find Maxwell had ordered men to smash open his office door with a crowbar! Maxwell had decided not only to assume total control of the *European* but to move his entire office staff into the *European*. The journalists were none too happy having an angry, obnoxious Maxwell breathing down their necks day and night.

One day Maxwell went too far. He pulled the senior executives to his office and began ripping into them, only days before the first edition was due out, telling them they were a load of incompetents. Then he went from person to person, in his awful way, asking people questions, then not letting them answer, shouting at them, cursing them, calling them 'cunts'. I saw three people visibly shaking. For a brief second he rested and I asked if I could have an urgent word. We went outside.

'You have a paper to get out in two days,' I said. 'These people don't know you. They can't take that treatment. If you continue like that they'll go to pieces.'

He nodded and walked back in. Putting on his most Churchillian voice, Maxwell intoned: 'This is the most important day in newspaper history and you are the people I have chosen to carry through this task. Good luck to you all.' And the meeting ended. No decisions whatsoever had been taken.

One week after the *European* launch Maxwell called me to his suite in the early morning. He threw a copy of the *European* on to the desk and I realized he was not in a good humour. 'It's shit,' he said. 'It's not the paper I wanted produced at all. You must go down there and take over. You will be my Exocet missile.'

I told Maxwell that I thought Ian Watson had done a good job under very difficult circumstances and that any new paper had to be given time to get over teething troubles.

'Balls,' came the reply, 'if it takes any more time to be sorted out there won't be a *European*. You have my absolute authority to go down there and sort out the place; more than that, it is an order.'

I went immediately to Watson and told him what Maxwell had decreed. We agreed to work together. I suggested I would put forward the ideas and he would provide the authority; in that way his editorship would not be undermined.

'Thanks,' he said.

After calling an editorial conference some changes were immediately implemented, one being that those journalists whose job it was to scour the European newspapers for story ideas would provide a preliminary list of the top stories of the day within two hours; they had been taking all day.

When word came out that Maxwell had deputed me to take charge of the editorial content of the paper there was a mini rebellion, led by deputy editor Peter Millar. A deputation went to see Maxwell and then he called me up.

'I've had a deputation,' Maxwell intoned, looking sad, 'and they are all threatening to walk out if I don't give them their jobs back. We can't have that after only one edition of the paper has come out.'

'What are you going to do, then?' I asked. 'You know they are only bluffing. One or two, like Millar, might go but the rest wouldn't.'

Maxwell thought for a split second. 'Ian Watson believes it would be better for morale if they all stayed – and he did make most of the appointments.'

I replied: 'OK, but I do feel rather stupid having done the job for just four hours.'

Maxwell blurted out: 'You feel stupid; I feel an absolute cunt.' And we both laughed. It was the only time I heard Maxwell describe himself like that.

A couple of weeks later Maxwell told me that he was promoting me, giving me another two jobs. He said that my two main jobs were at the *European* and the *Daily Mirror*. His idea was that I should work until 4 p.m. at the *European* each day and then switch to the foreign editor's job at the *Mirror*. Worse was yet to come. He also decided that he wanted me to become foreign editor of the *Sunday Mirror* and the *People*, which meant effectively I was working seven days a week. I knew what he was doing. He just wanted to have me spend as much time as possible working to make sure I would have no time to see Andrea Martin.

His other ruse was to send me all over the world to keep me away. He sent me on the most ridiculous trips and would talk to me each day, pretending the work was of vital importance, trying to convince me the trips were legitimate. The money spent didn't matter a damn.

One such 'important' story was to cover the travels of Mrs K. Prunskiene, the delightful divorced mother of two, the archetypal housewife from Lithuania, who had been catapulted into the presidency as that tiny Baltic country struggled to shake free the shackles of the mighty Soviet Union.

It was during an editorial conference at the *European* in the spring of 1989 that Maxwell, putting on his most serious voice, said: 'Nick, I have the most important task for you. This woman is the most important person in the world today, a symbol of a little nation's fight against the Great Bear. I want you to go and follow this woman, wherever she goes in the world; stay close to her, become her friend.' Then he added: 'You had better go immediately,' and he stood up and shook my hand dramatically as though I was some knight from the Middle Ages going off to battle.

Every day he phoned me, telling me that wherever Mrs Prunskiene went, I must follow. I travelled all over Scandinavia and had orders to follow her to the United States, but fortunately that trip was cancelled. Then he made me wait to obtain a visa to the Soviet Union while he tried, allegedly, to get one for me through 'his' channels. It never arrived and I returned to London after a most pleasant ten-day trip around sunny Scandinavia. Except for one interview with Mrs Prunskiene, it wasn't exactly journalism. But it had succeeded in keeping me out of London.

But there were new ambitions on the horizon. Maxwell was now the owner of Macmillan, the prestigious American publishing firm, and the profitable Official Airline Guides, as well as the Mirror Group. He had launched his *European* newspaper and picked up a clutch of ailing East European newspapers as the Eastern bloc countries threw off the shackles of Communism and searched around for Western publishers to rescue their ailing newspapers. He was on his way to becoming one of the world's top ten publishers, but it was getting more difficult.

At this stage, in the late 1980s, Maxwell thought he could do anything. He became involved in trying to save the ailing *Sunday Correspondent* when it looked like folding in the summer of 1990, and he agreed to put up some money in an effort to save it; but in return he wanted editorial control. Understandably, the *Sunday Correspondent* backers and senior editorial staff didn't want to know. At the time I was on holiday in the Lake District and Maxwell phoned me from the *Lady Ghislaine* somewhere near the Turkish coast.

'How would you like to become editor of the *Correspondent*?' he boomed when I picked up the phone in my hotel room.

I told him that I thought it would be a very good idea.

'Good', he replied, but before I could ask any further questions, he said, 'I'll be in touch,' and put down the phone.

He called three more times during the next couple of days but his last call was negative; I could tell he was not being allowed to provide the new editor for the paper. Later he was to tell me: 'If they had only let us take over, the *Correspondent* would be alive today.'

Maxwell tried everything in his power to make it successful. When the *Correspondent* finally collapsed Maxwell bought the title and some of its debts, and he came up with a plan to merge the *European* and the *Sunday Correspondent* and bring out one paper on a Sunday. That meant readers of the *European* in Europe would not get their paper until the Monday, when the whole idea of the *European* was to provide people with weekend reading. Watson thought it a crazy idea and told him so. Maxwell didn't like that sort of opposition to his ideas and it cost Watson his job. With the *Correspondent*'s debts Maxwell also found himself responsible to its last editor, John Bryant, a former *Times* man, who had agreed to take over as editor at the enormous salary of £300,000 a year. So Maxwell decided to use Bryant by offering him Watson's job as editor of the *European*. Watson was devastated.

He commented: 'Maxwell had promised me three years. It was my baby. When he told me over Sunday lunch in February 1991 I just went back to my office and slumped in the chair, unable to take in what he had just done. I was determined to resign. I stayed there for four or five hours, chain-smoking and thinking how to tell the staff and my family. Then Bob came over and tried to take me to his apartment for a drink but I refused. He saw my overflowing ashtray and said: "I've told you before I would fire you if I caught you smoking."

'I replied: "You knew I was a smoker when you hired me. In any case you can't fire me twice."

'Maxwell replied: "Don't bet on it."

'I told him I was resigning and he told me I couldn't. Why not?

'Maxwell then played his next hand, saying angrily: "If you don't accept the job of editorial director which I am offering you then I will call the staff together tomorrow and close your fucking paper down." He told me I must accept

144

the position as editorial director and help him make it a success.

'What could I do? I was stymied. I couldn't let down the staff who had worked so hard and I didn't want to see the paper die. I felt I was looking down the barrel of a loaded shotgun. I agreed to stay, there was nothing else I could do. But I never forgave him.'

Driving home that night Watson took a call from Ian Maxwell, then managing director of the *European*: 'What have you said to so upset my father?' he asked. 'He's hopping mad.'

Watson told him briefly what had happened and then asked: 'Do you think he'll close the paper down?'

Ian replied: 'I wouldn't test him on that one; I wouldn't risk it in the mood he's in.'

A typical example of Maxwell's interference was after Saddam Hussein ordered his troops to invade Kuwait. In that week's paper the respected diplomatic correspondent, Ian Mather, wrote a page-one story and Watson headlined it 'War Inevitable'. When Watson returned from lunch he was told Maxwell had ordered the front page headline be altered to read 'War Imminent'. Watson objected, only to be told by Maxwell: 'What do you know about the Middle East? I have changed your pathetic headline because I have just talked to President Gorbachov who told me he expects the Americans to launch an attack in a few hours.'

To his credit Watson altered the headline back to the original, but he had missed half the print run. In fact it was months later that the Allies launched their attack. But Maxwell's interference had lost the *European* credibility.

Watson was also privy to some of Maxwell's paranoia. On one occasion Maxwell sacked a teenager who had, quite accidentally, destroyed a roll of film showing Maxwell with the Duke of Edinburgh. Watson went to plead for the youth to be reinstated. Maxwell roared at him: 'That was no accident.

Have I an editor who doesn't recognize industrial espionage when he sees it? Why was it my film? Why do you support people who are out to injure me?'

The outburst was nonsense and eventually the youth was reinstated.

Maxwell's first love was always newspapers; he couldn't resist becoming involved whenever given the chance. He had always wanted to become involved in a major American newspaper or magazine but the right opportunity had never emerged. He had nearly taken over America's *National Enquirer*, the largest-selling weekly tabloid in the United States, but after several months of haggling in 1989, that had come to nought. Then, out of the blue, came manna from heaven – the *New York Daily News*. Maxwell needed a new victory; his massive ego needed a further boost and for some time he had missed the applause and acclamation of clinching a big deal. As though on cue the *Daily News* hove into view searching for a saviour – and it found Maxwell.

The *Daily News* is as much a part of 'the Big Apple' as yellow cabs and bagels. Started in 1920 and for decades America's bestselling paper, it has featured in Broadway plays, been sung by Frank Sinatra and even starred in *Superman*, where it was renamed the *Daily Planet* and employed Clark Kent. No one in New York wanted the paper to fold but the problem was finding someone to take on the debts, take on the unions and support the paper while it struggled back to profit. The Chicago Tribune Group, which owned the *Daily News*, had had enough; the paper had been wracked by industrial problems, appalling overmanning, a corrupt labour force, old machinery and crippling restrictive practices.

The whole scenario was made for 'Cap'n Bob' – as New Yorkers insisted on calling Maxwell who, in fact, had dropped his rank fifteen years before. And Maxwell was confident that he would soon be flush with funds, for he had just taken the momentous decisions to sell the two jewels in his crown: his beloved Pergamon, the founder of his empire, and a forty-nine per cent stake in Mirror Group Newspapers. Maxwell hoped those sales would restore his battered finances.

Once again Maxwell produced one of his trite old remarks, the one many people had heard a dozen times from his lips: 'It's lucky I wasn't born a woman because I can never say no.' Every other publisher who had looked at the possibility of taking over the *Daily News* had walked away from the deal, although the Tribune Group was offering $60 million to anyone who would take it off their hands quickly.

Not Maxwell. From his Holborn headquarters Maxwell held one ten-minute conversation with the paper's union leader, George McDonald, in which McDonald agreed to give concessions, and Maxwell was hooked. McDonald, it seemed, understood how Maxwell worked, for he said: 'You know, owning the *Daily News* is like a visiting card for sheikhs, kings and queens. It opens the door for people and I guessed he wanted it that bad.' He was right.

Once again he couldn't say no and the *New York Daily News* was to prove a major loss-maker. But Maxwell enjoyed New York. It seemed as though New York City and Maxwell were made for each other; for once he didn't look totally incongruous with his baseball hat and huge belly, strutting around town and beaming with delight at everyone who shook his hand and welcomed him to 'the Big Apple'.

In Chicago, Charles Brumback of the Tribune Group watched as the negotiations balanced on a knife edge. But he was to say later: 'The difference between us and Maxwell was that we were looking for a fifty-year investment; he was sixty-seven years old and wanted to enjoy a piece of his lifetime's ambition.'

Playing the poker game he so loved, Maxwell demanded

more and more concessions but the unions knew he wanted the prize. Maxwell had been warned that McDonald was impossible to deal with, that he was a man not to be trusted; yet Maxwell found him amiable and likable. Finally, with thirty-six hours to go, the deal was struck and Maxwell signed, knowing owning the *Daily News* was going to cost him at least $1 million a week, money he hadn't got.

'Cap'n Bob Bites The Big Apple' screamed the *Daily News* headline, while an opposition paper headline screamed: 'Brit Saves *Daily News*'. The saving of the *Daily News* in such grandiose, spectacular fashion won the genuine affection and admiration of the people and the powerbrokers of New York. They loved Maxwell for riding like a shining knight to the rescue of their paper and they gave him the sort of reception he loved – adulation!

Maxwell ordered his own picture be put on the front page alongside an editorial, signed 'Maxwell': 'This is a great day. For me, for newspapers and, above all, for New York.'

There was just one shock for New Yorkers the next day – without telling anyone Maxwell had ordered a 5 cent price increase to 40 cents. When someone complained he yelled back: 'Tell them I put the price up because I need the money.' No one realized at the time he was telling the truth.

Maxwell took to the streets the next day, selling papers at a news-stand, playing to the cameras, kissing babies, talking to New Yorkers and pressing the flesh, until cops had to ask him to move on because he was stopping the traffic. Nothing could have been more fantastic for Maxwell than to stop the traffic in New York – he revelled in every minute of his glory.

'We were mobbed like Madonna,' Maxwell boasted.

Back at the *Daily News* he was brought five television advertisements for the paper's relaunch; three featured Maxwell on screen, the other two showed historic *Daily News* front pages. Maxwell passed only the last two, saying:

'They are approved as long as you keep my mug out of it.' Such reticence from Maxwell was out of character. Then he commented: 'I learnt my lesson in England. *Private Eye* stuck it to me for having my face in the paper every day, so I'm shy of that.' Those newspapermen around Maxwell who had known him some years raised their eyebrows; it wasn't often Maxwell admitted to being wrong.

At the end of that fantastic week, fantastic, that is, for Maxwell's ego, he had learned that it was the annual Gridiron dinner at the Capital Hilton in Washington, hosted by America's leading satirists for their special guests – including of course the President, George Bush. Maxwell was determined to receive an invitation and he did. It had been Maxwell's ambition for years to meet the US President. He had managed to obtain a single meeting with Ronald Reagan but, until buying the *Daily News*, he had conspicuously failed in his innumerable attempts to meet George Bush.

Nothing was more important to Maxwell than the Gridiron dinner. Maxwell was going to look every inch the quintessential British press baron, resplendent in white tie, tails and his impressive array of military medals. Back in London his faithful retainer Bob Cole was woken by his boss and told to catch the next Concorde flight to the States and bring with him Maxwell's tails and the military medals. No expense would be spared to make Maxwell look the part.

He did look the part but the white tie he wore had been purchased only minutes before for $10 from a waiter! Cole had arrived in New York with everything Maxwell demanded, but no white tie. Maxwell sent him out to buy one. Minutes later Cole returned from shopping with the $50 white bow-tie which Maxwell had to tie himself. Thirty minutes later Maxwell called Cole and ordered him to report to his suite immediately.

'I walked in,' said Cole later, 'and saw a very red-faced Maxwell struggling with the bow-tie. I had forgotten that despite all the bow-ties he wore, Maxwell never learned to tie one himself. He looked desperate.

'"Can you tie these fucking things?" he asked.

'I told him I could, but not on someone else.

'"Well, go and find a proper one and make it quick. I must not be late for the President."'

Cole went down to the hotel kitchens and bought a ready-made tie from a waiter for $10.

Maxwell made the dinner, adorned with his medals, and bowed to everyone as he was introduced as the man who saved the *Daily News*. Not only had he received an invitation but he was given pride of place, sitting next to the President – a privilege he would never forget. And, typical Maxwell, he spent most of the dinner earbashing poor Bush about the necessity of America bailing out the former Soviet Union. Maxwell also tried to secure a privileged position as the President's special unofficial secret envoy. He told the President that whenever there were delicate matters that he felt should not go through the normal diplomatic channels, then he would gladly be the messenger, flying wherever the President required him to, in the interests of a peaceful world. President Bush apparently thanked Maxwell for his kind offer but promised nothing.

Never in Britain had Maxwell ever received the kind of respect and adulation that he experienced in New York and Washington. In Britain, Maxwell had never been accepted by the Establishment, whether it was in the City of London's financial centre or by society or the nation's political heart. He had tried time and again but had always found himself an outsider. Even his money hadn't worked the oracle for him – and it rankled. Furthermore, Maxwell had indeed always been the butt of jokes, particularly in the satirical magazine *Private Eye*, where for decades he was referred to as 'the bouncing Czech'.

Maxwell was on a high, enjoying himself more than he had for years. People actually wanted to see him, to talk to him, to be a part of his scene in a way he had never experienced before. But it was more than that; for a few days he felt at home, he felt wanted and he felt loved.

I spoke to him on a couple of occasions during those hectic days.

'You should come over here,' he said enthusiastically, 'New York is a wonderful place, everyone is so friendly and open, nothing like Britain.'

'You sound as though you're enjoying life,' I quipped. But he could not accept that.

'There is much work to be done here,' he intoned, 'the time for celebration is over. I may have to stay over here for some months.' Before I could comment further he did one of his favourite tricks. 'Bye,' he said and put down the phone in an instant. He had often told me about this: 'Always put down the phone quickly as soon as you have said what you want; never give people a chance to say what they want. It is very sound advice I'm giving you.' He pulled that trick with many, many people.

He held a cocktail party aboard the *Lady Ghislaine* which was moored not far from the United Nations building. It was attended by David Dinkins, New York's mayor, and a bevy of leading American journalists. Maxwell was at the height of his ambitions, the Randolph Hearst of the 1990s, entertaining the great and the good of New York society on board his magnificent yacht which was bedecked with photographs of Maxwell with world leaders.

But it was a different story for the workers of the *Daily News*. Maxwell was determined to deal with the unions and the workers with even more determination and speed than he had shown at the *Daily Mirror* seven years earlier. In Britain, unsure of the power of the Fleet Street unions, he had trodden gently until he had the confidence to strike. In New York he believed he could strike immediately, and did so, firing 130 security men within days of taking over,

151

followed by a host of middle managers and others he believed were unnecessary; those sackings on top of the hundreds of redundancies he had formally agreed during his negotiations to buy the paper.

The Mafia mob, however, did not mind too much if they sold a few hundred jobs but kept the paper going, for they made their money through illegal racketeering with the sales and distribution of the paper, no matter how few people were employed.

Maxwell announced that he would spend the next three months in New York, as a 'hands-on' publisher, revitalizing the paper with his energy, motivation, ideas and drive. He seemed convinced that he could succeed with the *Daily News* in the same way he had with the *Daily Mirror*, turning it into a very profitable enterprise. As he flew out of New York a couple of days later to attend to urgent business in London, Maxwell looked like the cat that had eaten the cream. He proclaimed: 'Within a year the *Daily News* will break even, eventually it should end up being a licence to print money.'

At that time, he did not know to what extent the Mafia controlled vital areas of the *Daily News* nor how they ripped off the sales for themselves every night of the week, stealing millions of dollars a year. It meant that Maxwell would find it very difficult indeed, if not impossible, to bring the *Daily News* into profit.

Thrilled by his success in New York, Maxwell decided to launch the *European* on the American market in a bid to increase sales and encourage advertising. As editorial director, Watson was given the task of organizing the printing of the paper and its sales distribution. As the launch date, October 1991, grew nearer, Watson and others noticed Maxwell's increasingly strange and nervous behaviour, despite the fact that Watson had secured a remarkably good deal for the printing of the *European* in the United States and set up a distribution system for 50,000 copies a week.

152

Watson had organized a big celebration party at which the first US-printed edition of the *European* would be presented. More than six hundred had agreed to attend, including fifty European ambassadors to the United Nations along with the great and the glamorous of New York. An orchestra had been organized and Moët et Chandon had agreed to provide the champagne free. Everything was arranged for another Maxwell success story in America.

Yet, Watson commented later: 'Maxwell's nervousness about the New York launch increased as the date approached. Two weeks before deadline Maxwell summoned me to his office. He was in a filthy mood and told me the launch would have to be postponed. I protested, saying everything was arranged, but he insisted.

'When I asked why, he told me that the *New York Daily News* people had discovered the arrangements for distribution of the *European*, and were very unhappy. What they objected to was never made clear to me but their objections were strong enough to make Maxwell think twice. I had refused to involve the *New York Daily News* in the distribution of the *European* in America. I had set up another distribution system with another American Maxwell paper, the *Racing Times*.'

Maxwell told Watson: 'You have angered the unions over there, you know, with your distribution arrangements. They're not pleased at all. You've no experience of New York. You don't appreciate they don't like being cut out.'

Surprisingly, Maxwell relented and agreed to let the launch go ahead. Within weeks, sales of the paper had tripled to 25,000 copies a week. What Maxwell did not tell Watson was that the Mafia mob who controlled distribution of many of New York's newspaper sales had objected and had told Maxwell in no uncertain terms that he would have to allow them to take over distribution of the *European*, or else!

SEVEN

'I'm not like ordinary men; I don't have time to take care of myself.'

Maxwell was always an early riser. He would order his Filipino maids to wake him at 6 a.m. but his personal valet, Simon Grigg, would be expected to be there by that time each morning to wake his employer with a glass of orange juice and a large cup of coffee. Maxwell would usually sleep in an old-fashioned nightshirt bought for him by his ever-loving wife.

Often Maxwell was awake and had been so for an hour or more. He hardly ever slept through the night. Usually, he would have gone to bed, exhausted after a hard day's work, by nine o'clock in the evening. After an hour or so's sleep he would wake, get up and restart work, often phoning New York, where it was around 6 p.m. He was also most particular about receiving the next morning's newspapers as soon as they arrived at the Mirror building. Many were the nights he would get on the phone by 11 p.m. to the *Daily Mirror* night newsdesk demanding to know the reason why he had not yet received his papers. And, depending on his mood, he would accept the answer or demand that something be done immediately and his papers sent up that instant, despite the fact it was nothing whatsoever to do with the poor man to whom he was speaking. Many were the times that I heard his voice booming from the newsdesk phone as the desk man tried to placate his boss.

'Yes, Mr Maxwell,' and 'No, Mr Maxwell,' were the only answers the veteran desk men gave after they realized it was useless to argue with the boss with whom they could never reason – because he would not listen to any explanations. Maxwell never wanted to hear reasons or explanations, and he would tell them so in no uncertain terms. What Maxwell demanded from the moment he stepped into the Mirror building on July 13, 1984 was action and obedience, but above all obedience. He never wanted to know if there was a good reason why something had not occurred, something as trivial as his newspapers being five minutes late on a filthy, cold, icy January night. The elements didn't interest him; only the fact that his papers were late.

Maxwell liked having the *Daily Mirror* newsdesk at his beck and call. It operated 24 hours round the clock, 365 days a year, meaning he could keep in contact with the outside world from his ivory tower next door at the top of Maxwell House. Wherever he was in the world it seemed comforting to him that he could have access to someone he could appeal to for information, assistance or just someone he could speak to, order about or bully.

By midnight or 1 a.m. Maxwell would have read through all the papers, particularly *The Financial Times* and the *Sun*. He read the *Sun* so that he could compare it to his *Daily Mirror*, and so he could play at being 'editor'. He loved finding stories, different angles, promotions, sports stories that the *Mirror* had decided not to print that night, or play down or treat in a different way. Every *Mirror* editor, or anyone sitting in the editor's chair on duty, would wait for the customary nightly telephone call – and no one would know what sort of mood he would be in: challenging, pleasant, angry, affable, jokey or turbulent, demanding or irrational.

155

Sometimes, if Maxwell had a bee in his bonnet about some story, he would be on the phone five or six times demanding to know whether his ideas – his orders – had been followed up, what had been done, who was doing the story, and what he always wanted to know was the name of the particular person responsible if there had been what he described as a 'fuck-up'. It seemed to me sometimes that Maxwell loved 'fuck-ups' simply because he could vent his rage, make the wretched person on the end of the phone jump to attention and become worried and agitated, just so there would be no complacency, no resting on work well done, no feeling of confidence among his senior executives.

And because he was so fascinated, so interested in the newspaper business, and because he loved being the publisher of Mirror Group Newspapers, his papers were ninety per cent of his life, despite the fact that they only amounted to ten per cent of his business empire. It was also the reason that his editors always had immediate access to him, no matter where he was or what he was doing. He loved to know what was going on at any time, anywhere; he loved domestic politics, and perhaps more so international politics, and that was why Maxwell and I formed a relationship. I read prodigiously, not just newspapers and magazines but also reports of foreign papers and embassy notes that arrived daily on my desk. I needed to, because Maxwell either knew a great deal or he was brilliant at making one believe he knew a great deal.

After shaving and showering Maxwell would be dressed by his valet and would then sally forth to start the day. The first duty receptionist would be at her desk at Maxwell House, sitting immediately outside his office, by 7 a.m. and he would usually start by ordering some phone calls. By 7.30 both Ian and Kevin would be in the office, and in trouble if they were not there by that time. A twelve-hour day faced them, if not a lot longer. He would have a fifteen- or twenty-minute meeting with them, discussing the order of the day, and they would wait patiently for their father to finish speaking. Only after he had said everything he wanted to would he look at them with the question, 'Anything else?' That was their opportunity to raise whatever matters they thought should be dealt with. Often the questions they raised were dismissed by Maxwell with a flick of the hand, and the sons would have to accept that his decision was final.

Most mornings, however, it was Kevin who was called in for private meetings with his father while Ian could relax, waiting for the dreaded call, and enjoy an orange juice and a cup of coffee while planning his day, and, if possible, find time to read the morning papers. During the years, Peter Jay, the former British Ambassador to the United States, who had previously been talked of, unenviably, as the 'cleverest man in Britain', worked for Maxwell, he also was expected to be in his office by 8 a.m. However, that was not usually the first contact of the day; that had been made either as Jay was shaving and showering or on the car phone while he was driving to work in the Jaguar Maxwell provided him with as his chief-of-staff.

Maxwell was pleased as punch when Peter Jay came to work for him; he felt he had achieved a formidable victory for his position and his prestige when a man of Jay's undoubted ability and reputation agreed to work for him. Jay's acceptance gave Maxwell yet another bona fide person to whom people would look when ascertaining whether Maxwell was a person they should or should not do business with. Even in 1984, before Maxwell began to hit the world headlines, there were many who believed he was a man, and particularly a businessman, whom they should avoid like the proverbial plague.

Jay provided a link with the outside world giving testimony that the very best brains would and did work for him. Two of Jay's undoubted qualities appealed to Maxwell; one was his ability to contact the most senior members of the Civil Service whenever necessary and the natural ease with which he could also contact senior and junior members of the Government. He was also wonderfully diplomatic when dealing with foreign embassies and foreign governments – which to Maxwell was most important. Third was Jay's great ability to write the perfect letter of apology – something which he found he had to write time and time again due to Maxwell's appalling disregard towards commitments and appointments which he hadn't the slightest intention of honouring. Every week Maxwell reneged on numbers of such appointments and invitations with complete unconcern for what problems or inconvenience he may have caused.

It was Jay who so often had to handle the complaints that came in when arguments arose over major accounts. The more I witnessed the treatment Jay took from Maxwell the more surprised I became. It appeared to me that the longer Jay stayed the more he was smoking and drinking and the more ragged and harassed the man became. He was amazingly stoical, which didn't seem to go with a man of Jay's undoubted ability. He was brilliant at presenting a flawless résumé of meetings within minutes of a gathering ending, with all the points unerringly in their correct order of importance.

No one had forgotten the albatross that hung round Maxwell's neck to his dying day – the 1971 DTI report that had branded him as 'a person who cannot be relied on to exercise proper stewardship of a publicly quoted company'. The two other DTI reports of '72 and '73 were just as damning. The DTI inspectors' report of April 1972, which examined his encyclopaedia business, was a severe criticism of Maxwell's management style and his deliberate overstating of profits; they cited evidence where employees had been 'bullied' by Maxwell into stating 'unrealistic' profits, and 'phoney' documents and 'bogus' invoices had been given as evidence by Maxwell. In their third report in November 1973, the DTI inspectors reported on his private companies and produced another damning report with accusations of fake and backdated invoices and rewritten board minutes; they also showed confusion between Pergamon and his private companies. The inspectors also did not hide their surprise that despite their indictments Maxwell gave no appearance of being crippled, that the 'criticisms had not abashed him or affected his fixation as to his own abilities'.

Maxwell had appealed against the DTI reports, and in a celebrated judgement, Lord Denning emphatically rejected Maxwell's appeal, stating that in the case of each criticism the inspectors had indisputably put the facts 'fairly and squarely to Mr Maxwell'. Despite losing the appeal 'utterly' Maxwell had, however, won a victory. The accounting profession changed its practices in the wake of the Pergamon revelations and procedures for all future DTI inquiries were changed. In future, a provision was instigated that those criticized in a report had to be given the opportunity to comment before publication. It was that question of natural justice that had been Maxwell's challenge to the authorities.

It was Maxwell's ability to attract such luminaries as Jay to work for him that helped rebuild his prestige, image and reputation that had been all but destroyed in the 1970s. Another to join was Sir Thomas McCaffrey, a former Labour MP and press spokesman for Prime Minister James Callaghan. He accepted the same job working for Maxwell but not for long. And the Labour peer Charles Williams was employed as a financial adviser to the Mirror Group. Later, Lord Donoughue, financial adviser to premier Harold Wilson, was to join Maxwell, but on the financial side. Lord Rippon, the former Conservative Cabinet Minister, was another to be lured by Maxwell. There were to

159

be others who accepted prestigious jobs the bigger the empire grew.

Maxwell's ability to attract the great and the good was vital to the success of his ability to borrow more and more money. One such person was Robin Leigh-Pemberton, former chairman of National Westminster Bank and a friend of Maxwell's for many years, friend of Prime Minister Margaret Thatcher and lately Governor of the Bank of England. Then there was Sir Michael Richardson, a man of great integrity in the City, non-executive chairman of stockbroker Smith New Court, who acted for Maxwell in the flotation of Mirror Group Newspapers. Maxwell's private phone book, which was marked 'Strictly Confidential', the distribution of which was strictly limited, was full of the most senior City figures, including bankers, merchant bankers, stockbrokers and accountants. And not just their office numbers and direct numbers but on most occasions their home numbers as well.

Peter Jay tried to bring some semblance of order to Maxwell's business life but to no avail. Like a first-class civil servant Jay believed that he should employ the same tactics of order as are practised throughout the civil service. And he tried to educate Maxwell to conduct his business in the same disciplined way as a minister of the Crown. To that end he instituted 'the Box' – literally a large wooden box that Jay had positioned on Maxwell's desk which was divided into categories: immediate, urgent, priority and routine. Every morning Jay would go through the work of the day and the mail and place the various papers in the appropriate part of the box. Jay also allocated time on his diary, usually an hour to ninety minutes every day around 11 a.m. when Maxwell would have the time to go through the box with his PA and Jay and deal with everything. Maxwell hated the box. He would do everything in his power to avoid having any time at all to look into it, let alone read anything there. It wasn't the way he had ever conducted business – and he hated the discipline Jay was trying to instill into his life.

I remember being in Maxwell's office one morning when Jay came in, apologetic at disrupting his boss. As Maxwell and I talked, Jay hung around waiting for the moment to say something.

Finally he did, saying: 'Bob, just to ask whether you have seen a note I put in the box this morning which is very urgent?'

Maxwell replied: 'What note? I haven't seen any note.'

As diplomatically as possible Jay replied with an awkward smile: 'Well, I did put it in the box.'

That infuriated Maxwell. He shouted at Jay: 'Well, if it's so fucking important why did you put it in a fucking box? Why the hell didn't you give it to me like any sane person would?'

Jay simply took the cursing and the violent attack, went to the box, fished out the piece of paper and handed it to Maxwell. 'I'll see you later,' he said to me.

It was obvious that the piece of paper was indeed urgent, if not immediate. That was typical Maxwell, typical of the way he behaved, blaming others for something he had not done. In the end the infamous box was to go and Maxwell returned to his way of ordering his business affairs, attention to the panic of the moment and utter disregard for the ordered business which should have been executed with discipline every day.

Jay also tried to sort out Maxwell's mail, which, understandably, was vast. Because of the enormous pressure on Maxwell's time, Jay devised a system whereby he would check all the incoming mail and, where appropriate, reroute it to other senior executives to deal with. The executives would either return the correspondence with their recommendations or deal with the matter themselves. Maxwell didn't like this procedure one little bit. Angry at what Jay

161

was doing with what he perceived as his mail he screamed at Jay one day: 'Why do you send my mail all around this fucking company when it is addressed to me? I want to see my mail, all the mail, do you understand?'

That led to disaster. Already he had not the time to check the important mail that Jay, quite rightly, sent to him, but now he insisted on seeing everything. Of course he never had the time to deal with and answer it all, leading to confusion, with urgent matters being neglected. In turn, that would cause Maxwell to fly into rages, screaming and shouting, cursing and blinding everyone in sight, but particularly poor Jay, when all along it was Maxwell's own fault, his inability to delegate any authority to anyone.

Maxwell's favourite habit was ordering his senior executives who ran his business empire to report to him for meetings at the Holborn HQ, which he of course renamed Maxwell House. They would be asked to attend either early in the morning or afternoon. These men were holding down responsible jobs, most of them paid in excess of £100,000 a year with generous Christmas bonuses to keep them sweet. And yet he would leave them pacing up and down, waiting outside his office for perhaps two to four hours until he was ready to see them. It was the most ludicrous situation. On pain of being fired they were not allowed to leave under any circumstances without his permission, but they could not get in to see him, even for a second, for permission to return later. It was one of Maxwell's most devilish, and stupid, schemes to show his top men who was the boss. And it happened virtually every day. The executives were understandably furious, but they put up with it. Those exempt from this treatment were his sons, his editors and a privileged few such as Haines and myself.

His treatment of these senior men caused major problems for Andrea Martin, for many believed she held the key to his door and therefore was partly responsible for their frustrating, humiliating experience whenever they were called to see him. There was nothing she could do, primarily because most of the time he was on the phone to various people in various parts of his empire, or the world, and to him those phone calls were more important than the matters he had called his subordinates in to discuss. But his treatment of those executives caused untold bad feeling towards him. He didn't care a damn!

It was the same with telephone calls. The first hurdle was to get from the telephonist to Andrea, and then to Maxwell. Among those privileged to be put through immediately were his stockbrokers, his merchant bankers, his bankers, people he listed as VIPs, and his editors. For everyone else it was a case of leaving messages and hoping the great man would return their calls. Sometimes people complained of waiting for weeks for a return call.

He would always take telephone calls during meetings and loved to chatter away on the phone, to whoever, while those attending the meeting had to sit and wait patiently for him to finish. Sometimes, he would pick up his direct line – 3333 – before the telephone receptionist had time to answer it, he so loved receiving phone calls. On other occasions he might pick up the phone at reception if it was ringing while he walked past, and answer it himself.

For some reason wrong numbers often came through on his direct line and he loved to tell the caller that the person they wanted had just joined the army; and then he would put down the phone, roaring with laughter. The telephone number of London Zoo was very similar, and calls would often come through asking questions about the zoo. Maxwell loved that. He would roar like a lion down the phone, and on other occasions he would bark like a dog then hang up without saying a word. But his favourite trick was to quack like a duck. For some unknown reason Maxwell loved ducks, and one of the Reichmann brothers – the Canadian property developers of Canary Wharf fame – gave him a small, green, carved-stone duck as a paperweight for his desk. He liked that. It was just one of the little games which he loved to play.

Maxwell would spend days and often weeks paying not the slightest attention to the business affairs he should have dealt with in his capacity as head of a multi-billion-pound publishing empire. Maxwell always had a travelling box full of papers and a large ministerial-type briefcase which went wherever he went, whether Moscow, New York or Tokyo. It was packed and unpacked a dozen times before Maxwell could be persuaded to sit down and go through the papers, and often he would not bother to make any decisions. His secretaries or Jay would try to go through important papers, seeking decisions, but Maxwell would simply turn away and refuse to pay any attention.

Memos were also a problem. I was often asked by various people, from different parts of Maxwell's empire, whether I could advise them on how to make Maxwell respond to their notes. They would also ask me if I would look through their memos to see if their approach to Maxwell was the correct one. I always offered to help. Usually, these memos were two or three pages long, in single-space paragraphs of perhaps five hundred to a thousand words. 'That's no good,' I would tell them, 'he will never read it.'

Usually they would reply: 'But he has to, it's really important. I've cut it down dramatically.'

And I would explain: 'The only memo Maxwell will ever read is a single page, preferably with four points on it and each point no more than ten words long – a total of perhaps forty to fifty words.'

They would reply: 'That's impossible; it can't be done.'

And invariably I said: 'If you want him to read it, take the advice.'

The reason I knew this was because I regularly saw him

164

at work, particularly when we were overseas for a few days, with Andrea Martin, Judy Welsh or another secretary trying to persuade him to tackle his papers. On a few occasions I sat in and saw that he would ask his PA what the particular memo was about and would only read it himself if short and to the point. I remember one occasion in Paris: he read a memo and passed it to me; it was a single A4-page close-typed memo and he glanced at it before passing it to me to read. It was a reasoned argument from one of his financial companies why this head of department should be allowed to hire more staff.

'He wants more staff,' I said.

'I thought so,' Maxwell replied, 'I've told him a dozen times he can't.' Then he called to his PA and asked her to get the man on the phone. 'Ah, I received your memo,' Maxwell began in a kindly voice and I heard what I took to be enthusiasm on the other end of the line. Then Maxwell said: 'I've told you before that you can't have any more staff, mister. Why are you wasting my time sending me another memo?' I didn't hear the reply but Maxwell cut him off, saying: 'You, mister, are a cunt and you have sent your last memo. See me when I return.' And he put down the phone giving the man no opportunity to reply.

I didn't know the man or his job but I commented: 'That was a bit harsh, Bob.'

He turned, looked at me and said: 'He's a cunt, we don't need him.'

Perhaps the most important people Maxwell called to see him each and every day without fail were those involved in the financial side of Maxwell Communications Corporation (MCC) and the Mirror Group. After seeing Kevin every morning the next in line was officially Jay, but Maxwell often postponed his early morning appointment until later in the day. At 8 a.m. most days Maxwell would see his money men. These were always private meetings with Maxwell inviting only one or two and sometimes three directors into his office at one time, but never altogether. These included the men who were to have to unravel Maxwell's devious financial activities after the administrators, the DTI inspectors and the Serious Fraud Office were called in to check every area of Maxwell's financial affairs and operations. Two other younger men also joined the list of frequent visitors to Maxwell's office, both university lecturers of political economics: the American, Larry Trachtenberg and Andrew Smith, who were directors of London & Bishopsgate Holdings. They had discovered a way of tracking Japanese stock market indexes by computer which they maintained would earn huge profits if they had a large enough investment vehicle. Maxwell was to provide that vehicle for them.

Throughout the morning Maxwell would always take calls from his bankers and his stockbrokers, no matter who was in the room. Maxwell always kept the Reuters dealing screen on his desk and would refer to it frequently throughout the day. Most times it seemed when I was in his office the phone would go and he would answer with the usual words: 'Put him through.' Frequently, Maxwell would then ask, 'What's the closing price?' He was referring to MCC's share price, but later, after the *Mirror* was floated on the stock market, he would naturally ask that price also.

In his office Maxwell was remarkably fussy. He banned ordinary paper clips because his fingers and thumbs were so big he couldn't manipulate the pins, so they were done away with in favour of plastic ones he found easier to handle; he banned biros as well, demanding people only use Pentels; and no cover sheets were allowed on any faxes – because they were 'a bloody nuisance' and 'a waste of paper'.

The number of people waiting outside his office became so large that Maxwell banned them waiting there and ordered double doors to be erected so everyone had to wait in a corridor twenty yards from his office near the lifts. And the mêlée in that corridor often seemed like musical chairs, as there were only two seats for the large number of frustrated executives. The only consolation was a water machine. Usually, the waiting time was only an hour or so but some were kept waiting, unable to leave, for more than six hours.

Stephen Clackson recalled being one of those people made to wait with other *London Daily News* executives during the early morning. He commented: 'At that time everyone associated with the *LDN* was called to the morning meetings, somewhere around 9.30 in the morning. There were not just editorial people but also production, financial, advertising, marketing, about sixteen in all. We might wait ten minutes or more than an hour for Maxwell. People would become agitated and nervous; a couple would tell Maxwell jokes, others would try to impersonate his voice; it was all mortuary humour, all waiting for his arrival, not knowing what he would say or do; not knowing whom he would pick on, but the nervousness increasing as the minutes ticked by.

'Then Maxwell would come in and sit down, pick up the typed agenda, look at it and put it on one side. Everyone would have their relative files to go with the agenda, waiting for him to start the meeting. Invariably, however, he would pick on something entirely different, something not on the agenda, some minor, trivial little point. He always seemed to do that, to find a piece of trivia, go for something insignificant, so he could torture someone, attack someone, make someone at the table feel incompetent.

'Everyone would then be left in a state of confusion and nervousness which he would end by telling one or two dreadful jokes which we all laughed at, but only because he was telling the joke and your job might depend on it. Then the phone calls would start and Maxwell would be pressing the intercom, "Get me Kissinger" or "Mitterrand" or "Gorbachov", and conversations would take place in

167

various languages which we presumed were carried out to impress.

'Quite often there would be a stranger none of us had met at the meeting but whom Maxwell had ordered to attend. You soon became aware of why that person had been summoned; the poor man had been brought in for the cabaret. When there was a stranger at the table you knew he was the victim for the day, looking so nervous. Maxwell would walk in and say 'Which is Mr So-and-So?' and the poor man would stand up. Maxwell would move round the table to him and just start laying into the poor man.

'I remember one man who had been with a major British company who had something to do with personnel and had been ordered to send out letters to all employees of Pergamon subsidiaries. Maxwell begins by saying to this man who he has never met before: "This letter you have sent out; this is shit, cunt. My old grandmother, who could never speak a word of English, brought up in the mountains of Carpathia, could write better English than this." And that was just the start. Maxwell went on for perhaps a minute, reducing the poor man to a wreck. He tried to reply but Maxwell just ordered him to shut up. "You're not listening to me; watch my lips when I speak to you," he shouted at him.

'Maxwell then ordered this poor guy to leave the room, go to an adjoining office and write down his job description and say exactly why he should continue to be employed by Maxwell; and the poor bastard left the room, nearly in tears, to go off and write this letter prior to his execution.'

Clackson went on: 'The moment he left the room everyone round the table was thinking, "Phew, thank God that's over, thank God it wasn't me that was the sacrificial lamb," and Maxwell would roar with laughter at his own bullyboy tactics as the man left the room. Then, to lighten the atmosphere, he would tell a dirty joke, perhaps about a female traffic warden being fucked by a camel, and he would get the punchline wrong; and yet despite that, everyone, so relieved at the events of the day, would laugh with him, laugh out loud. It was awful and inside you felt awful for laughing, for sitting there while Maxwell had monstered some poor innocent. And his meetings went like that. That was no extraordinary meeting. It would be like that perhaps two or three times a week.'

Maxwell adored being important. He loved inviting important people to his office and perhaps having three or four ambassadors, chief executives and overseas politicians come to his headquarters at any one time. That made him feel important, bolstered his confidence. He told me one afternoon: 'You would have enjoyed it here this morning; you should have come up. I needed you. I had the French Ambassador in my apartment upstairs, one of my bankers in my office and Ian and Kevin were looking after visitors. So I sent Andrea to talk to the Ambassador because she speaks French fluently. Next time that happens I shall call on you.'

Maxwell had one pet hate – signing cheques. It was anathema to him and I remember sitting there on several occasions while he would ask his PA why he should sign the cheque and if the person authorizing the payment was sure it had to be signed that night. Only when told he had to sign that night would Maxwell scribble his barely legible 'M', the letter that had to be on everything, otherwise nothing would get done throughout his empire. He loved the power of withholding that famous letter 'M'.

I remember the time when Jay came into the office while Maxwell and I were chatting one evening. He was trying to persuade Maxwell to sign a cheque towards the Commonwealth Games, the games that Maxwell allegedly saved, but which later he tried all in his power not to fund. Jay said: 'I need you to sign this cheque.'

Looking up at him, Maxwell enquired: 'What is it?'

169

Jay replied: 'The cheque for the Commonwealth Games.'

And he came over and tried to hand him the cheque to sign, but Maxwell stopped him: 'I will decide when I sign that cheque, not you.'

Jay persisted: 'It is my duty to bring this to your attention and the cheque must go out before midnight.'

Maxwell would have none of it. 'I will decide when that cheque is paid, it is none of your business; now fuck off out of here.'

And Jay, downcast again, left the room without another word.

Maxwell always tried to evade signing cheques, making excuses, ordering checks to be made on accounts and invoices, which resulted in weeks of delay before the money had to be paid out. Throughout the building, heads of department would make repeated apologies to clients and suppliers that their account had not been paid, giving innumerable different reasons and excuses, until towards the end they would just admit they had problems persuading Maxwell to sign the cheques. More than that, Maxwell would decide that a bill was too high and invite the chairman of the relevant company to his office to discuss the invoice.

One such invitation was to Young & Rubicam who had been given a budget for the launch of one of his greatest pets, the *European*. Y & R worked long and hard on the launch, having to submit each and every advertisement to Maxwell for his approval, which usually ended in him changing his mind and ordering total rethinks on the ad he had been responsible for in the first place. But when it came to paying the bill Maxwell didn't want to know, and he refused to pay the original amount which he had agreed. Finally, after months of waiting and argument on the telephone, a meeting was arranged at Maxwell House which resulted in Y & R agreeing a much lower fee. It was typical Maxwell, refusing to honour an agreement he had made.

Maxwell received scores of invitations each week, demanding to see each and every invitation; and although he had no intention of actually attending the lunch, dinner, cocktail party or event he would accept the invitation. Usually Jay, Andrea or one of his secretaries would have the unenviable task of phoning hours or minutes before an event to apologize for Maxwell's non-attendance, due to pressure of work or international obligations.

Maxwell's other trick was to accept an invitation and then, at the last minute, order Mrs Maxwell, Kevin or Ian to go in his stead. This often led to arguments when they had made other arrangements for that day. But Maxwell would brook no argument and, on nearly every occasion, the person he deputed to attend would swallow hard and do as they were told.

In the summer of 1990 one such event took place, when Maxwell had not said that he would or would not accept an invitation to an important Jewish event. Mrs Maxwell had told Maxwell's secretary, Judy Welsh, that she really wanted him to attend, because it was of some importance. When the appointed day came nothing was done or said by Maxwell or his wife and an horrendous row broke out between them. As usual, Maxwell blamed everyone else for the mix-up when, of course, it was totally down to him, and after the storm had subsided Mrs Maxwell wrote a note saying that she would 'never disobey an order from Mr Maxwell' and would have attended the dinner if only she had known he wished her to attend. To those secretaries caught in the crossfire it was a minefield.

Most of Maxwell's day was spent in his office or his apartment conducting business. He hated leaving the office, going to meetings or lunches. He always liked to call the shots, he liked to feel he was the most important person in any meeting and he secured that by demanding people come to see him. And most of the time they did. He did

171

leave his ivory tower to go and see Mrs Thatcher or Robin Leigh-Pemberton, or indeed the chairmen of any banks that invited him. But that was about all. He wanted to feel like the emperor summoning his advisors and counsellors and those who wanted to deal with him.

It didn't matter what cost was involved in sustaining that image. He would send his Gulfstream overseas, usually to Europe, to bring in a celebrated guest or to impress someone; he would frequently send the helicopter to Heathrow, or anywhere else to pick up and bring guests to Maxwell House; he would send his Rolls anywhere in the City, the West End or to embassies, to bring visitors back. And he would usually greet them in his most charming manner.

I was often called upstairs to meet one or other of his guests. I would watch as Maxwell decided how each should be received. Some he would kiss enthusiastically on both cheeks and hug them, bear-like, as he welcomed them, as though they were long-lost brothers; yet I knew he hardly knew them, perhaps having met them once or twice. Others he would greet at the door as they were ushered in, put an arm around their shoulders, engage his most ingratiating smile and tell them how kind it was of them to go to all the trouble to come and visit him. To most guests Maxwell was the perfect host, the immaculately behaved gentleman, generous to a fault. They would thank him profusely for sending his plane, helicopter or car to fetch them, touched by Maxwell's generosity of spirit. Maxwell knew the trick of making people feel important. He was a past master at flattery, an expert in ingratiating himself if he thought he would receive some benefit from his fawning behaviour. Sometimes I would stand and watch Maxwell at work, embarrassed at the way he behaved to some of his guests.

I watched one day as he received Shimon Peres, the former Israeli Prime Minister, in the ornate drawing room of his apartment. He threw his arm around him and kissed him on both cheeks, saying how wonderful it was to see him again, how wonderful he looked and what a great privilege and pleasure it was for him to go to all the trouble to come and see him in London.

There were the frequent visits of Leonid Zamyatin, the Soviet Ambassador who in the end was recalled by Moscow in disgrace after he supported the abortive coup against Mikhail Gorbachov a few months before Maxwell's death. I met Zamyatin on a number of occasions both at the Soviet Embassy and Maxwell House. Fascinated by Maxwell's close relationship with Iron Curtain nations, I would pay great attention to this relationship. They were always on the most friendly terms, always joking and smiling together whenever I saw them, and always over-attentive in their responses to each other whenever they met. Maxwell indeed was more effusive towards Zamyatin and it seemed to me that Zamyatin always treated him with the greatest respect, as everyone in Moscow did whenever they met Maxwell.

On occasion it appeared to the suspicious side of my journalistic nature that Maxwell was over-interested in some of the Iron Curtain ambassadors, for they would often arrive with small, inoffensive presents for him for no particular reason. There were bottles of vodka, tins of caviare, occasional books, odd little presents that didn't amount to much but which seemed to be an effort on the part of the ambassador to show his appreciation towards Maxwell; what I tried and failed to determine was what Maxwell was doing in return. I could only guess but whenever I spoke to the ambassadors they were always full of the utmost praise for the work Maxwell was doing for their country.

There were the Bulgarian ambassadors whom Maxwell always fussed over, as well as those from Czechoslovakia, Poland, Hungary and Yugoslavia as well as from Israel. All would come to see Maxwell, most of them arriving in Maxwell's Rolls, which they enjoyed and appreciated. I met

173

most of them from time to time when Maxwell would call me up to chat with them, often while he was involved in talking to someone else in another room.

Sometimes there were the most hilarious occasions in Maxwell House when he had invited numbers of people, all totally separate, to attend at the same time. Perhaps the most remarkable was an occasion when I was called in at the last minute to chat with two Japanese gentlemen from one of Japan's leading newspapers while having lunch in his small, intimate study. Maxwell asked me to go and have some sandwiches with them because he was very pushed and had to attend other lunches.

Champagne was produced and lovely, delicate smoked salmon and other sandwiches were served by Joseph who kept running in and out. What I didn't discover until later was that Maxwell not only had a full lunch for twelve going on in the main dining room; but others were sitting having a small lunch in the drawing room upstairs, while another small delegation were having sandwiches in his office. Maxwell went from room to room, having one course here, another there, a drink in a third; but he kept moving, making apologies all the time to his visitors until the business was completed. I remember him walking into the study as though these two Japanese newspapermen were the only people he wanted to see and talk to; and minutes later, having snaffled three sandwiches which he ate in one bite, he made his apologies and left, returning twenty minutes later for a quiet cup of coffee. In those circumstances Maxwell was a remarkable actor, giving neither his guests nor myself an inkling of the chaos elsewhere.

As his day wore on, Maxwell would have meetings with the directors of Mirror Group Newspapers, checking on production, finance, advertising and circulation, one reason being that the Mirror Group, with its generous cash flow, provided Maxwell with much-needed income to pay off debts accumulating on the private side of his business. His meetings were usually perfectly normal affairs but sometimes they would bring out the worst in him.

I remember meetings in his office when plans for the *European* were being drawn up. They would be held once or twice a week. Most of the time Maxwell was perfectly pleasant but you could tell when he did not like someone and wanted to embarrass or humiliate them. One person he took a dislike to, for no apparent reason, was David Bradbury, a journalist of the old school, around fifty, a little scruffy in appearance, who liked a glass of good wine. A rotund, jovial man, he was a political animal of the old *Mirror* days and a friend of Mike Molloy who had been working on planning the early stages of the *European* from the outset. Whenever Bradbury was asked by Maxwell what he was doing for the new paper the poor man could hardly get a word out before Maxwell lunged at him, telling him what he should be doing. When Bradbury spoke, Maxwell interrupted; when Bradbury tried to explain, Maxwell cut in and ordered him to shut up. As a result Bradbury became tongue-tied and Maxwell became more obnoxious, rude and offensive. Maxwell wanted Bradbury out and told me so, saying he was 'useless'. I discussed the matter with Molloy who did the decent thing and found another job for Bradbury away from the limelight where he was not exposed to Maxwell's abusive behaviour.

Stephen Clackson told of an incident during the planning stages of the *London Daily News* when Maxwell would hold similar planning meetings with senior executives of the paper. Clackson said: 'Maxwell seemed to delight in embarrassing people. On one occasion he told everyone around the table they were incompetent and he would sort things out. He called in one of his new lawyers, a young woman by the name of Debbie Maxwell who had apparently only been with the firm a very short time. When she walked in the room, looking very cool and sophisticated, tall and slim, Maxwell introduced her and then told a really filthy story involving fornicating elephants, but I can't remember the exact joke, which was not at all funny, simply embarrassing. It was the sort of joke that no one would tell in mixed company, particularly in an office in front of a young woman who had been asked to come into a meeting where only men were sitting at the table. Everyone was deeply embarrassed by the joke but we had to laugh because it was Maxwell, their boss, telling the joke. And we did laugh. Yet we all felt embarrassed that we laughed at this appalling joke in front of this sophisticated young lady who was a complete stranger. It was in awfully bad taste and we had gone along with it. That's how embarrassing he could be.'

Maxwell had a knack of being either charming to his staff or dreadful. When he wanted to hire someone it was amazing the lengths to which he would go to impress that person, that 'together they could do whatever was needed'. To that end he would use his plane, his helicopter or his Rolls – simply to impress. He would offer salaries far in excess of what he needed to offer, to let the person believe how important they were to him and how important he believed they were. And people felt flattered, extremely flattered, that this apparent ogre was so sweet, charming, understanding and generous. The honeymoon period, as everyone who worked for Maxwell described it, might last for an hour, a day, a month or a year, but it nearly always came to an end. And yet he didn't seem to like firing people himself, not people to whom he had become close, whom he had invited into his inner circle.

When the time to part arrived Maxwell was most generous in handing out pay-offs, particularly in the last few months of his life. He usually asked Jay to fire staff around the office that he no longer wanted to have around, getting rid of secretaries, receptionists and telephonists nearly every

week. The time had to come when Jay himself was fired
– and he was dumb-struck when Maxwell told him he was
to be axed, explaining that he thought it time they parted
company. Maxwell had given him no inkling that he wanted
to be rid of him. In fact, Maxwell had become suspicious
of Jay and spent months tapping his phone before the axe
fell. Maxwell felt Jay had too many influential friends, that
perhaps he knew too much of what was going on, and
that perhaps he was too bright to keep around. Jay won
a month's reprieve while he looked round for another job
and Maxwell was surprised, and actually delighted, when
Jay told him he had been appointed Economics and Business
Editor of the BBC, a prestigious job with a good salary.

Sometimes Maxwell was genuinely shocked at the reaction of some people when he told them he was to fire
them. One such surprise was a managing director of one
of Maxwell's companies. I walked into Maxwell's office
shortly after he had fired the man and Maxwell seemed
genuinely distressed: 'He started to cry', he said, 'and I
didn't know what to do. All I did was sack him and he
broke down and cried . . . I'll look after him . . . I'll make
sure he doesn't starve.'

Despite the enormous numbers of hirings and firings Maxwell sailed on as though nothing mattered in the world
except his own personal life. Every half hour throughout
the day Maxwell would be handed something to drink, a
glass of orange juice, a large steaming cup of black coffee
or tea. And he would get angry if the glass or cup wasn't
removed from his office after ten minutes because he hated
to see a dirty cup around the place. From six in the morning
that would be his diet, except for lunch, which he invariably
ate. But he did try to eat sensibly, to keep to a diet in an effort
to get down his enormous weight which varied between

nineteen and twenty-two stone, depending on whether he had been strict with himself or not. And when he was on a diet he would try and survive throughout the day on coffee and clear soup.

An hour or so after lunch on most days Maxwell would need to take a siesta and would retire upstairs to his bedroom, change out of his day clothes into his nightshirt, and go to sleep. He never let on. He hoped it was one of his closely guarded secrets. His secretaries were ordered to tell everyone who called that he was in a business meeting and could not be disturbed. Often, he would just go to bed because he was fed up and over-tired. Maxwell would sleep soundly for perhaps two or three hours, occasionally waking and calling for Kevin, Ian, Andrea or one of his personal secretaries to go up and see him, to issue an order, dictate a letter, sort out correspondence or see the latest faxes.

Maxwell enjoyed his big bed. He often liked to work from his bed, something his secretaries hated because it meant they had to run up and down stairs every five minutes because everything he needed to know about was downstairs and they never knew what papers he would want. It didn't worry him a jot that he was making life very difficult for his personal staff. Then at about 6 p.m. when everyone was ready to go home for the day, Maxwell would arrive downstairs ready and eager to restart work. He would have changed into a fresh shirt and suit. Indeed, most days he changed his shirt three times. That was one reason why he kept a Filipino maid just to wash and iron his clothes and do virtually nothing else!

Throughout the years I knew Maxwell he was most prone to colds and we occasionally discussed his health when he was feeling low and under the weather. In Prague on one occasion we were in his hotel suite and he was feeling sorry for himself. 'I don't know why I keep getting colds,' he complained, 'I don't seem to be able to shake them off like I used to. Maybe I'm getting old.'

I commented: 'One of the problems may be that you don't get enough fresh air. You live your life in air-conditioning, in the office, in your apartment, in the aircraft and in the hotel suites where you live overseas. It can't be good for you, especially as you only have one lung.' He wasn't convinced but just nodded his head as though agreeing, and continued to look sorry for himself.

It was in 1955 when Maxwell, who was then smoking forty cigarettes a day, developed severe pains in his chest. It was diagnosed as secondary cancer of the lungs. Maxwell was told that he only had four weeks to live. His eldest son, Michael, then nine, was brought to the hospital to say goodbye to his father and later the other five children – Anne, Philip, Christine, Isabel and Karine (who herself died two years later) – were brought from home to say goodbye.

It was decided to obtain a second opinion and this was more hopeful. Further tests were made and during an explanatory operation the surgeon found he only had to remove the upper left lobe of Maxwell's right lung. It was benign. Maxwell knew he had been near death and immediately stopped smoking cigarettes completely. To the end of his life he hated cigarettes and would forbid any employees or members of his family to smoke in his presence, ever. It is true that Maxwell took up smoking Havana cigars but less so during the last few years of his life.

He was never without his inhaler due to this and would often take courses of antibiotics to clear a particularly nagging cold. But he would never complete the course of antibiotics, a necessity, and as a result the cold would return and he would take more pills to try and alleviate the symptoms which did undoubtedly drag him down. Stupidly, if one lot of pills didn't work he would try something different, and then be surprised that he wasn't instantly getting better. I remember the odd occasion when he would actually lose his voice and be unable to speak except for a hoarse whisper. Quite naturally that caused much hilarity among his staff, but not many people were privy to such occasions for he would just go to bed and stay there until he was better.

Because of his weight and his age, Maxwell suffered quite often from back-ache for which he would take strong painkillers, not just the odd aspirin. And if the symptoms persisted then he would call his osteopath from Oxford to come and 'fix' his back. During the last few years Maxwell would send his helicopter to Oxford to pick up his osteopath and then fly him back home again after treatment. The osteopath would arrive on the top of Maxwell House with his portable table, which was difficult to bring down the awkward stairs leading from the roof. Maxwell would demand he came at a moment's notice, in the evenings or at weekends if he was in pain.

And yet despite the enormous pressure of work, despite the incredible financial problems and the most demanding schedule for a man in his late sixties, Maxwell hardly ever suffered from a headache. It seemed that his entire life was one long headache yet he never complained of having one. Indeed, I remember him boasting to me: 'I never get headaches because I have a remarkable brain.'

One major problem Maxwell did suffer from was obesity. As a young man, over six feet tall with a good physique and with his good looks and strong face, he caught the attention of many a young woman. He undoubtedly had character and personality and could ooze charm at will. Even in his forties he was not overweight. From the age of fifty, however, Maxwell began putting on weight at an enormous rate and would sometimes reach twenty-two stone. He did diet, or said he did, and was embarrassed about his weight. One morning in Tokyo, dressed only in his white bathrobe, I remember him saying to me, as he patted his vast girth:

'I really must do something about this; it really is not very good.'

I asked him naively: 'Do you ever diet?'

He didn't reply, but gave me a filthy look and disappeared into his bedroom.

Maxwell did indeed diet. On a number of occasions he tried the famed Cambridge diet but after a few days he forgot it and went on a binge, eating anything he could lay his hands on. He often tried to eat nothing but fruit, which he loved. Before he felt rich enough to stay in the Ritz or the Georges V in Paris, Maxwell stayed in his little apartment in the rue des Écoles, where he would love to go out to the local market and buy fruit. He loved exotic fruit, like wild strawberries, and would often eat fruit ten times a day, but leaving the skins, the peel, pips and stones wherever he was, never bothering to put them on a plate or in a wastepaper bin.

In December 1987, fed up with being unable to stem his weight, he decided on drastic action – he went into a London clinic and had his stomach sewn up by a Harley Street specialist. But he told no one of the operation. He should have had the stitches removed after three months but chose to keep them in, convinced he was eating less. Finally, after repeated calls from the specialist, he did go back into the clinic to have the stitches removed – and promptly went back to eating huge meals again.

Another way he tried to stop eating was by ordering the lock on his kitchen to be changed in 1988. Maxwell confessed that he would get up in the middle of the night, wander into the kitchen and gorge on a whole cold chicken or a leg of lamb, scoffing half a loaf of bread and finishing off with loads of fruit. Then he would go back to bed. But his idea of locking the kitchen door didn't help for he ordered the locksmith to give him a spare key. In the middle of the night he would creep into the kitchen, gorge himself

181

anyway and then lock the door afterwards, pretending he hadn't been there. And next day, despite the fact that bones and half-eaten food were strewn all over the place, he would deny that he had been anywhere near the kitchen. 'How could I?' he would protest. 'I haven't got a key.'

Stories of Maxwell and his gargantuan appetite are legion. He knew where he could get something to eat in London twenty-four hours round the clock. He would send out his staff, usually the faithful Bob Cole, at all hours whenever he wanted something special. One night he called up Cole at 10 p.m. and said, 'Go and get me some fresh fruit.'

Cole explained the time and said no shops were open; it was impossible.

Maxwell told him to go out and buy some from a barrow-boy. Again Cole told him it was impossible. 'Go to the Haymarket Theatre and outside you will find a barrow with fruit on it. Go and buy some Cox's pippin apples and plums.'

Wearily Cole obeyed and was surprised to find Maxwell was absolutely right. There was a barrow-boy outside the Haymarket Theatre.

Sometimes, late at night, he would ask Cole to go out and buy a £10 bucket of Col. Saunders Kentucky Fried Chicken and lots of chips; other times he would send him to the exclusive Poon's Restaurant to buy Chinese food and order him to bring back £50 worth which he would consume himself!

And there was one wonderful night when Maxwell with his chauffeur Les Williams found himself in Batley, Yorkshire, renowned for the best fish and chips in Britain. He told Williams to drive round until he found a fish and chip shop. Together they walked in and Maxwell said to the woman behind the counter: 'What have you got?'

She replied: 'Cod, haddock, plaice, rock salmon, scampi.'

Maxwell said: 'I'll have two of each and 50p worth of chips because I'm slimming.'

And when they had finished their massive meal, which must have done Maxwell no good at all with all the batter surrounding the fried fish, he wrapped everything up in newspaper and threw it out of the window as they drove out of Batley!

And yet Maxwell was obsessed by tidiness and cleanliness, especially in the kitchen. In many ways he was fastidious whenever it concerned anyone else, but not about his own habits. He demanded the kitchen was spotless and yet he was a complete slob when it came to eating, raiding a kitchen, or leaving half-eaten food around. Once he had started eating something he would never bother to put it back unfinished; never bother to clean up after himself; never tidy anything of his own personal belongings. He always demanded totally fresh food and wouldn't tolerate any fruit that was more than a day old. He sacked one Filipino maid for keeping some food which was more than a day old in the refrigerator!

In public Maxwell was never a big eater, but in private he seemed unable to control his appetite. In Sofia, Bulgaria, on one occasion I remember walking into the kitchen of his suite one morning and watching as he stuffed food into his mouth at an enormous rate, picking up five or six small sandwiches at a time and cramming them into his mouth so that he could hardly chew the food. It was like watching a starving man, driven mad by hunger, unable to control himself as he forced handfuls of food into his mouth. He must have sensed me there, because he turned and saw me standing in the doorway. For a split second he was like a cornered animal, as though I had caught him thieving. He stood up straight, drew the back of his hand across his bulging mouth, picked up some food and put it in the refrigerator. I just said: 'Good morning,' and never

183

alluded to the sight again. That single incident revealed the fight Maxwell had with the appetite that he was obviously unable to control.

Maxwell was also generous with anyone when it came to food and drink. On flights overseas he would always enquire if people had eaten; if one came to see him for more than a few minutes he would ask if one needed a drink or something to eat. He made sure secretaries had eaten and would tell them to stop work and go and get something to eat if he discovered they had skipped lunch or it was getting late in the evening. I spoke to him about Ethiopia and the starving children there. He said: 'I can remember going hungry when I was young; I can remember being hungry at night when I went to bed. No one should go hungry.'

Yet he did like going for walks, but not proper, long walks. I remember in Finland persuading him to go for a walk one evening in beautiful sunshine and the most lovely clear atmosphere, so different from London or New York. He was standing outside the hotel enjoying the clean air and I chanced by.

'Let's go for a walk,' I suggested and he agreed.

'I don't walk enough,' he volunteered and I nodded, saying I thought that would do him more good than anything and chastizing him for not getting enough fresh air. 'I like walking but I don't get any time. You don't realize I'm not like ordinary men; I don't have time to take care of myself.'

I disagreed with him, telling him it was the only way to live a longer life.

'You may be right,' he admitted, 'but before I could enjoy real walking I would need to get rid of this bulk.' For about ten minutes we strolled, rather than walked; he climbed on to a wall like a young boy and walked along the top of it putting one foot in front of the other, having to balance himself on the narrow bricks. I followed, but when we had walked about thirty feet along the sloping wall, we were then ten feet above the ground and he decided we had done enough. But he had problems turning round and nearly fell off the wall. I remembered that he had suffered a broken ankle only a year or so before, when getting out of the helicopter, and dreaded the idea of Maxwell falling down, breaking his ankle again. Fortunately, he managed it and we walked back again. When we got back to the hotel he took a deep breath and said: 'That's better,' as though we had done a five-mile hike. We had walked a few hundred yards.

He was a vain man in every sense of the word. That was why he had his hair – and eyebrows – coloured every two weeks by George Wheeler, a former hairdresser at the Savoy, who would come to Maxwell House and spend two hours washing, cutting and colouring Maxwell's hair. Officially, it was a closely guarded secret. Hardly anyone saw Maxwell while this operation was going on. I remember being in Exeter when Maxwell was to make a speech the next day and George Wheeler, then in his seventies, was summoned from London. I walked into his small hotel suite that morning and called out, 'Bob, I need a word.'

Maxwell's booming voice replied: 'You can't come in, it's private. If you want to ask me something stay out there and shout.'

So I did.

Then he said: 'Go away.' I knew he was having his hair done but he didn't want me to know.

Wheeler would often complain that he could never get Maxwell to sit still long enough for his chemical colouring process to take effect; that he would become impatient and tell him to finish the job quickly. To make sure his hair stayed 'just right' Maxwell would go to bed most nights with a hair net on his head.

185

Maxwell would call for Mr Wheeler, as he called him with some respect, wherever he was in the world. Sometimes he would be flown to the *Lady Ghislaine*, while it was moored in Sardinia or the Canaries, flying club class, or to Paris or wherever. He also had his nails manicured and colourless polish applied every few weeks by his own private manicurist.

His vanity knew no bounds. The only time I ever saw Maxwell panic, and it was always for the same reason, was when he realized he was heading out without his powder puff. He kept it in his jacket pocket, a very ordinary, inexpensive Rimmel powder. For some reason he always thought he had a shiny nose and I would see him dabbing away at his nose before meeting important people. To carry out his powdering he would always turn away, embarrassed. And he was too shy to refer to his powder puff by name. He would tap his pocket, realize it wasn't there and turn round to Simon or Joseph or his secretary as though in a minor panic. 'I haven't got my, you know,' he would say and he would turn on his heel and go and fetch it himself rather than have the ignominy of asking aloud for someone to go and fetch his puff. Those who travelled with him all knew his little secret but no one alluded to it. Sometimes I felt embarrassed for him because he would apply so much powder that it was not only obvious but looked ridiculous, and yet because no one was meant to know, no one would point out that too much powder had been applied.

And he applied so much aftershave – which he would splash on whether or not he had just shaved – that you could smell he had passed by some time later. But he didn't keep to one special cologne, preferring different ones.

He always had his shirts made for him at a New York custom shop, with his initials IRM on them; he had his rather loud suits tailored for him in Savile Row, but his very loud ties, which he loved, came from Harrods. Often they were sent on approval and Maxwell would decide to buy a few and send the rest back. He contemplated having his shoes made for him but when he discovered what he considered to be an astronomical price, he shied away from the idea, content instead to wear rather ordinary slip-on casual shoes. He wore these for ease of putting them on because, with his bulk, he could not bend down low enough to tie shoelaces. He always had close by him, in his bedroom, on the plane, in his travel bag, long shoehorns, which meant he didn't have to bend too much to put on the shoes.

Sometimes at night he would go to bed at around 10 p.m. and lie watching television or one of his favourite movies on video, a Clint Eastwood or a James Bond film. Usually, the volume was turned up loud. He would watch the news and CNN, the American cable news network, as well as soccer matches, and, when bored, would constantly flick from one channel to another trying to find something to interest him. He would hardly ever have dinner with anyone, not even his sons. He was happier going to his bed and having his dinner served there, waiting for the next day's papers to be sent up to him so he could read them before going to sleep for the night.

Sleeplessness was one of Maxwell's problems despite the fact that he was often exhausted by the end of the day. There are wonderful stories of people holding long overseas conversations with Maxwell, conversations of the utmost importance, when the person at the other end would suddenly hear grunting and snoring – Maxwell had simply fallen asleep. I witnessed one such incident at about nine one evening in London. There were two or three of us in his drawing room and his head suddenly slumped back and he began to snore heavily, his mouth wide open, which was not a pretty sight. His son Ian came in, went over to him and shook him gently: 'Come on, Dad, wake up, it's time for bed,' and with a start Maxwell woke up, a little embarrassed, and got up and went to bed.

He began taking the sleeping pill Halcion, which became the world's top-selling sleeping pill during the 1980s. He would take one or two pills before going to bed for the night to make sure he got a full night's sleep and didn't wake up too early, as he was prone to do. He began to rely on them, always taking them with him when flying, often taking a pill while flying the Atlantic, and would sometimes arrive rather drowsy as the effect of the pill hadn't totally worn off. Towards the end of his life he was taking more pills as he found it more difficult to sleep. He knew the risks of Halcion but chose to ignore them.

He had been informed that there were certain risks to Halcion; that doctors were receiving reports that people taking Halcion were prone to 'psychiatric effects' more common than other benzodiazepine drugs such as Xanax, Valium and Dalmane. Research undertaken in the United States showed that people were prone to daytime amnesia. Upjohn, the US company which made the drug, have always defended Halcion as a safe and effective drug with similar side-effects to other benzodiazepines. And they claimed that the drug was safe to use at the recommended dosages. But in October 1991, one month before Maxwell's death, the drug was withdrawn from sale in Britain after it was banned by the UK Department of Health, which claimed Halcion was associated with a much higher frequency of side-effects than other sleeping medications. It had been banned in Holland. However, the pill continued to be on sale in the United States. A panel set up by the US Food and Drug Administration cleared Halcion in May 1992 after recommending changes in labelling to underline the dangers of side-effects.

Professor William Asscher, Chairman of the UK Committee on Safety of Medicines, said in 1991: 'We are not banning Halcion because of the withdrawal symptoms, which are common to all these drugs, but because Halcion appears to lead to more insomnia, depression, memory impairment, hallucinations, sometimes aggressive behaviour and more paranoia than other, similar drugs.' Many people who knew Maxwell closely would indeed agree that many of those side-effects could well have been a description of his behaviour during the last year or so of his life.

Dr Samuel Pisar, a distinguished and respected French lawyer and friend of Maxwell's who knew him well during the last few years of his life, had a background similar to Maxwell's. A Jew like Maxwell, he actually lived through the horror of Nazi death camps but somehow survived the gas chambers. The families of both men were murdered in Auschwitz. Those experiences, and the fact that both men were raised in the all-pervading fear of the holocaust, brought them close. Some months after Maxwell's death, Dr Pisar told me: 'Something must have gone desperately wrong. I have read all the allegations against him; I have read the reports that he plundered his companies and the pension funds of more than a billion pounds; but all this does not equate to the man I knew. Of course I did not know him that well, or for very many years, but I do believe that something must have gone desperately wrong for him in those last few months. I must tell you that I found him very odd during the last few months, doing some very odd things that didn't make sense.

'It is very painful for me to know that he did these appalling things I have heard and read about. I do believe that something went wrong with his mind. Towards the end I would sometimes speak to him and he was incoherent, not making sense in some of the things he said. I have tried to think, but I cannot put forward anything that could be a

189

greater good to mitigate what he did. All I can say is that what I have read does not make any sense whatsoever. It pains and hurts me that I became close to him when it seems obvious that all these awful things were about to happen, and he made them happen. Now we shall never know but it may be that something went wrong with his mind.'

The European Commission Proprietary Medicines Committee suggested that Halcion should only be prescribed for 'severe' sleeping disorders, that it should not be used for more than two to three weeks and that the dose should not exceed 0.25 mg for adults and 0.125 mg for elderly patients. It also advised that patients with psychiatric disorders should not be prescribed the drug. Maxwell had been taking the drug for years, not just for weeks, and he had been taking higher doses than that recommended by Upjohn or the EC Committee.

Throughout the years I knew Maxwell there was very little enjoyment, very little *joie de vivre* about him. Always he appeared restless, agitated. His irrational outbursts of anger, his childish temper and tantrums, were not of a mature, balanced, ordinary human being, especially one who had achieved many of his ambitions. Maxwell kept making new ambitions for himself, pushing himself to new goals, but he never became the world-respected statesman and international power-broker he wanted to be; nor did he make the world's top ten publishing companies – both ambitions of which he spoke to me and others. He was always intolerant, more often than not irritable and impatient, certainly headstrong and enormously arrogant, but there was more than that to his behaviour. There was an emotional restlessness about him, a deep-rooted obsession, if not an unnatural urge to dominate and rule, and I wondered whether his excitability and irrational behaviour amounted at times to a madness.

Frequently when he was alive, and certainly since his death, I have been asked by many people whether I thought Maxwell was genuinely mad – insane, unsound of mind, or suffering from intellectual unbalance. I was not competent to judge such a condition and yet I have to say that some of his behaviour, some of the actions I witnessed, some of his violent mood swings, made me wonder whether he was always of sound mind or whether, occasionally, his reason was undermined or disordered. He certainly suffered from paranoia, a deep suspicion of everyone, including his personal staff, his employees, his fellow directors, if not members of his own family. For the vast majority of the time, however, he was normal, sane, totally in possession of his faculties and entirely rational. Most of the time I spent with him I did respect his undoubted intelligence, his reasoning, his lateral thinking. Sometimes I thought him a genius but I never considered him an intellectual, because I don't know whether he was capable of original thought.

In the last few years of his life Maxwell was probably only really happy when he was on his yacht, the *Lady Ghislaine*. To Maxwell, his yacht was the culmination of all his life's endeavours, all the trials and tribulations he had been through to make the millions so that he could buy the boat of his dreams. On board, he was far away from his worries, his anxieties, his problems – and yet, whenever he wished, he was in touch with the world through fax or phone.

He took pride that it was one of the largest and most luxurious yachts in the world. He would frequently order the skipper to moor the yacht in harbours where it would attract the greatest attention and where it would put to shame the yachts of other world magnates and personalities. The *Lady Ghislaine* was some ocean-going vessel, 155 metres long, with five luxurious cabins, four with double beds, as well as its own stateroom with two adjoining bathrooms and a dressing room. An office, fully equipped with computers, printers, a fax and phone links, as well as a shredder, adjoined Maxwell's stateroom. There was a dining room, which was rather dark, which Maxwell hardly ever used, and two large reception rooms. The boat had three sundecks and the top sundeck was the only place which had no surveillance from the bridge. There was a sauna and a gymnasium which led off the top sundeck, but Maxwell was never known to step inside the gym, let alone use any of the equipment.

The seventieth birthday bash of the late American billionaire Malcolm Forbes, gave Maxwell a chance he couldn't resist – to show off his splendid yacht. The owner of America's foremost business magazine, collector-extraordinary, balloonist, motorcyclist and a squire of filmstar Elizabeth Taylor, gave the blow-out of a lifetime when he invited four hundred and fifty of the world's wealthiest people to a three-day party in Tangiers in 1989. Total cost, including the hiring of six hundred dancers and two hundred Berber horsemen, was about £2 million.

With such a constellation of guests, collectively worth around £20 billion, protocol was a potential nightmare, so to avoid any embarrassment Forbes decided to provide the same accommodation for them all – rooms in the smart Solazur Hotel. But not Maxwell. Fearing he might be lost among the crowd of billionaires Maxwell refused the invitation to join everyone else and fly out in one of the four chartered aircraft. He insisted on flying in his own Gulfstream and ordered that the *Lady Ghislaine* should move to Tangiers and moor in the harbour there.

More embarrassment was to follow. The invitation demanded black tie and 'exotic dress' for the women. To make sure he would be noticed by one and all Maxwell decided to go in exotic dress and ordered Mark Booth, the handsome young chief executive of Maxwell Entertainment Group, to find him an appropriate costume. He provided the most amazing and bizarre outfit – the bright, colourful robes of a genuine Arabian pasha, replete with turban. With every other man smartly dressed in black tie, Maxwell looked totally out of place.

On arrival in Tangiers Maxwell decided he wanted to go and see Forbes but had no invitation. Not put off, he headed for Forbes's residence, but was not allowed entry by the guards. Undaunted, he clambered over the railings and arrived at the house. Eventually, Forbes made an appearance, looking distinctly put out by the intrusion, accepted graciously the birthday present Maxwell gave him, but never invited Maxwell into the house. After only three minutes Forbes made his apologies and shut the door.

The day after the party Maxwell discovered that Rupert Murdoch, who had also brought a yacht to Tangiers, was hosting a party, and he managed to get an invitation for himself and Mrs Maxwell. But before leaving the *Lady Ghislaine* Maxwell ordered his chef to prepare a sumptuous lunch for about twenty people. He intended to scupper Murdoch's party by inviting all Murdoch's guests over to the *Lady Ghislaine*. But his plot failed. No one would leave the Murdoch party. In the end, two hours later, Maxwell returned with just three guests who only wanted coffee. When Maxwell returned, minutes before his hijacked guests, he ordered the stewards to remove the splendid buffet lunch as quickly as possible. It was amazing that Maxwell appeared to take not the slightest notice of such rebuffs.

Most of the time on board, however, Maxwell would love to disport himself on the top sundeck where no one could see him, strip down to his swimming trunks and smother himself with suncream. In a basket on the deck he kept about twenty different suncreams. He would help himself to drinks from the fridge in a corridor leading to the gym, which was always stocked with Dom Perignon, pink Krystal champagne and beer. He took a nefarious delight in spying on other ships with his powerful binoculars, seeing if he could recognize anyone and spot what they were doing.

This was his headquarters during the day and he loved the feeling of power and privilege that came from controlling his vast empire from the sundeck of his magnificent yacht while he cruised through the Mediterranean or some other blue tropical waters. He would order Andrea Martin to come to the sundeck and sunbathe while taking notes, getting phone calls and acting as his secretary. All the calls would go through the bridge and Maxwell adored lying in the sun talking to his minions around the world, slaving away in their offices, helping him earn another million!

Lunch would be served on the sundeck. Masses of food would be brought up the two flights of stairs by three or four sailors whose job it was to keep the fridge replenished and the food trays full of delicacies. Vast quantities of seafood would be served, including salmon, lobster, crab, mussels, clams and other shellfish, lashings of caviare, pâté de foie gras and delicious cheeses. All this Maxwell would consume followed by ice-cream and fresh fruit. Despite the fact that the chief steward and one or two assistants would serve lunch to him, Maxwell insisted on serving himself, so that he could pile more on his plate without people realizing he was being greedy and gluttonous. Usually he would wash it all down with a bottle or two of iced pink champagne. Sometimes he would also drink a bottle of white wine and after lunch would be tiddly, unsteady on his feet, but never actually drunk or incapable. He was in his element and he revelled in the absolute luxury, spoiling himself rotten. It was everything he had ever dreamed of for himself and he was living it to the full. There was nothing more he could want for on those long summer days and he was relaxed and happy.

Maxwell truly lived life like a monarch during those days

and weeks at sea, as his servants – the sailors – ran up and down to the sundeck bringing him faxes and messages and answering to his every whim and command. He kept a hand bell on the deck which he would ring for attention, and would insist the stewards removed the dishes the moment he had finished eating because he hated being surrounded by dirty plates.

He was also extremely fussy about what he ate. He hated garlic or onions and told the chef he would be sacked immediately if he ever discovered an onion in the yacht's kitchen. On one occasion he did fire a chef – because he had put a cheese in the refrigerator! He hated sauces or gravy because he believed they polluted the food. Everything had to be fresh that day and vast amounts of food were thrown away, and money wasted, because of his demand for fresh food.

On the *Lady Ghislaine* Maxwell would forget all about diets or watching his weight. He would eat food that in London he would order never to be served to him, like chips or lashings of ice-cream. Any food he disliked he would describe as 'camel's dung' or 'monkey's crap' and throw it away for the birds.

And then there was dinner. During the afternoon he was shown the menu for dinner with a choice of two or three first courses and a couple of main courses. He always insisted dinner was served inside with low lights and music. He loved Gershwin and would often order the same music to be played and re-played throughout the evening when he would reminisce about his life, his mother, his childhood, as he drank too heavily. Maxwell would drink a bottle of white Burgundy for the first course, a bottle of his favourite Petrus, which cost about £250 a bottle, with the main course and perhaps another bottle with the cheese. Then he would finish with a couple of schooners of vintage port, some bottles more than one hundred years old.

He didn't like having visitors on board. He preferred the entire yacht to himself, with the exception of Andrea Martin and the thirteen-man crew. He didn't even like having his family on board either. He would usually arrange to hold one business meeting on board whenever he visited the yacht so that the trip could be put down against tax as a necessary business expense. Otherwise he didn't invite people to join him on the yacht except on special occasions. People did visit him on board, but only by his invitation, so that he could show off to them; and the more important the person the more he smiled and joked with them as he showed them round. He liked throwing occasional lavish parties on board when no expense was spared; and he held a few prestigious press conferences so the world's press could admire his magnificent opulence and wonder at his wealth. That was why he launched the *European* on board and threw a party in New York to celebrate buying the *Daily News*. Whenever strangers, such as journalists, came on board, Maxwell's paranoia would surface: extra security men were hired to patrol the decks, all cabins were locked, all papers were shredded or locked away and all telephone lists removed out of sight. He wanted no one to share the privacy and secrecy of his life on board. But those occasions were few and far between; most of the time he preferred his own company.

Usually Maxwell walked around the yacht barefoot wearing brightly coloured shorts and T-shirts, often with a baseball cap. His wardrobes on board were full of clothes, mostly bright, summery clothes and outfits Mrs Maxwell had bought for him and sent down to the yacht, so that when he visited the boat he hardly brought any clothes with him. He would often swim early in the morning, at six o'clock, and sometimes in the late afternoon. He loved to swim naked and nearly always did so. A sailor would always be standing by watching Maxwell in the water, for safety's sake, and, if necessary, to hold the telephone for him. Maxwell was a good, strong swimmer and could float for ages without moving a muscle. And yet, to be safe, he had a ring which was attached to about fifty feet of rope from where he would never swim too far. When he walked up the steps after swimming he would say to the sailor watching over him: 'Not bad for a pensioner, eh?'

After a morning swim and a good breakfast Maxwell would usually take one of the two tenders to collect the morning newspapers from the nearest port. He would buy not just the British newspapers but also the French and German as well as the *New York Herald Tribune*. Maxwell nearly always steered the tender, powering the boat as fast as possible in a reckless fashion to call attention to himself. He claimed to one and all that he was a very good sailor and loved the sea but he always had seasickness pills on board and would often use them when he arrived at the boat.

On board the *Lady Ghislaine* Maxwell became so relaxed he sometimes reverted to what can only be described as his 'baby talk'. He would refer to a 'swim in the sea' as a 'twim in the tea'; he would say 'trightened' for 'frightened', 'minkey' for 'monkey', 'deaded' for 'tired', 'losted' for 'lost' and called his pockets 'sky rockets', as well as other such childlike words which he would make up. It was all part of his bizarre behaviour pattern when he was off-guard.

For some reason Maxwell often loved to substitute 'ch' for 'sh' when he was indulging in baby talk. For example he would say 'chip' for 'ship' when referring to the *Lady Ghislaine*; he would call 'shirts' and 'shoes' his 'chirts' and 'choes'; he would say 'chop' for 'shop'. Another favourite was to replace 'r' with 'w' so that he would say 'Wussia' for 'Russia'.

He did the same with people's names. He loved making up names for his employees and acquaintances, as well as giving people nicknames and pseudonyms, for those whose

197

identities he wanted to keep secret. For example, he always referred to the black American Democrat politician Jesse Jackson as 'Mr White', referring in fact to all black people as 'white' and laughing when he did so, an example of Maxwell's odd sense of humour. One of his solicitors, Mr Philip Morgenstern of Nicholson Graham & Jones, he called 'Mr Morning Star' (after the newspaper); Mr Clive Chalk, executive director at bankers Samuel Montagu he called 'Mr Cheese' and he called the libel lawyer Peter Carter-Ruck 'Peter Carter-Fuck'.

If there was a really good restaurant where the yacht moored for the night Maxwell would sometimes go ashore for a change of scenery and to stretch his legs. He would try to make sure the *Lady Ghislaine* was moored so that everyone in the port could see and admire his yacht. He would take a walk along the harbour, and a sailor from the yacht would walk ten paces behind, for Maxwell's personal protection. And he would always take his walkie-talkie set with him, to keep in touch with the bridge. Occasionally, he would go to a casino and gamble for two or three hours, always the centre of attraction as he demanded to play two roulette tables at a time, gambling hundreds if not thousands of pounds at the single throw of the dice. Sometimes he won, sometimes he lost, but it never worried him. He just liked the challenge of playing two tables and having other gamblers watching him play.

In his earlier days Maxwell had been a keen gambler, often visiting casinos in London and overseas in a bid to challenge the tables and illustrate that his intelligence was capable of beating the odds. In his younger days Maxwell was an inveterate gambler but in his later years, certainly since taking over the Mirror Group in 1984, he only gambled occasionally. Primarily he played roulette but would sometimes try his luck at other games like black-jack.

In 1989 he walked into a casino in Nice but wasn't sure

whether he would be allowed to play because it was strictly members only. Maxwell asked to see the manager and turned on the charm, telling the man that he had played at the casino once before, but that was more than twenty years ago. The manager returned a few minutes later and happily told Maxwell that he was correct, he had played there, and, what was more, he was still a member.

When we were playing the tables in Paris once, I asked Maxwell whether he had ever been a big gambler. He gave me an old-fashioned look, suggesting I shouldn't have the temerity to ask such a personal question, and said: 'Yes. And I discovered it was a fool's game, but it does have a certain fascination, a challenge. I liked to play when I was bored.'

There have been stories that Maxwell would gamble hundreds of thousands of pounds a night but that is difficult to verify. He was certainly a member of several clubs in London, and his favourite was Maxims, but people who accompanied him gambling only saw him win or lose around £50,000 at an evening session. A lot of money, but not by Maxwell's standards. Undeniably his kick was to show off at a casino, but he wasn't a good gambler, throwing chips on to the tables, apparently haphazardly, and seeming not to care whether he won or lost. However, he did like to leave a casino with money in his pocket, or better still, one of the casino's cheques, simply so he could say he had won. But these were in the late 1980s when he seemed to be playing out of boredom, not a feverish gambling urge.

But to those back at base Maxwell was determined to keep up his customary reign of terror. He spent half the day on the telephone calling his lieutenants and his editors, making suggestions, demanding changes, throwing his weight around. On one occasion, after a very good lunch, he phoned Jay in Holborn only to find he was out to lunch. When Jay returned his call, Maxwell turned up the heat, demanding to know why he had had the temerity to leave the office without permission when the chairman (Maxwell) was abroad. He demanded Jay write an explanation immediately giving reasons for his absence and fax it to him on the yacht. When he received Jay's long explanatory note Maxwell read it, roaring with laughter at what he saw as a huge joke. Then he phoned Jay back and tore into him again, pretending to be furious.

Maxwell would behave like this whenever he was bored. Every Friday, virtually without fail, when Maxwell was abroad he would phone Joe Haines. The reason was that Haines only came into the office from Monday to Thursday, staying at home for the rest of the week. This infuriated Maxwell who believed that Haines should come into the office at least five days a week for the money he was being paid. So, to punish him, Maxwell would phone most Fridays with some task or other he wanted him to perform, making him do something which would take time and trouble and interrupt his long weekends. Then he would put down the phone with great amusement.

On board Maxwell would while away the hours when he wasn't eating or working by watching videos, often spy thrillers. At night he would play chess, backgammon or cards with Andrea and would always cheat if he thought he was about to lose. He would become totally ruthless at any game and refused ever to admit he had lost. And when challenged that he had cheated, which he frequently did, he would categorically deny it, prepared to do anything to win the game.

In reality, except for occasional important phone calls, Maxwell's time on the yacht was spent relaxing, eating and enjoying himself. To everyone else, especially his wife, he pretended that Mrs Maxwell could not accompany him there because he would be working most of the time. Indeed, the family were hardly ever invited, but they weren't unhappy about that. Kevin and Ian were happy away from their father, for on board he would just spend time attacking them for no good reason; Ghislaine knew that she would simply be used for secretarial duties. For most of the time on board the yacht Maxwell behaved like a spoiled child, loving every minute of it.

All the time, however, Maxwell was paranoid about security. This was unusual for him, for whenever we travelled overseas, no matter where, he would always say he didn't need, or want, any security whatsoever. He was often asked before going to a foreign country, particularly in the Eastern bloc, whether he wanted security and he always refused it. But on board he was remarkably wary at all times as though he feared an attack on his life. He ordered his first captain, an Englishman, Mike Insull, to buy guns which were to be kept on board. In his liking for secrecy Maxwell always referred to them as 'vegetables'. And he ordered Insull to train the crew in how to use them 'just in case it might be necessary one day'.

Whenever he came on board Maxwell would ask Insull: 'How many carrots and potatoes have you brought on this trip?'

No one was meant to know to what he was referring but he told Andrea – to see her reaction to living near possible danger. He would always watch any other ships sailing nearby to check if people were tracking him and he ordered Andrea never to hold up faxes when she was reading them in case any nearby ship might have such sophisticated surveillance equipment that they could read the faxes from hundreds of yards away. Nothing revealed Maxwell's paranoia more than his behaviour when on the yacht, but it did reveal his state of mind, and undoubted fear of a possible attack on his life.

EIGHT

'You have my word that you can trust me.'

Robert Maxwell was a born traveller. He loved movement and hated to be stuck in one place for long, even his own home. Travel, mobility, action were like drugs to Maxwell, an urge, seemingly a necessity, whether it was moving from one chair to another or jetting off across the world. He was forever restless. And yet during all the times I travelled with him, Maxwell never seemed to learn anything from his journeys as most travellers do; he never showed any interest whatsoever in his surroundings; though spending much time in the world's capital cities he would never go to operas or concerts, ballets or plays, art galleries or museums; he could just as well have been in the middle of Moscow, Manchester, Munich or Minneapolis, for all the difference it made to him.

It was due to his innate sense of boredom. He could never sit still at a dinner, at a concert or an opera, for any length of time without becoming fidgety and bored. You could tell in an instant that his interest had waned for he would never make any pretence at idle chatter, never make any effort to stimulate or interest himself. His boredom threshold was low and he made no secret of the fact. And it was the same with his travels. He felt that movement was action and he had this compulsive need to be active. He would occasionally go for a short stroll but never to see shops or explore a city, rather to snatch a little fresh air and to escape the confines of his hotel suite.

Maxwell travelled with one objective – to get to his destination in the shortest possible time. He would cause chaos with his staff by the demands he made on them, time and again, rearranging his schedule without a thought to the enormous problems he was causing. Often, his four-seater Aerospatiale Twin Squirrel helicopter, registration G-RMGN, would be waiting on top of Maxwell House in New Fetter Lane to whisk him away to his waiting Gulfstream at Heathrow. Maxwell knew that he had to abide by time slots, particularly at certain times of the day, but he never seemed to care.

He knew there were restrictions on the flying of helicopters at dusk and dawn, and during the hours of darkness, over metropolitan London – for sensible safety reasons. And yet he would often try to order his helicopter pilot to take off as darkness fell.

Maxwell knew there were strict conditions about flying too and he tried all in his power to suggest that he was above such orderly regulations. Time slots control the airways, especially at such congested airports as Heathrow, the world's busiest international airport, but Maxwell would just shout at his managers on the ground to sort everything out for him so he could take off the moment he climbed aboard his Gulfstream. Incredibly, Maxwell did seem able to squeeze his take-off into slots that the authorities at Heathrow had said were not available. Of course, he loved doing that, making his own rules, disregarding regulations and restrictions, having people realize that Bob Maxwell was a Very Important Person indeed!

He had spent much of his early business years in the 1950s and 1960s flying around the world trying to sell Pergamon's scientific books, journals and encyclopaedias. He would issue press statements that he was about to embark on selling trips and at each capital he visited he would call on the prime minister's office or the president's residence and issue further statements, announcing great orders and sales. Sometimes he would meet those in power, and there are photographs to show he did, but not all those meetings he boasted of actually took place. He hyped his sales and his deals and always returned to London having achieved a dramatic success, which he instantly announced to the press. The shocks were reserved for his senior staff who would rush around reorganizing their production schedules in light of the sales, only to be told by Maxwell that the sales hadn't actually been made; it was simply his way of helping to stimulate them.

I remember one of the first trips I made with Maxwell to Japan. I was going on two weeks' holiday to Florida, a promise to my teenage daughters that I had made two years before. Peter Jay telephoned a couple of weeks before to tell me that I would be accompanying Mr Maxwell to Tokyo in September. I asked why and Jay told me: 'I don't know; but he wants you with him.'

I explained my predicament to Jay who told me that I had better take up the matter with Maxwell.

Later Maxwell phoned: 'I hear you have refused to come to Tokyo with me?' he began, which seemed an odd approach but presumably was intended to unnerve me.

'Not true,' I replied and told him of my promise to my daughters.

In classic Maxwell style he came back: 'You have a choice. You can either put your family first or the company. Your future with Mirror Group rests on your reply. If you say "no" then that will be the end of the matter.' And the phone went 'click'.

The end of what matter, I thought, but I knew the answer; to say no to Maxwell on this occasion would mean an end to my career and he would make sure it was. I checked dates and times and flights and discovered that by rearranging everything I could take my daughters to Florida for ten days. I called Maxwell back and left a message saying I had been able to rearrange my holiday with my daughters and would be pleased to accompany him. But I regretted that I had to refuse his invitation to fly out with him on his private jet. It was his first small private plane, and I knew the journey in that would be horrendous because of the necessity to stop and refuel every few thousand miles. I booked on a BA jumbo instead.

It did mean leaving Miami, flying to New York, on to London to drop off my daughters and then two hours later flying straight to Tokyo. I made it, arriving just hours before Maxwell. I had time to shower, shave and change before he arrived at the hotel and, though a little jet-lagged, I was there to welcome him. He walked straight past me as though I wasn't there. I smiled to myself; all that flying, rush and struggle and he hadn't even said 'Good morning'.

He hadn't briefed me and I did not know why I was there. I waited for orders, my first mistake.

The next morning the phone rang: 'Where the fuck are you?' were his words.

'In my room,' I replied tamely.

'What the fuck is the use of being in your room; you are meant to be here with me at the Stock Exchange,' and he hung up.

Thirty minutes later I was at the Tokyo Stock Exchange. He then proceeded to explain to me in some detail the workings of the Tokyo stock market, as though he was giving me a lesson.

Maxwell and his entourage, accompanied by ten or more Japanese officials running in his wake, went everywhere, including the places forbidden to all but traders and officials and he instructed me to walk by his side while he asked questions, explained the market, and told the Japanese that they needed to modernize their exchange, 'Otherwise you will be left behind the rest of the world.' Technically, he was right, but I did think it a little rich telling the Japanese to modernize! They accepted everything he said with a smile, with agreement, with a nod of the head and a great deal of bowing. He liked that; it appealed to his sense of importance.

That trip Maxwell took me everywhere with him. He failed in his attempt to meet the Prime Minister but we did meet the political powerbrokers of the ruling Liberal-Democrats.

Japanese was one language that Maxwell could not speak and he became irritated at having to listen to interpreters all the time. Maxwell offered to be the go-between for the Japanese Prime Minister and Mrs Thatcher, telling the ruling Liberal-Democrat leaders that he was very close to Mrs Thatcher and that he would often take her messages from world leaders. I was surprised to hear that and feared that Maxwell was trying to con his Japanese hosts, claiming that he had far more political clout in Britain than was the case. They shifted in their seats when Maxwell announced that he would deliver personal messages to Mrs Thatcher, as though they had failed to realize until that moment how important Maxwell really was back home in Britain. From then on Maxwell's reputation seemed to be boosted in Tokyo and he was treated with even more respect and subservience than before. He pressed the necessity of meeting the Prime Minister again, but he did not succeed, though personal messages from the Japanese premier were delivered to him later.

Maxwell was in Tokyo on a roadshow which had been organized by Nomura, the Japanese finance house, to sell MCC – Maxwell Communications Corporation – to the Japanese. Maxwell wanted to persuade the Tokyo Stock

Exchange authorities to list his MCC stock on their exchange. During our few days in Tokyo there were numerous presentations, at which highly professional, spectacular, glossy videos of MCC, its products, its ambitions and its boss, Maxwell, were shown in a very good light. And Maxwell, flanked by senior Nomura executives, would answer questions asked by financial and corporate analysts and financial journalists. As always, he came over well, speaking impressively, and the reports were positive.

I remember walking back into his hotel suite after one such major presentation: 'That should make the little slit-eyes buy some shares,' he quipped as he kicked off his shoes, threw his jacket on a chair and sat down on a sofa with a contented smile on his face. His lack of tact amazed me because walking into the suite behind us were one or two Japanese managers working for Pergamon in Tokyo, and I was convinced they must have heard, but their faces betrayed not a sign.

As always the Japanese were generous hosts and keen to entertain us. We attended lunches and cocktail parties and dinners and Maxwell didn't like having to spend so much time out of his suite. But he did seem to quite enjoy all the bowing and scraping. Maxwell knew the rules of bowing (i.e. that on meeting, the person with the lower social or business standing bows slightly lower than the person he is meeting and the women always bow lower than the men). He would sometimes try to flatter his more important hosts, political leaders and Japanese ministers by bowing lower than they did, as if in supplication to their superiority and I couldn't help smiling as the huge, twenty-odd-stone, 6ft-2in Maxwell would try to bow lower than the small, 5ft-4in slim gentleman before him. I realized Maxwell was only doing so to ingratiate himself with his hosts because in private he didn't seem to like the Japanese one jot.

As the four-day visit wore on, Nomura's chiefs grew

worried as Maxwell talked of his plans for the immediate future, expanding in every known direction until MCC was one of the ten biggest publishing and printing groups in the world. The worry for Nomura was that no listing on the Tokyo exchange is permitted within one year of a major change in the company to be listed. A number of them spoke to me of their concern, telling me they tried to speak to Maxwell but he would not listen or take any notice of their warnings. 'If he makes one major purchase in the next twelve months the authorities will simply not allow a listing and he will have to wait another twelve months. Please,' they asked me, 'would you tell Mr Maxwell? It is most important.'

So I told Maxwell of Nomura's concern and their wish to speak to him about this matter which they feared could become a real problem.

'Why don't they approach me themselves, why do they tell you this and not me?' he asked.

I explained they claimed they had tried to raise the matter but Maxwell had brushed them aside.

Disingenuously Maxwell said in a hurt voice: 'Brush them aside? Me? Never!'

Later, one of Nomura's partners came to me and bowed. 'Thank you very much, Mr Nick' – which is how they addressed me – 'Mr Maxwell had spoken to us and told us he will make no purchases for one year to comply with our regulations. We thank you.'

I couldn't let them believe Maxwell would keep his word, so I joked: 'But you had better keep a watch just in case; he might forget his promise.'

Naïvely the man, who was surrounded by three other Nomura men, smiled broadly. 'No, no, never, not Mr Maxwell.'

One night Maxwell and I went off to a sumptuous Japanese meal at a geisha house. This was indeed trouble for Maxwell because it meant he had to eat Japanese fashion, sitting cross-legged on the floor at the table which was about twelve inches off the ground. He didn't mind slipping off his shoes as we entered the geisha restaurant but he landed with an almighty thump on the cushion on the floor as he tried to sit down discreetly, knocking everything for six on the table. There were only six of us at dinner that night, in a tiny, private dining room served by three geisha girls. Maxwell looked like a fish out of water. At the best of times he doesn't like eating small little items of food but prefers to dig his teeth into something substantial, or use his bear-like hand to shovel food into his mouth. When any item was placed in front of him Maxwell would immediately pick up the lot and push it into his mouth, finishing in seconds, while the Japanese would use their chopsticks, delicately picking up each tiny morsel one at a time. As a result Maxwell would become bored, impatiently waiting for the Japanese to finish. I knew the dinner could not go on for long like this and the Japanese were obviously embarrassed by his eating habits. What I didn't realize was that this dinner was on Maxwell and after ninety minutes, unable to hold his patience any further, Maxwell got up to leave. He turned to me, told me to settle the bill and walked off. My heart sank because I wasn't sure how much money I had. Luckily, it was £800 for the six of us, and I just had that amount.

The following morning I told Maxwell that I was totally out of money. He turned to his valet and asked for one of his briefcases. He opened the case and I saw it was stuffed with US dollar bills. Maxwell just put his giant hand in, picked up a handful and gave it to me, not counting the money. 'Thanks,' I said and discovered later he had given me $3,000.

It was during the 1987 trip to Tokyo that Maxwell renewed his relationship with one of the most powerful and amazing characters of modern Japan – Ryoichi Sasakawa. I do not believe it was mere coincidence that Sasakawa was also one of the richest men in Japan. His wealth was based on contracts that he had won during the Japanese occupation of China before World War II, providing the Japanese army of occupation with many of its needs and winning lucrative contracts to supply Japanese industry with all the Chinese raw materials they needed during those years. After World War II Sasakawa began power-boat racing in Japan, a game with speedboats about three feet long being raced by remote control round a course, which was to become the main form of gambling in post-war Japan. And Sasakawa held the sole rights. It amassed him a formidable fortune and Sasakawa became one of the most influential political king-makers in modern Japan. His wealth supported both the Liberal-Democrats and the Opposition Labour Party; he set up trusts to distribute his wealth and formed Sasakawa Foundations in many countries of the world. Sasakawa donated $12 billion to industrial, social and public works projects in Japan and around the world. He has been the biggest individual donor to the work of the United Nations and has contributed vast sums to the World Health Organization to support programmes aimed at eradicating disease and malnutrition.

Maxwell organized the Great Britain–Sasakawa Foundation to promote cultural links between Britain and Japan, and its London offices were housed in the Mirror building in Holborn Circus. Its patrons were Sasakawa and Lord Wilson of Rievaulx, the former Prime Minister. The management council included Maxwell, who decided he would be chairman, as well as Sir Edward du Cann, David Corsan and Brandon Gough of accountants Coopers & Lybrand, Angus Ogilvy, husband of Princess Alexandra, Dr David Owen, James Prior and Maxwell's old friend Gerald Ronson of Heron International. The foundation was launched in November 1984 with a gift of £10 million from Sasakawa.

210

Maxwell had been introduced to Sasakawa in 1983 by Mr Itaru Tanaka, a journalist and broadcaster of distinction in Japan, whom Maxwell took on to his Pergamon staff in Tokyo. During that visit to Tokyo, Sasakawa, then a sprightly eighty-eight years old, invited us to his ultra-modern, stylish palace for dinner. No expense had been spared. The entrance was magnificent, something out of a James Bond movie. Vast glass doors, fifty feet high, opened silently as we drove up to the front of the modern building. The cars entered the building and stopped next to a pair of escalators, fifty yards long, leading to the next level; liveried men came rushing to open the car doors, three to a car, and they ushered us up the escalators.

We were met at the top by two of Sasakawa's sons and taken to meet their father, a squat little man, full of energy and *bonhomie*, who smiled and laughed a lot. Ian Maxwell was with us, frequently chided by Maxwell for not speaking immaculate Japanese, as Maxwell had sent him to Tokyo years before to learn the language. Maxwell was fidgety and impatient because he couldn't understand what was being said without the interpreter, and, to make matters worse, he couldn't understand the interpreter's English very well either.

This dinner was a social event and no business was conducted, unusually for Maxwell. It was also one of those occasions, and there were very few of them, when Maxwell behaved most respectfully to the little man whom he knew was one of the wealthiest people in the world. It was amusing to see Maxwell, trying to listen intently to every word Sasakawa said, pretending to understand everything and hardly understanding a word. I thought then: 'What an actor!'

The meal was unbelievable. The table, set for twelve, was like the contents of an Aladdin's cave: all the cutlery and the plates were solid gold; the glasses covered in gold leaf; the condiment sets were gold and the overhanging chandeliers appeared to be solid gold. The walls were covered in a light-coloured silk. And throughout dinner Sasakawa kept the proceedings alive by frequently leaping to his feet and shouting, 'Campie!' the Japanese word for 'cheers' which should be uttered with a shout. We all followed suit and Maxwell began to enjoy himself, throwing back quite a lot of Krug champagne as he entered into the spirit of the evening. The food, all ten courses, was delicious.

The day we were due to fly out Maxwell said he had a surprise for me.

'We are going to have breakfast with Henry Kissinger in China,' he said.

I was pleased. I had met Kissinger, the former Secretary of State, once before in 1979 when he had kindly come to my rescue. Some years before that, Ian Smith, the former Rhodesian Prime Minister, had put me in jail for forty-eight hours and expelled me from the country over the editorial policies the *Daily Mirror* took towards white Rhodesia. I had been trying to get back into the country because Rhodesia, at that time, was one of the most important stories for the British papers, and the *Mirror* was missing out. I managed to ask a Kissinger aide if he would ask the Secretary of State to intervene on my behalf and, having explained the problem, hoped for the best. Within forty-eight hours I received a phone call in my Johannesburg hotel telling me that Kissinger had spoken to the Rhodesian authorities and all I had to do was show up in Salisbury, the capital, and apply for a press permit. It worked better than I had dared hope. When I arrived, full of trepidation that I might end up in jail again, I was treated like a VIP. Met at the airport, guided through Customs and passport control, put into the VIP lounge by officials, and after all the preliminaries were dealt with, my baggage was collected and I was taken by an official chauffeur-driven car to the Rhodesian Ministry for

External Affairs to meet the Foreign Minister, Mr Piet van der Byl.

Shaking me warmly by the hand and smiling broadly, the minister apologized for the fact that I had been thrown into jail, that I had been arrested at all and asked that I should accept the full and official apologies of the Rhodesian government as well as his own personal apologies for the way I had been treated. He called for tea and poured it himself, offering me cake and biscuits in a remarkable show of contrition. A few weeks later I had the opportunity of meeting Kissinger in person and thanking him. In his customary deep growl, he replied: 'Anything to help the press.'

We flew from Tokyo, over the beautiful snow-capped Mount Fuji volcano and on to China. Maxwell introduced me to Kissinger as the man he had rescued from jail. It wasn't exactly accurate but I just smiled. The three of us sat down to breakfast after the obligatory photographs for the Maxwell library. The discussion was far-ranging but most of it concerned the changes taking place in the Soviet Union and the need to back Gorbachov at all costs. Kissinger went along with Maxwell's argument that the West had to put its faith behind Gorbachov if there was to be no breakdown in law and order in the Soviet Union. And Kissinger agreed that the West would probably have to fund the change, if there was to be a fundamental change, from Communism to Western-style democracy and a modern market economy. They talked of the breakdown that seemed imminent among the Eastern bloc nations, but neither suggested Communism would collapse so speedily throughout Eastern Europe as it eventually did. Both were convinced that East Germany would remain a bastion of Communism under the hardline Honecker.

The next visit to Japan, in December 1990, proved rather embarrassing for Maxwell. We had arrived at Anchorage for a refuelling stop and the pilot, Captain John Macullum, announced that we could not continue the final lap of the journey to Tokyo because the seal on the door had been damaged by ice during the previous stop at Frobisher Bay, where the temperature had been –40°! Maxwell ranted and raved but Macullum stood his ground, saying the only solution was for him to fly the plane back to California for a new door seal. 'If you can fly the fucking plane back to California then you can fly us to Tokyo first,' Maxwell shouted at Macullum. Macullum refused so Maxwell fired him on the spot.

Fortunately there was a Japan Airlines flight scheduled to leave Anchorage within the hour and there were just enough seats, with one first-class seat available. Maxwell turned to Andrea as he booked the seats and asked for his American Express card. He handed it over to the smiling Japanese girl who was making out the tickets. She came back ten minutes later saying there was a problem – Maxwell's American Express card was not acceptable.

'What do you mean,' he asked, 'not acceptable?'

The girl explained that the machine would not accept the card.

'Phone up American Express headquarters in New York and tell them Robert Maxwell is here,' he said.

The girl went away and returned with the local airline manager and his assistant.

'I'm very sorry, Mr Maxwell,' the manager said, 'but we cannot accept this card. Is there any other way you can pay?'

That really set off Maxwell. He flew into a rage. 'Do you know who I am?' he thundered. 'I am the chairman of Thomas Cook, the worldwide travel firm. I know the chairman of American Express. Get him for me on the phone this instant.'

Shaking but still calm, the manager said he could not do

214

that and asked Maxwell how else he would like to pay. That was like a red rag to a bull.

'Don't you tell me what I should do. I have told you what to do, now do it,' he roared.

Time was ticking by and the flight had been called. I took out my Mirror Group Newspapers British Airways credit card and put it on the counter saying diplomatically: 'As the flight is about to take off perhaps we should use this for speed.' Maxwell looked at it, nodded assent and turned away, leaving me to sign the $10,000 bill. Once on board Maxwell was determined we should all enjoy ourselves. He kept ordering bottles and bottles of champagne and then passing them back to us sitting behind.

During that 1990 visit to Tokyo, Maxwell did manage to have a meeting with Prime Minister Kaifu and he spent most of the discussion advising the premier of what he should do during his planned tour of Eastern Europe early in the New Year. Maxwell talked of the need for financial aid that the East European countries, struggling to shake off forty years of Communism, needed desperately, and he urged Kaifu to be as generous as possible. Kaifu spent most of the time listening intently to what Maxwell advised. We also held talks in a tiny, cramped room with the leader of the Opposition Socialist Party, Madam Doi; the shelves of the room were crowded with stuffed owls. It was surprising to note the difference in Maxwell's behaviour between the two talks; to Kaifu he was attentive, keen, razor sharp and obsequious, and to Madam Doi he was paternal and patronizing, seemingly asking questions because he thought he should to be polite.

We flew back to London via Ulan Bator, the capital of Outer Mongolia. This once beautiful city had been ruined by awful, boring Russian architecture, grey eight-storey blocks of identical flats everywhere. We were entertained by typical Communist officials who had been installed by

Moscow, educated by Moscow, the quintessential grey-suited Politburo types. For some unknown reason Maxwell had decided to enter the cashmere business, an industry of which Mongolia was proud. With a sweep of his hand he guaranteed to buy all their export production for the next five years! To me it seemed Maxwell was behaving as he had seen his grandfather behave, bartering and dealing in the mountains of Ruthenia in the 1920s when Maxwell was still a young boy; but he was now capable of buying up a nation's entire production, whereas his grandfather had only been able to deal in one hide at a time.

Maxwell wanted to corner the market in Britain for Mongolian cashmere and had offered the Mongolians a stupidly high price. Over a formal, stuffy lunch Maxwell asked Sir John Morgan if he thought it was a good deal for MCC.

Sir John replied: 'No, Chairman, I totally disagree. I don't think there is a market in Britain for this wool, especially at this price. And, furthermore, cashmere has nothing whatsoever to do with MCC's core business.'

Maxwell looked downcast at this but said he was still determined to go ahead. He instructed the American financial expert Larry Trachtenberg to investigate the deal, who also advised that Maxwell should have nothing to do with the wool. Months later Maxwell pulled out of the deal, leaving the Mongolians in the lurch.

In February 1988 Maxwell told me I would be accompanying him to Davos, Switzerland, for the World Economic Forum held there annually so that prime ministers, finance ministers, and big business can mingle in an informal atmosphere, exchanging ideas, meeting each other without any civil servants present. And to safeguard the quality of the forum only government ministers and presidents and chairmen of international companies are permitted to attend, not their deputies.

Maxwell was in his element. He chaired the discussion group on the media, spending most of the time talking himself rather than throwing the debate open to everyone else. During cocktail hours he moved around the hall searching out those he wanted to nail and ignoring those who wanted to talk to him. And he had his PA phone everyone of importance inviting them to his hotel suite so that he could hold court. It was chaos.

The following year Maxwell, who loved going to Davos so he could meet so many important people at one gathering, sent me ahead and then couldn't make the three-day get-together. I received a phone call from him: 'I want you to take messages to the following people, tell them I cannot be there this year and give them my kind regards. Make a fuss of them, then phone me to tell me what progress you've made.'

The following day I called back having spoken to nearly everyone.

'Good,' he replied, 'are they missing me?'

I didn't tell him that the management were not displeased that he hadn't come because he always caused chaos, so I gently massaged his ego with the kind remarks delegates had made.

'Good,' he went on, 'well, you had better stay there a couple of days in case I need you, and go skiing.'

In 1990 Maxwell was back at Davos. One evening he invited a number of grandees to come to his small suite for informal chats over drinks. But stupidly he had invited them all at the same time although each meeting was meant to be private. In his bedroom were the Prime Minister and Deputy Prime Minister of Czechoslovakia sitting on the bed; in the sitting room was the Deputy Premier of Hungary and standing outside on the landing was the Deputy Prime Minister of Quebec being jostled by various television crews waiting to film their man talking to Maxwell. Maxwell arrived late at the same time as word came that General Jaruzelski was waiting to see him in his suite downstairs. Without a word to anyone Maxwell turned on his heel and went downstairs, abandoning his guests. An hour later Maxwell returned – but his guests, not at all happy, had finally given up waiting and left.

At the main session when all the European leaders were on the stage addressing the three hundred or so delegates, Maxwell arrived late after the meeting had started. He walked straight to the front row of the auditorium and sat down. Five minutes later he got up, walked out, went to his hotel and announced we were flying back to London, the meeting had become boring. What had actually happened was that Maxwell had demanded that he should be allowed to address the meeting but was told he could not, as government ministers only would be speaking – and he was miffed. He just wanted to show his displeasure publicly.

In the spring of 1989 I visited Brussels with Maxwell and he addressed the commissioners at a private meeting about the plans for his *European* newspaper. Questions followed his speech which was well received, for it was an idea they all applauded and welcomed. In his answers, however, Maxwell totally overstated the plan for the *European*, saying it would be on every news-stand and in every newspaper shop throughout Europe from day one. He envisaged the paper being delivered to every hotel guest in Europe and to every airline passenger. My mind boggled; that was millions of copies every issue. Maxwell didn't bat an eyelid as he became carried away in his enthusiasm for his grandest project. Later, Maxwell, as usual, wanted to give a press conference inside the EC building. He had brought with

218

him two people responsible for marketing the paper and told them to put up a large *European* poster behind him so the TV cameras would see it. That was totally against EC rules but it made no difference. An official hurried over and told him to take it down. Maxwell nodded and the official went away.

'Put it up immediately,' he told the two young women with him.

'But . . .' one began, looking anxious.

'No bloody but,' he said, 'just do as I say. Put up the poster just before the cameras start. I will take full responsibility.' It worked and no one said a word.

It was in 1988 that Maxwell told me I would be accompanying him to Kenya to see the newspaper he owned there and hold talks with President Daniel arap Moi. It struck me at the time as an odd trip for Maxwell because he never showed any interest in Africa.

A few days before we were due to go I received an anonymous phone call in the office from someone who told me: 'Listen. This is serious. I have information from the Israelis that the KGB plans to assassinate Mr Maxwell when he goes to Kenya.'

My mind raced ahead, as the call had shocked me. The one fact was that Maxwell was going to Kenya, so, in an effort to gain more information, I asked the caller: 'Why do you think Mr Maxwell is going to Kenya?'

The voice replied: 'He is going next week. You must warn him.' And the phone went dead.

One's first reaction to any anonymous telephone call is to ignore it, but the mention of Kenya made me realize this information could not be ignored. I phoned and told Maxwell I had to give him some very important information. As I told him of the call, he seemed surprised and unnerved by the news. Then he said: 'I don't take any notice of anonymous calls, but thank you. Keep this information a secret between the two of us; tell no one.'

Half an hour later Maxwell was back on the phone. 'I have some people I want you to meet.' So I went up to Maxwell's drawing room, and was introduced to the Israeli ambassador and a man whom I presumed was Israel's Mossad chief in London. I told them what had happened. As I spoke everyone looked at the carpet and when I had finished they each raised their eyes to note reactions. 'Thank you,' Maxwell said, 'not a word to anyone,' and I left the room.

Two days later he called me upstairs and told me he had decided not to go to Kenya 'because of pressure of work'. He added: 'I want you to go in my place. Go and see the President, give him my best wishes and apologies and tell him that I am still studying the plan for the newspaper office block. Also go and see my newspaper out there and report back on the staff, how they are working and how well the newspaper is doing.'

I was ushered in to meet President arap Moi the day after my arrival. It was a totally private meeting, no one, not a single guard or civil servant, was present. That was odd. We sat and took tea from lovely bone china cups. After exchanging pleasantries the President said to me out of the blue: 'Where's the money?'

I was stunned. I didn't know about any money. I hoped he was referring to the money needed to fund the office block which was also to house the staff of his political party.

I asked: 'You mean the money for the office block?'

The President replied: 'The money Mr Maxwell promised our country.'

I knew of no promises of money and wondered what Maxwell had thrown me into, so I simply ignored the President's question and talked of Maxwell's plans to build the promised office block which he was studying back in London.

220

The President changed tack: 'The office block will cost a great deal of money. Does Mr Maxwell realize that land values are going up all the time?'

I assured him Maxwell would employ the best brains to evaluate the project and that Maxwell was confident he would be going ahead in the not too distant future.

I could see the President wasn't pleased with the talks and the subject was changed to discuss Maxwell's newspaper in Kenya and his continued support of the pro-government newspaper. I was only too happy when the meeting was over but I could tell the President was not a happy man. It appeared that Maxwell was up to his legendary tricks – making promises that he had no intention of keeping.

Back in London I called to make a report to Maxwell, but he didn't want to know. We were never to discuss my visit to Kenya or my talks with President arap Moi, but, to cover myself, I wrote him a succinct one-page report. I don't suppose for a moment he ever bothered to read it.

It was in 1988 that Maxwell began to woo Bulgaria in earnest. He had instructed me to go to a couple of cocktail parties at the Bulgarian Embassy where I was briefed on the Lyudmila Zhivkov Foundation that Maxwell sponsored, a charity set up in 1982 to promote the principles of 'truth, beauty and education'. (Todor Zhivkov, the hardline Communist dictator of Bulgaria, had asked for the foundation to be named after his daughter, Lyudmila, who died in mysterious circumstances in 1981, aged thirty-eight. It was rumoured that Lyudmila, Zhivkov's strong-minded daughter whom Zhivkov was training to succeed him, had been murdered, but it now seems she committed suicide.) Maxwell had become friendly with Todor Zhivkov and had published his speeches as well as a directory of Bulgarian achievements. But it didn't mention the one fact for which Bulgaria had

221

become famous – the killing in a crowded London street of the Bulgarian dissident writer Georgi Markov with a poison-tipped umbrella in 1978.

It was at about this time that Maxwell put together his entourage for his overseas travels. Wherever we went he would make a point of introducing his team to the officials and heads of state, prime ministers and presidents. He loved to march ahead of us, like a prime minister attended by his civil servants, head held high, and walk into gatherings awaiting him, with the words: 'Hello, I'm Robert Maxwell,' while we stood in a row behind him as he shook hands and, as often as not, kissed the presidents on both cheeks in true Continental style. Then he would conduct the introductions. He revelled in his position as a powerful international publisher-cum-statesman, the friend of world leaders, the rich and powerful. He recruited Sir John Morgan, a former British Ambassador to Poland, South Korea and Mexico, whom he would introduce to the heads of state as 'my Foreign Minister'; he had recruited one of Europe's top bankers, a former managing director of Credit Lyonnais, Jean-Pierre Anselmini, whom he would introduce as 'my banker'; he always introduced *Mirror* photographer Mike Maloney as 'my Royal photographer' and he usually referred to me as 'my editor'.

Maxwell wanted Sir John Morgan to head his interests in Bulgaria, then still under Communist rule. Sir John was sent to Sofia to thrash out an agreement for a business management school, to be called the Maxwell Management School. Arrangements were made to acquire beautiful buildings up in the hills outside Sofia, which had been a sanatorium for old agricultural trade union officials. It boasted an indoor swimming pool and gymnasium, tennis courts and other facilities and was situated at the bottom of a ski lift. With the assistance of the highly regarded Cranfield School of Management, providing the services and managing the school, it really was a first-class idea for a nation emerging from the rigours of forty years of Communism. It was Maxwell's second gesture to Bulgaria, cementing his relationship with the Old Guard Communist regime.

Then calamity. Maxwell's buddy Zhivkov was deposed in November 1989 by so-called Socialists, former Communists who knew their only chance of political survival lay in dumping Zhivkov and proclaiming themselves Socialists. On a couple of occasions I had seen Maxwell and Zhivkov together and they were very matey, with lots of kissing and hugging and back-slapping whenever they met or said farewell. It was obvious Maxwell was on the make but I didn't realize at that time how big a fish he was trying to catch. Maxwell waited to see how the dice landed and who would really be in control. As the dust settled Maxwell saw his chance of running to the aid of the tiny Balkan nation and offering his services. In the spring of 1990 Maxwell informed me we were going to Bulgaria to witness that nation's emergence from Communism.

In Sofia, Maxwell was treated like royalty, given the use of two large villas in a compound of luxurious diplomatic chalets on the outskirts of Sofia and a fleet of Zil limousines.

We had a number of meetings with the Prime Minister, Andrei Lukanov, a former Communist who was committed to holding free democratic elections in the summer. It was during one of these meetings that Maxwell turned to Jean-Pierre Anselmini and with a flick of the hand ordered him to leave the room. Anselmini looked stunned at the order, but had no option but to obey. That left just Maxwell and me in the room with the Prime Minister and his advisers. It was then that Maxwell came up with three ideas: one, he wanted to found his own bank, to be called the Maxwell Bank of Bulgaria; two, he wanted to take a stake in Bulgaria's Agricultural Credit Bank; and three, he wanted one of his companies, Bishopsgate Investment

Trust (nothing to do with Bishopsgate Investment Management which was involved in the pensions scandal) to organize Bulgaria's entire foreign debt, then running at US $11,000 billion. He boasted that Bishopsgate was already handling other East European nations' foreign debts and he promised that Bishopsgate would pay better rates of interest than anyone else.

'You have my word that you can trust me,' Maxwell began, 'you can trust me absolutely to take care of Bulgaria's foreign debt, better than anyone else. Remember, I have been a friend to your country for many years now and we can trust each other.' I had sat in on many of Maxwell's talks but this was the first time I had heard him wanting to found his own bank, take a stake in a major national bank or service a nation's foreign debt. He further proposed managing Bulgaria's overseas currency reserves, which were said to stand at about $100 million. But Maxwell had yet more surprises.

During the next couple of days we travelled all over the country searching for new, crazy ideas for Maxwell to invest in. He was like a small boy in a toy store, knowing he could have anything he wanted. Travelling around Bulgaria was like going back to the Europe of a century ago; there were hardly any vehicles in the countryside, just horses and carts; the farmers wore sacks on their backs to keep off the rain and the women wore long dresses; on their feet they wore sandals made of old tyres and the peasants' homes were hovels which they shared with their sheep, pigs and chickens.

We checked out a dreadful old chemical plant which appeared highly dangerous to me, like a leftover from the 1950s, so very ancient compared to a modern Western plant of 1990. I wondered what on earth he was doing thinking of buying it, but he never explained. He agreed to buy the principal former Communist newspaper; he invested in Balkan Film, producers of the cartoons *Cuddles & Orvill*, and told the Prime Minister he wanted to start Bulgaria's own *Yellow Pages*. During one dinner Maxwell told Lukanov: 'I want to settle down here in Bulgaria, here in the Balkans. I would like to buy a country estate and have it as my summer residence; somewhere I could station my helicopter and work from.'

As I am sure Maxwell hoped, Lukanov had the answer: 'Why don't you view one of the former presidents' palaces, they are all for lease to people such as yourself.'

Slapping the table, Maxwell said: 'An excellent idea. When can we view?'

Zhivkov's former homes, lodges and summer palaces were dotted all over the country and all in the most wonderful surroundings. In all, Zhivkov had thirty-two separate lodges and palaces. Maxwell suggested he should take a lease on six different ones, so it was decided we would fly from one to another viewing them. The one Maxwell was most interested in was on the Black Sea coast at Perla where, he anticipated, he could moor the *Lady Ghislaine* – and officials measured the harbour to see if the yacht could moor there. It could.

I remember walking around the summer palace with Maxwell, watching him taking a seat in Zhivkov's private cinema; examining the bathrooms, strolling through the lounges, dining rooms and kitchens, inspecting the beautiful Roman-style indoor swimming pool with the cantilevered roof, and sitting on Zhivkov's king-sized double bed and bouncing up and down with a broad grin on his face, checking the springs! And then we sat out on the balcony overlooking the Black Sea, sipping drinks and watching the seagulls soaring overhead.

'Going to take it?' I asked Maxwell.

His reply surprised me: 'Do you think Andrea would like it here?' he replied.

'I don't know,' I answered, 'but it's a little remote for her, I would imagine.'

Maxwell came back: 'But it would be very peaceful for her, I could see her working out here on the balcony in the sunshine.'

Later that day he telephoned Andrea at her London home telling her what a wonderful time everyone was having in Bulgaria, telling her that she was missing a great adventure and beautiful sunshine. Then he asked if there was any message he could pass on to me. The next day he told me: 'I had a chat to our friend last night; I told her she should be here; I offered her her job back but I don't think I am very popular at the moment. She didn't want to know.'

I asked him: 'Are you surprised?'

He looked glum and said: 'Well, these things occasionally blow up; she'll get over it soon enough and then she can come back and we'll have the old team back again.' Gone were all the accusations against me, the apparent impossibility of working together.

Then Maxwell discussed with me his idea for Bulgaria: 'This place could be the film-making centre of Europe; the scenery is wonderful, the climate is warm, the labour is cheap and I have founded Balkan Film Enterprises. The stars could come and stay in my palaces and they could rent my film studios, my equipment and staff.' Shortly after his return to London, Maxwell sent out his East Europe financial expert Brian Cole, and one of his first investments was £250,000 in film production equipment.

During our stay in Bulgaria Maxwell held talks with the Opposition leaders of the United Democratic Front, the coalition which eventually threw out the Communists in October 1990. Talks were held in a stuffy little over-crowded office in the centre of Sofia. Maxwell immediately took off his jacket and asked them what he could do to help their cause in the forthcoming elections. They asked for paper, to enable them to print leaflets, and sufficient for a small four-page tabloid news sheet. He promised to supply paper for posters to both the Socialists (the former Communists) and the Front. He told the Front he wanted to be fair, that he supported their cause, that he wanted them to be victorious in the elections, and form the next government. But he did not.

On his return to London he called in Haines and told him he wanted him to go to Sofia and advise the Socialists on how to run their election campaign to ensure a victory for the Old Guard Communists. Haines said he should take Helen Liddel along as well as she had been responsible for running highly successful campaigns for the Labour Party in parliamentary elections in Scotland. Haines told me he was embarrassed flying out to Sofia to work on the side of former Communists, in an effort to ensure their victory against the Democrats. But he went none the less – and the Communists did indeed win that first parliamentary election.

Maxwell wanted the Old Guard Communists back in power so they could ensure his investments went ahead in Bulgaria with the minimum of fuss – and the maximum of support from the old Politburo. And after those first elections Maxwell speeded up investments; he took an eight per cent interest, investing about £1 million in the Agricultural Credit Bank; he pushed forward his interest in the Economic Bank of Bulgaria but he put most of his effort into establishing his own bank.

Maxwell despatched his 'banker' Jean-Pierre Anselmini to Sofia with Brian Cole to arrange the banking licence through the Governor of the Bank of Bulgaria, and find premises. There was, however, a snag: before any licence was granted the directors insisted Maxwell deposit $30 million. Maxwell insisted the licence be granted and the bank registered before parting with the money. Eventually, during another visit to finalize the plans, Maxwell and the Governor shook hands on the deal, but it was not to be. Maxwell never received his licence.

227

His two advisers were also told to go ahead with Maxwell's most ambitious deal in Bulgaria – the Rodina complex
– a development site on the road to the airport where
Maxwell planned to build a printing works, a newspaper
office block and a business park, costing in total £100
million. But there was a debate over the ownership of the
site, which was allegedly owned by the former Communist
Party. The deal came to nothing and Maxwell lost interest
by the end of 1990.

Maxwell also decided to purchase on behalf of his highly
successful Israeli company, Scitex, Bulgaria's most successful
antibiotics company, Razgrat. He immediately gave the
company a $7 million loan just as a sweetener for his
planned takeover. When he returned to London he told
Scitex of the magnificent deal he had done on their behalf;
but Scitex directors didn't want to know and they refused
to go ahead, much to Maxwell's chagrin. The deal was
dropped and eventually, in 1991, Maxwell got back his $7
million loan.

Maxwell did sign a contract to build a printing works in
Sofia for £1.72 million in a joint project with the International
Foundation of St Cyril and St Methodius. Everything was
signed and sealed. But for no apparent reason, in June 1990,
Maxwell welshed on the deal, refusing to go ahead or send
the money. He gave no reason, but the former Communists
had just won their election victory; and maybe he didn't
need the goodwill any more.

Yet he did continue with plans to buy up a number
of major businesses in the country. He despatched Brian
Cole once more to Sofia to ferret out more possible projects
which he could take over. His list of interests was bizarre
to say the least – Balkan Airlines, a major wine-producing
company, a petrol company, development land, the large
Tsum department store, two other newspapers, *Potkrepa* and
168 Hours, a hotel with a golf course, a UK–Bulgaria transport

company and a major stake in the rose oil industry. But not one was to eventually reach fruition.

Maxwell didn't miss a trick to promote himself in Sofia; to show goodwill and make sure the people, as well as the former Politburo, realized that Maxwell was a true friend of Bulgaria. He sponsored a pop concert – in conjunction with the Communist Party – just two weeks before the elections. And he gave Slavia, Bulgaria's oldest football club, $100,000 and a set of shirts with 'Maxwell' written on the front.

At the annual party to celebrate his birthday, this time his sixty-seventh, at Headington Hill Hall a few days later, he was given a T-shirt with the words 'King of Bulgaria' emblazoned on the front and a paste crown. Jokingly he was crowned King of Bulgaria, while everyone sang 'Happy birthday'. Maxwell loved it, beaming from ear to ear with pride.

After the Bulgarian Old Guard Communists and Socialists were forced out of office in December 1990, following strikes and demonstrations, Dimitar Popov, a sixty-three-year-old lawyer with no political affiliations, took over as prime minister of a coalition government until new elections could be held. Four months later no elections had been held so Maxwell decided to go ahead with his plan for Bulgaria and try to win the support of the coalition government. In April 1991 he wrote to Prime Minister Popov claiming his previous support for the Communists had been misinterpreted.

He wrote: 'It is my deeply held conviction that I should help people, not governments or political parties.' In his attempts to win over the new government he went on: 'Bulgaria is now irrevocably on the path to democracy and a legitimate government is in power, which I believe we can trust . . .' It was Maxwell at his most insidious.

Maxwell dreamed up the most amazing pie-in-the-sky

plan to forge a relationship between the Bulgarian government and Maxwell's group of companies to run the country
together! He had never suggested such a proposition before
in any dealings in any other country.

His remarkable seven-page letter to the Bulgarian Prime
Minister outlined his extraordinary proposals:

> After thorough consideration, I have come to the conclusion
> that certain proposals may well be mutually attractive to the
> interests of the Bulgarian people and those of some of my
> partners who I am confident will wish to participate. These
> partners include some of the leading Western banks, finan-
> cial institutions, insurance companies and other companies
> specializing in investments and acquisitions.

In a blatant effort to bolster his plan, and give himself
credibility, Maxwell wrote:

> In this extremely important matter I shall be personally
> active, and shall make use of my excellent relationships
> with Prime Minister Major, President Bush and Secretary
> Brady, Chancellor Kohl and Minister Genscher, President
> Mitterrand, Prime Minister Kaifu and others.

Maxwell's letter explained in detail his eight point plan:

> 1. To unite the efforts of the Bulgarian Government and its
> associates with those of the Maxwell group of companies and
> its partners, in order to make it possible to reduce Bulgarian
> debt to foreign governments by seventy per cent.
>
> 2. To restructure Bulgarian debt, starting with the equiva-
> lent of US $500 million and finally achieving US $2 billion.

Included in the other six points was that a remarkable twenty per cent of all money received should be capitalized in the Maxwell Foundation, Sofia, 'for the benefit of nobody but the Bulgarian people'. A further thirty per cent would be used for direct investment in Bulgarian industry and services. And the remaining fifty per cent would primarily be used 'for the improvement of the economic situation of the people'.

Maxwell also brazenly suggested that one third of all investment funds should be provided to promising local businessmen through the European Bank of Bulgaria (the bank Maxwell intended to found in Sofia).

In the remarkable document Maxwell outlined in some detail the advantages his plan would accrue to Bulgaria and his partners. He then added:

> As for my personal motives, I have made my fortune and I now participate in many non-profit-making operations all over the world – in Europe, America, Japan and also in Bulgaria. It is my intention that at least twenty per cent of the operations proposed shall be financed by some of my Foundations – this amount corresponds to the amount I wish to invest in the new Maxwell Foundation in Sofia.
>
> So for me it will be a no-profit no-loss operation – I shall merely transfer money from one Foundation to another, and in this manner I shall be able to distribute my contribution to the East and West more evenly.

He ended his outrageous letter by urging the Prime Minister to treat his proposals in the 'strictest confidence' for fear that wider knowledge could bring pressure on him from other Central and East European countries for similar arrangements to be offered which, he wrote, 'I am unable to afford at this time.'

231

But, despite another visit to Sofia in the spring of 1991, just six months before his death, he was unable to convince Mr Popov or the other Bulgarian ministers that he was the person they should do business with. He had failed again. This was a bitter pill for Maxwell to swallow, because he had been determined to achieve an important ambition in Sofia – a substantial stake in a bank, which would make his foreign exchange dealings easier and more profitable.

One of Maxwell's more subtle visits was to Finland. We flew there ostensibly to chat to the Finnish government and the Prime Minister. It was an informal chat around an oblong table with the Prime Minister at the head; I was sitting next to Maxwell, taking notes. It lasted exactly one hour during which time Maxwell quietly lectured the PM on how he should run his government, the economy and the nation, and what his relationship should be with the Soviet Union, and President Gorbachov in particular. At the end the Prime Minister shook hands, said goodbye and then turned to one of his aides: 'It was very nice meeting Mr Maxwell, but he never let me speak.'

The talks with the premier were not the primary reason for the trip. We flew north to the huge modern paper mills and were taken on a detailed tour of the entire works, at the end of which Maxwell began talks with the chairman and directors about future supplies for Mirror Group Newspapers, and the bargaining over price began. When it was all but over and the deal was struck, Maxwell then ushered everyone out of the room and only he and one other person remained in the room.

'What's that for?' I asked naïvely of one of the directors.

And he explained: 'That is a little Finnish tradition. When big buyers like Mr Maxwell buy newsprint there is always an agreement afterwards, a reward for the purchase whereby the purchaser arranges for a small percentage of the price to be paid into a private bank account somewhere else in the world. Many of the big publishers do this, that is why they always come to Finland personally to conclude these newsprint deals.' I nodded knowingly and wondered how much Maxwell had taken for his 'percentage'.

Afterwards we enjoyed another Finnish tradition: a real sauna, where everyone strips off, both sexes in the same sauna room. And whether it was for Maxwell's predilection or not I don't know, but, as if by magic, some beautiful young Finnish girls happened to be there, also enjoying the sauna at the end of their day's work – and with not a stitch on. I had wondered why our hosts had tried to persuade Maxwell so enthusiastically to take a sauna that day. They had all done so but Maxwell declined. Later I told him what he had missed.

'Next time I shall remember,' he said.

Maxwell's affairs with Erich Honecker of East Germany and General Jaruzelski of Poland – the two hardline Communist leaders of the Eastern bloc – were perfect examples of Maxwell's total disregard of public opinion in Britain, and his naïvety in thinking that such visits had no effect on his reputation in Western Europe.

Throughout the summer and autumn of 1990 the world had seen and heard nothing of the ageing East German leader, Erich Honecker. There were rumours that he was seriously ill, that he had contracted cancer, that he had undergone operations for cancer and even that he was at death's door. It therefore came as a great surprise when Maxwell phoned me at the end of September to say we were going to East Berlin to see Honecker. To me, a newspaperman, it seemed that this was one of Maxwell's trips out of which we were going to get a good story, perhaps a very good one.

On October 2 we flew to East Berlin, taking with us two beautifully bound red leather volumes of the *Encyclopaedia of the German Democratic Republic*, priced at £110 per set, a present for Honecker on the eve of the fortieth anniversary celebrations of the founding of the Republic. Honecker and Maxwell greeted each other like long-lost brothers, hugging and kissing – three kisses – as the TV cameras whirred and the cameras clicked. Far from looking ill and tired, Honecker looked in fine form, especially for a seventy-seven-year-old man. After his initial greeting the East German leader sat very upright behind his large ornate desk as we talked, as though he were a cardboard cut-out. But his mind was sharp and his comments lucid. I looked for any signs of illness but saw none. After the cameramen and officials had left the room we sat and talked for perhaps an hour.

Of course the bulk of the conversation revolved around events unfolding in Moscow and other parts of the Communist bloc. Surprisingly, Honecker was confident that the reforms sweeping Eastern Europe would not reach East Germany for perhaps a decade. He argued that the United States, Britain and France would not want to deal with a reunited Germany and would much prefer to maintain the *status quo*. Maxwell agreed, telling him that he would produce another encyclopaedia for the fiftieth anniversary of the GDR in ten years' time. Even at that time the Communists of East Germany, the Communist showcase of Eastern Europe, seemed well entrenched, and yet in a matter of months, Honecker and his hated secret police, the Stasi, were to be swept from power.

After the visit the world wanted to know how Maxwell had found Honecker; whether rumours of his impending death were true or false. Quite correctly Maxwell dismissed the rumours as 'nonsense', commenting that Honecker, whom he claimed had been 'a reformer all his life' was 'in very good nick'. I disagreed with Maxwell, however, over Honecker's state of health for I had noticed that the old man's hands were shaking when we were talking to him, that age was showing. Maxwell ordered me to take out this comment in the story I wrote for the *Mirror*. After a discussion, however, I eventually won the point, stressing that the *Mirror* had to be totally accurate as we had been the only newspapermen to see the East German leader for four months.

After looking through the magnificent encyclopaedia, Honecker asked Maxwell if it would be possible to fly over further copies because he would like to present a copy to each of those participating in their anniversary celebrations the following week, which was to be attended by Gorbachov. Maxwell said he could supply the two thousand extra copies but only if Honecker chartered Maxwell's own plane. Honecker agreed enthusiastically and the extra sets arrived in time for the celebrations. What was more surprising was that despite the fact that Honecker was removed from office only weeks later, the GDR did indeed pay for the books and the cost of chartering the plane.

It was while heading home to London that I saw Maxwell in a mild panic. He had instructed Sir John Morgan and the rest of us to check in at the East Berlin airport and he would catch up with us later. Minutes before the scheduled take-off, Maxwell arrived.

'Where's Andrea?' he enquired.

'I thought she was with you, Chairman,' Sir John replied.

'She didn't come with me, you were meant to look after her,' Maxwell said to all of us, trying to remove the blame from himself.

Suddenly a change came over Maxwell. He was looking around earnestly, not sure of himself, not sure what to do. Then he sprang into action. He turned to the East German officials who had been assigned to us and told them to call the Chief of Police, to call the Stasi headquarters and to put a call through to the office of Herr Honecker and inform · them that his PA, Miss Martin, was missing and must be found. 'It is of paramount importance,' he said. It seemed strange for Maxwell to react in this way. The officials went off to phone and Maxwell paced up and down, chiding each of us for not taking care of Andrea, as he alleged he had instructed. Fifteen long minutes later a call came through from Honecker's office saying Miss Martin had been found, still in the hotel suite where Maxwell had ordered her to stay until he phoned. He had completely forgotten. When she arrived Maxwell turned to me and said: 'If you ever lose Andrea again I shall fire you, do you understand?' Andrea tried to explain to Maxwell that she had only obeyed his orders but he didn't want to know – he was embarrassed but refused to face the truth that it was entirely his fault.

Maxwell's involvement with Poland had provided the British press and particularly *Private Eye* with much anger and amusement. In 1985, when Maxwell seemed to fly around Europe as a roving ambassador, he first met General Jaruzelski, the military leader who had ferociously put down the shipworkers' rebellion in 1981 resulting in the loss of many lives. But despite the introduction of marshal law Jaruzelski had been unable to dim the light of the Solidarity movement or its leader Lech Walesa. After his meeting with Jaruzelski in 1985, Maxwell announced at a press conference that the Solidarity problem had been 'solved' and that his newspapers would be devoting less space to the protesters in future. Privately, when he returned to the *Mirror*, he instructed that no mention of the word 'Solidarity' was ever to be made in the *Mirror*. As Foreign Editor that could have caused me problems but I decided to ignore his edict and carry on as before. I did write about Solidarity after that and Maxwell never mentioned it.

Maxwell was invited by General Jaruzelski to attend the fiftieth anniversary commemoration of the beginning of World War II, which began at Westerplatte on September 1, 1939, when Hitler's navy bombarded the Polish fort. Maxwell loved the idea and was determined to wear his old British Army captain's uniform for the occasion. He invited along Field Marshal the Lord Bramhall of Bushfield, who had been Chief of the Imperial General Staff and one of Britain's most senior Army officers. He worked for Maxwell as an adviser to Brassey's, the defence publisher, and complained to me that he was rather embarrassed as Maxwell never paid him unless he actually asked for his salary, despite having a contract which stipulated payment each and every month. None the less, the Field Marshal agreed to come, for this was to be an occasion attended by all the nations that fought together against Hitler's Germany.

The Ministry of Defence was contacted and asked whether a former Army officer from World War II was permitted to wear a uniform on such an occasion and it was explained quite firmly that it would be incorrect for Maxwell to do so and against Army regulations. Maxwell was determined. To get around the Ministry ban Maxwell instructed Sir John Morgan to try and hire a captain's uniform from London theatrical agencies. Of course they had no uniform that would possibly fit Maxwell. So, finally, Maxwell called his own tailor and gave him just forty-eight hours to measure, cut and make the uniform in time for Maxwell to take it to Warsaw. Somehow he succeeded and before setting off Maxwell tried it on, complete with Sam Brown and peaked cap, and marched with his swagger stick around his offices showing off to everyone.

On August 31 we attended the service at the Tomb of the

Unknown Soldier in the centre of Warsaw, Maxwell march-
ing ahead of his delegation, and in front of Lord Bramhall.
Following behind were Sir John Morgan, Joe Haines, Andrea
Martin, Michael Maloney and myself. Naturally, we had
been allocated positions for the two-hour-long ceremony
but Maxwell had not been put in the VIP section. It made no
difference. He literally clambered over barricades dividing
the areas and pushed through the crowds of VIPs, turning
and waving to the Field Marshal and the rest of us to follow
him, as though he were leading a battle charge. Maxwell
also managed to upstage the delegation from the Ministry of
Defence, including the Army Minister who was representing
the British Government, and the ranking soldiers who had
been brought along, none of whom ranked as high as Lord
Bramhall. He then joined in the march past the tomb, an
event he was not meant to be taking part in at all, as it was
reserved for only the most important visitors. Maxwell was
in his element.

During our stay in Warsaw Maxwell had long meetings with General Jaruzelski and the Polish Prime Minister
Mazowiecki, but after the initial chit-chat, Maxwell asked
that their talks should be in private and no one, except
for Maxwell, Jaruzelski, his aide and an interpreter were
present.

At the Gala Concert that night, which was conducted
by the great Sidney Bernstein, and a slide and film show
about the holocaust which was narrated by Dr Samuel Pisar,
Maxwell was determined to be one of the star attractions. All
the international guests and the pride of Poland's governing
and social élite were present, but Maxwell wanted to upstage
everyone. So he waited to waylay General Jaruzelski and his
wife as they arrived. But he had a problem as there were
crowds awaiting their arrival and they could approach up
either side of the beautiful marble staircase. Still dressed
in his uniform, Maxwell kept moving from one side to

the other trying to catch their arrival. So I positioned myself way back enabling me to watch both staircases. As I saw Jaruzelski approach up the left side I shouted: 'Bob, go left,' and Maxwell rushed across, sending men and women flying as he pushed his way through the surging mass of people trying to get a glimpse of the President and his wife.

Then he went straight to Mrs Jaruzelski while the General looked on bemused, and bowed low, picked up the lady's hand and planted a long kiss on the back of her hand. He spoke a few ingratiating words to her, saying how beautiful she looked that evening and what a pleasure it was to meet her. Everyone just stood around in astonishment at the audacity of his behaviour. Finally, Jaruzelski went to where they were standing, took his wife's hand away from Maxwell and walked on up the next flight of stairs. Maxwell turned and beamed.

Back home, Maxwell received a letter from the Colonel of the Regiment, informing him that he had no right to wear the uniform without express permission from the regiment and demanding that Maxwell forfeit a day's pay – payable to regimental funds – for wearing the uniform, as was customary when permission was granted. Such a payment would normally be a maximum of £100 but Maxwell and the Colonel finally agreed on a £1,000 donation, which he duly paid. To Maxwell the experience had been worth every penny.

Desperate to forge new links with emerging nations, where he hoped to expand his political influence and snap up rich pickings, Maxwell turned his attention to South America, and decided to break new ground there by holding talks with the Argentine President Carlos Menem. Argentina was trying to emerge once more into the civilized world after elections which followed the collapse of the military juntas which had ruled Argentina since the Falklands War of 1982. The Argentine currency was weak at that time and Maxwell wanted to take advantage of this fact, hoping to pick up struggling TV stations and newspapers cheaply.

Argentina was made for Maxwell. Here was a chance to show his adventurous spirit, to be seen seizing the initiative by being the first major Western businessman to beat a path to Buenos Aires after years in which the economy of the country had aimlessly drifted as it tried to sort out its political future. In 1989 Britain still had no diplomatic relations with Buenos Aires, and that attracted Maxwell who always believed he was the man who dared to go where others feared to tread. As usual, Maxwell began his campaign to woo the Argentine leaders by distributing largesse, announcing he was donating $100 million in a package of benefits to help Argentina. We visited TV studios and a newspaper that he was particularly interested in, one reason being it had a helicopter pad on the roof. Maxwell did agree to support the ailing paper and handed over $50,000, but a week after he flew out the paper folded – and Maxwell lost his money. That was one occasion on which he did hand over the money immediately, hoping it would be a sprat to catch a mackerel. But he was wrong again.

Maxwell had sent ahead Sir John Morgan, Mark Booth, who was chief executive of Maxwell Entertainment Group, and Richard Marin of Citibank, who flew in from New York. Maxwell wanted not only to impress the Argentines but to show he meant business. His team did preliminary work dealing with heads of government departments and identifying potential purchases in TV and publishing. Two weeks later Maxwell and I flew down to Buenos Aires and rounds of intensive talks took place in a Plaza Hotel suite over three days and nights. He not only ended up trying to buy a newspaper and a TV station but also shook hands on a deal to buy a massive fish-processing plant and fishing boats! I remember at the time shaking my head and thinking he was mad. Yet one always had the sneaking suspicion that all was not what it seemed on the surface with Maxwell.

In talks with President Menem, Maxwell pushed hard trying to persuade the President that he should hand over all Argentina's foreign debt for Maxwell companies to manage, telling the President that he would give Argentina a better deal than anyone else in Europe or the United States. Maxwell also broached the possibility of opening up his own bank in Argentina or taking a stake in an Argentine bank. But none of these suggestions were taken up. I remember noting that President Menem looked rather sceptical when Maxwell, a publisher, said he wanted to open a bank!

After a splendid lunch attended by the glamorous Mrs Menem, a former film star, Maxwell, President Menem and a few of us played an impromptu game of football on the lawns outside his residence. Maxwell challenged Menem to send the top Buenos Aires football team to England to play his club, Derby County. Menem and Maxwell got on well together, laughing and joking like old buddies, and Menem offered to drive Maxwell to the airport in his new toy, a Ferrari Mondial. Naturally Maxwell accepted and two security guards had to help ease the giant Maxwell into the passenger seat as the short, sprightly Menem nimbly jumped in next to him and roared off at speed, with a security man hunched up in the small rear seat. Maxwell and Menem looked incongruous together and I thought of Laurel and Hardy.

Maxwell's forays into France were to prove embarrassing, both politically and financially. What began so promisingly in 1985 was to turn to disaster within four years. In a nutshell, Maxwell misjudged France, the French and his

241

'special' relationship with President François Mitterrand. Ironically, it was the French who first wooed Maxwell, offering him a twenty per cent stake in the proposed French TV satellite service. In France, the media, and especially TV, had been the preserve of the President, obedient to government control, and Maxwell believed his involvement in TV would quickly bring about a good relationship with Mitterrand himself.

The French president needed all the media allies he could rustle up with the presidential elections looming and the opinion polls indicating a right-wing victory. Mitterrand invited Maxwell to lunch and he was won over by this larger-than-life character who was prepared to invest his millions to support a left-wing presidency. In May 1986, France's second biggest news agency, the domestic ACP (Agence Centrale de Presse) came on the market. It had been losing the equivalent of about £100,000 per month and Mitterrand needed someone with deep pockets to bail it out. He turned to Maxwell to save 'this French institution' and Maxwell obliged, coughing up the necessary £2 million. He believed that by buying into TV and saving ACP he had won the admiration and political support of the French president.

Maxwell also came to the rescue when Mitterrand was desperately searching for sponsors to support France's bicentenary celebrations for the French Revolution. He agreed to commission the video-discs of the one million original documents of the French Revolution, stored at the National Library, for worldwide distribution. A presidential spokesman said: 'The celebrations needed money and Maxwell just opened his wallet for the President.'

Again Maxwell came to the aid of Mitterrand when it seemed the President's dream of producing a lasting edifice to compare with the Eiffel Tower, built to celebrate the bicentenary of the revolution, might be doomed to failure.

Two years before the 1989 celebrations Edgar Fauré had suggested that La Grande Arche, a massive office block being constructed by Bouygues near the centre of Paris, should be the symbol of the celebrations. With less than a year before the celebrations it appeared La Grande Arche might be a political embarrassment. Maxwell not only agreed to rent office space in the building but also purchased, in a joint company, the huge 16,000 metre-square windowless basement. The commitment cost him over £20 million.

The French were also looking for someone to finance the Rights of Man exhibition, and again Maxwell obliged, becoming, on the death of Edgar Fauré, the president of the organization. Maxwell loved the title though he had nothing whatsoever to do with the organization.

As plans for the French TV satellite had been crushed by the arrival of Conservative Jacques Chirac in the elections, Maxwell was keen to enter the fray again when the decision was taken to privatize TF1, France's most successful TV station. Much to Mitterrand's pleasure, Maxwell took a twenty per cent stake, costing £75 million, accepted the post of director-general and put his French-speaking son, Ian, into the company to represent his interest. It was not to work. To celebrate the launch of TF1, Maxwell threw a fantastic party on the *Lady Ghislaine* at Cannes, inviting all the French TV stars and celebrities as well as those who financed the new station. He announced he was investing an initial £20 million into a TV production company and the French believed he was made of money. Even the multi- millionaire Buoygues confessed that day: 'I'm a hardened businessman and I have a tough skin. But frankly, this man Maxwell is a mammoth . . .'

At the same time Maxwell was expecting to buy the Provençal group of newspapers in the South of France. He seemed to have the deal sewn up but his bullying attitude to those selling the group ruined his chances and the vendors refused his final offer, even though it was a staggering twenty per cent more than the one they accepted.

Determined to capitalize on the relationship with Mitterrand, Maxwell continued ploughing money into France, buying a stake in the celebrated Sygma photo agency and APEI, a small magazine publisher. But Maxwell needed TF1 to produce profits to support his French investments, and there was no sign of profits from the TV station. Once again Maxwell had not the time to devote to his new cash-hungry baby and control slid into the hands of the main financier, François Bouygues.

There were occasional lighter moments when one travelled with Maxwell. I remember being in his suite in the Ritz in Paris one afternoon and the phones would not stop ringing. Maxwell was on one phone, a secretary was on another, an executive from London had been waiting on a third line for ten minutes – and from the depths of his bedroom I heard a fourth phone ringing. I went in search of the phone and discovered it was in the spare loo in his suite, next to the bathroom. On the line was the Élysée Palace, so I asked them to hold and went to tell Maxwell.

'Follow me,' I said, 'you'll like this,' and he came through. 'There,' I said, 'I have not only got the Élysée Palace on the phone for you but you can have a seat at the same time.' That appealed to his sense of humour and he sat down on the 'throne' laughing and began chatting away to the Palace.

I was to visit France frequently during 1988 and attended the TF1 annual meeting. It was a frosty affair. On the stage were the two giants, Buoygues and Maxwell, who had been at loggerheads at every board meeting, hurling insults at each other in a bid for control of the TV station. There was obviously no love lost between them. After the meeting Maxwell left the stage without a word and walked outside to his waiting car to take him back to the Ritz while the other shareholders mingled over drinks. As we got into the car, Maxwell said between tight lips: 'I'm very angry, I can't speak. They have insulted me and insulted my son.' It was the beginning of the end of Maxwell in France.

It seemed that Maxwell had been outplayed and outwitted by numerous French people who were willing to take his money, use his financial muscle for their own ends and then dump him when he tried to throw his weight around. Maxwell pushed for another meeting with Mitterrand and he had a private lunch with him in the summer of 1989. Maxwell tried to win the support of the President against his rivals, but Mitterrand didn't want to take sides. Maxwell came back from the lunch an unhappy man; he slumped on the sofa in his suite at the Ritz and called for a bottle of champagne. He drank long and hard from his big pint-size glass but he wasn't in a mood to talk. 'We will leave first thing in the morning,' was all he said. 'I'm going to get some sleep,' the signal for everyone to leave him alone.

Within days he had pulled the plug on ACP and despite repeated pleas from the staff, from French journalists and from MPs, Maxwell was in no mood to continue to support the loss-making news agency. Two years later he was to sell his stake in TF1 at a loss – and he was never to see Mitterrand again. Once again Maxwell had tried to muscle in on another country, tried to gain financial advantage by winning over the most senior political powers; once again he had failed.

NINE

■■■■■■■■

'Gorbachov treated me like a Head of State.'

There were three other very important countries where Maxwell travelled in his business career which were to play vital roles in his life – Russia, Israel and the United States. The first, which he began visiting as far back as 1949, was the Soviet Union.

Throughout his life Maxwell's close involvement with Moscow was a tantalizing morsel to be brought up whenever Maxwell's name was mentioned. No one knew anything for sure, no one could prove anything against Maxwell, and yet the persistent rumours that Maxwell was a KGB man in the West persisted until, and even more so since, his death. In the 1950s and 1960s in particular, following Churchill's famous 'Iron Curtain' speech, any businessman dealing with the Soviet Union was suspect. That was understandable. Maxwell seemed to revel in the dubious reputation of being one of the very few Western businessmen dealing with the Communist regime.

Maxwell's background was more suspect than most. He was born in a part of Czechoslovakia which Russia grabbed at the end of World War II; he spoke Russian, though not fluently, as well as many other European languages, and from his earliest business dealings until his death he was a frequent visitor to Moscow.

It must be remembered, however, that Maxwell was a young Jewish boy who grew up in the 1930s in fear of Hitler, Fascism, the Nazis and their anti-Jewish hysteria which culminated in the holocaust and the murder of his parents and other members of his family. In Central Europe at that time the two major political ideologies – Fascism and Communism – were battling for supremacy. Though many Jews had no love of Communism they had an all-consuming fear of Fascism and many viewed Communism as the only counter-balance. Maxwell never appears to have had any second thoughts about travelling to Moscow, mixing with the Russians or trading with them.

There have been reports that Maxwell agreed to work with the KGB immediately after World War II when he was with the British army of occupation in Berlin. British officers confirm that he was very friendly with some of the Russian officers there and would go on drinking sprees with them. It may be, with the euphoria of defeating the Nazis and feeling a sense of freedom, he did sign up to work for the KGB, if requested, vowing never to let Fascism rise again; but there is no proof he signed such papers and certainly no documentary proof has ever come to light.

Ironically, when Maxwell first visited Moscow he was suspected of being a spy for British Intelligence. Files inspected in Moscow in the summer of 1992 reveal Maxwell's name in a hitherto secret document of the Strict Regime Office Number 32 of the USSR Foreign Affairs Ministry that registered arriving individuals suspected of being spies. He was given the nickname 'Bob Hoch' and the document revealed that Maxwell in fact first visited Moscow some time between 1947 and 1949. He stayed three days. But there was no date for his departure. KGB officials in Moscow concluded this meant that, although suspected of being a British spy when he arrived, he was not suspected of being one when he left the country three days later. There is no further information suggesting the reason for his visit or whom he saw.

It was about this time that Maxwell met the man who was to change his life – and set him on the road to becoming a millionaire. Paul Rosabaud was a middle-aged Austrian scientist who in the 1930s had been one of the Springer family's chief scientific advisers, a Jew who had fled the Nazis and worked for British Intelligence throughout the war. In 1949 Rosabaud became editor of the scientific journals to be published by a new company, Butterworth-Springer. Two years later, after Maxwell broke his relationship with Ferdinand Springer, Pergamon was born and Rosabaud took over day-to-day control.

Under Rosabaud the scientific publishing firm grew steadily in prestige and influence, but its turnover and profits only increased modestly. It was the 1955 United Nations Geneva conference on the peaceful use of atomic energy that transformed Pergamon from a small, élite publishing house to a major player. It was Rosabaud's scientific knowledge matched by Maxwell's entrepreneurial flair that made the breakthrough. Maxwell, accompanied by Rosabaud, went to Geneva and, having spent all his time talking to scientists and publishers, Maxwell realized that scientific publishing could make him the fortune he yearned for. Within months Pergamon hurried out a truncated version of the thousand UN papers prepared for the occasion, publishing them months before the UN version, and this at a time when the whole scientific world was hungry for them. Within two years Pergamon had grown into a major scientific publishing house – and Maxwell found himself courted when he returned to Moscow.

Maxwell learned from Rosabaud and other scientists who he spoke to at Geneva that the secret to establishing a prestigious and successful scientific publishing house was to appoint scientists of the highest calibre to the editorial boards responsible for publishing each journal and paper. For once in his life Maxwell, more or less, left his editorial boards, which he staffed with scientists of high repute, to do their job without interference. As a result Pergamon was to become not only such a highly regarded scientific publishing house but the cornerstone of his business empire.

Moscow wanted two things from Maxwell. Russian scientists wanted to publish their works in the West – to show off their own escalating knowledge – and they desperately wanted every item of scientific information, particularly nuclear information, that was being published in the West. The Americans, in the grip of fierce anti-Communist fervour, had stopped the flow of scientific information to the Soviet bloc and were putting pressure on Western nations to stop their flow of scientific knowledge to the Soviets. Maxwell happily agreed to the Moscow deal which he hoped would make him rich.

Bower, in his book *Maxwell: the Outsider*, reveals that Yuri Gradov, the Russian lawyer who negotiated the Pergamon deal, contacted the KGB to check out Maxwell and commented: 'They told me that Maxwell was all right. Otherwise they wouldn't have let him into the country.'

From that time on Maxwell was given special status in Moscow, allowed to stay in the prestigious National Hotel, and later, when I travelled to Moscow with him, in a suite in the Oktober Hotel, a privilege which was granted to very few foreigners. To represent Pergamon in Moscow, Maxwell was introduced to Victor Louis, a British journalist who had served time in a Stalin gulag and who was later to have close ties with the KGB. Louis, who died in July 1992, lived a privileged life in a lovely dacha outside Moscow complete with tennis court and swimming pool.

Maxwell was to have ever closer ties with Moscow and the KGB. Research carried out in Moscow in the summer of 1992 reveals the KGB had six separate dossiers on Maxwell, as well as one from the Bulgarian Secret Service, which always had close ties with the KGB Centre in Moscow. KGB officials explained that the importance of a person was gauged by the number of dossiers a person had on file – and six was considered above average for a foreigner. One dossier showed that Maxwell was considered to be a 'Great Friend of the USSR' – a title awarded by the KGB to those in the West whose sympathies in the cold war were on the side of the Soviet Union.

Another was a 'Spy Dossier' but that does not indicate that Maxwell was in fact a spy. Colonel Serge Alexandrovich Kurenkov of the KGB gave the following reply when asked whether Maxwell was a spy: 'That is a most complicated question and difficult to answer. No one can say if a man is a KGB secret agent or not; or simply an agent of influence or someone who works for the KGB as an amateur. Let me explain. There were three types of secret service collaborators who worked for the KGB – secret agents, agents of influence, and agents with an official status in foreign countries. And there are amateurs and helpers.' Despite the collapse of the former Soviet Union, there is no way that those who guard the KGB files today will allow any outsider to see them.

One senior KGB officer prepared to talk, Colonel Alexander Yevgenovich Koinkov, claimed he was responsible for introducing Maxwell to the recently promoted head of the KGB, Yuri Andropov, in May 1968. Koinkov also claimed, during interviews in 1992, that he was responsible for helping Maxwell construct his business empire and the web of secret stiftungs and companies in Liechtenstein, Luxembourg and Gibraltar. He also claimed that part of Maxwell's wealth was built on funds provided by the KGB. But there was no way to substantiate his claims and he was unable to produce any documentary proof.

Vladimir Nesterenkov, an officer of the GRU, the Soviet

military Intelligence organization, interviewed in July 1992, claimed the KGB had control over the Maxwell business empire and its dramatic collapse in 1991 proved the KGB's involvement. He said: 'When the time had come to blow it apart the billion-dollar business crashed in months. The mines had been well laid.'

Throughout the decades during which Maxwell and Pergamon traded with the Soviet Union, his companies were primarily paid by Gosbank – the USSR state bank – but not exclusively so. General Vitaly Petrov of the KGB Lubyanka headquarters claimed in 1992 that both Pergamon and Berlitz were involved in fund transfers by the KGB to the West. He also claimed that Berlitz was the only Western company that received secret KGB maps and satellite photographs for commercial use.

Vitaly Petrov also claimed that Maxwell was involved in the money scandal that rocked Moscow in 1990 when senior members of the Communist Party succeeded in transferring millions of dollars to the West when it seemed the Soviet Union was on the verge of collapse. Petrov claimed that thirty-five per cent of all the funds secretly transferred out of Moscow were moved through Maxwell-related companies. Other KGB officers, who refused to be named, disclosed that vast funds had been sent out of the country in 1990, and they claimed that Maxwell's companies were a conduit. The CPSU money scandal has never been resolved in Moscow, and may never be, because of the numbers of high-ranking former Communists, still in positions of power, who were believed to have been involved.

It does seem beyond doubt that Maxwell was seen by the KGB as an 'agent of influence', but there is no evidence to support any allegations that he was a secret agent, a spy for the Soviet Union. Nor is there any evidence whatsoever that Maxwell was ever accused of spying for another country or ever suspected of being disloyal to Britain. Maxwell was always passionate in his defence of Britain and he was always proud of the fact that it was he who selected to live in Britain and chose to live his entire life in the country of his adoption. During research in Moscow two KGB officers said they could produce documentary proof that would stand up in a court of law that Maxwell was an 'agent of influence' but they wanted $10,000 for the documents.

Maxwell's star burned brightest in Moscow when Yuri Andropov took over as head of the KGB in the late sixties and when he finally became General Secretary of the Party in 1982, though he was to survive for only fifteen months. Maxwell was given total freedom to publish whatever he wanted from Russian scientists, and in turn, Maxwell made sure that all the latest scientific journals and papers Pergamon produced were made available to Moscow. More than that, Maxwell struck a deal which gave Russian authors only thirty per cent of any monies earned from publishing their work in the West.

It was during those years that Maxwell began acting as the conduit for KGB funds in the West. The rouble was not convertible, and not traded in the West. No Soviet citizen was permitted to hold an account in dollars and never an overseas account. But for the KGB things worked differently. Those at a senior level were permitted to hold overseas dollar accounts, and the KGB needed dollars to pay its way in the world. In his unique position, trading as a publisher of Soviet scientific journals in the West, Maxwell would have been in receipt of monies from Moscow. But according to directors at Pergamon very little money ever came into Pergamon's British bank from Moscow.

With Maxwell's private foundations in Liechtenstein and his myriad of secretive stiftungs it was the perfect way for KGB dollars to find safe haven in the West. No banks were involved; no embarrassing accounts; no trace. Maxwell allowed the funds to travel through his secret companies, presumably, though there is no proof as yet, taking a good percentage for allowing the facility. It is very likely he had no idea where the money ever went, or was destined for. But in that way Maxwell would have amassed a small fortune for himself.

Maxwell's remarkable relationship with Moscow and the KGB was illustrated in September 1978 when he was permitted, with Mrs Maxwell, to return to Solotvino, the place of his birth. At that time the Soviets were most strict about allowing foreigners to move freely anywhere outside Moscow, let alone to a sensitive military zone near the Soviet border. Maxwell was escorted by officials from Moscow to Solotvino and taken on a guided tour of his old town. He found that little had changed since he lived there in the 1920s and '30s; the roads were still muddy, the houses were still wooden shacks, the people still lived in poverty and he didn't recognize anyone from his childhood. The visit was in fact a disappointment to him and he never wanted to return.

In 1983, six months after Andropov took over the ultimate reins of power in the Soviet Union, Maxwell was invited to Moscow and awarded an honorary doctorate from Moscow State University for his distinction as a 'well-known specialist in the field of economics who actively campaigns for the strengthening of friendship and mutual understanding between the Soviet and English peoples'. The signatories to that doctorate were the general secretaries of the Central Committee: Mikhail Gorbachov, then in charge of agriculture; Konstantin Chernenko, who succeeded Andropov as leader; and Nikolai Ryzhkov, who was to become Prime Minister of the Soviet Union.

Maxwell would often visit the Kremlin during visits to Moscow to brief senior Soviet ministers as well as the KGB chiefs and he was given privileged access to successive Soviet leaders. He would brief them on political thinking in the West, talk to them of the current political climate in Britain and Europe, and, at the same time, agree to publish their boring biographies in the West. According to former Pergamon directors the company hardly made any money out of publishing Soviet scientific journals and papers, nor out of publishing the tame biographies, which sometimes only amounted to the regurgitation of old speeches by Soviet leaders, that no one wanted to read, let alone buy.

Although Maxwell's star was in the ascendant when Andropov succeeded to the top job in November 1982 it was not to last long, for during most of his time as General Secretary he was an ill man. And the man who succeeded him, Konstantin Chernenko, had been Andropov's rival. He was also destined to last little more than a year.

Gorbachov's election as General Secretary was good news for Maxwell. For Gorbachov was an Andropov man, twenty years younger and his protégé. It was Andropov who had schooled Gorbachov; it was Andropov who during the late 1970s had realized that the Soviet Union's economy was heading for disaster – forecast by latest state-of-the-art computers which the KGB had stolen from the West and smuggled to Moscow. When Gorbachov took over the reins he knew the Soviet economy was tottering and the only way forward was to strike a deal with the West, enabling the state to reduce its massive expenditure on arms and missiles. Then he could turn his attentions to revitalizing the Soviet economy.

That was one reason why Gorbachov welcomed Maxwell in Moscow. He knew from the KGB that Maxwell could be trusted and this man seemed to have just what Gorbachov needed, offering to invest money, to produce independent newspapers, to start an independent TV station, promising things that Gorbachov desperately needed – a way to approach the Soviet people directly without the blocking instincts of the Communist Old Guard who ran state TV and the newspapers.

There was another reason. Oleg Gordievsky, the KGB colonel who in 1985 escaped to Britain from Moscow after years working for British Intelligence, attended the private meeting at the Soviet Embassy in London which Gorbachov addressed in December 1984. On that occasion Gorbachov stressed that one of the main interests in Soviet foreign Intelligence operations lay in the field of scientific and technological espionage. In his book *KGB – The Inside Story*, written in conjunction with the Cambridge historian Christopher Andrew, Gordievsky commented that it was clear Gorbachov regarded covert acquisition of Western technology as an important part of economic perestroika. Here was another area where Maxwell, with his worldwide scientific publishing empire, could be very useful.

Maxwell rose to the occasion with enthusiasm and energy. He saw himself as the catalyst between East and West, the successor to Armand Hammer, straddling the two ideologies like a wealthy, privileged Colossus; he wanted to be the honoured unofficial diplomat flying between Moscow, Washington, London, Paris and Jerusalem helping to solve the world's problems which he believed could be solved much more satisfactorily through intermediaries like himself, than through the usual diplomatic channels.

In the 1970s Maxwell had begun to see himself in this role and continued to develop the American side of his business, beyond Pergamon's narrow interests. He had stalwart old friends working for him there including Laszlo Straker, a man Maxwell could trust who had worked for him since the early 1950s. He was joined by Sheldon Aboff, a man who knew most of Maxwell's secrets, including most of what went on in Liechtenstein. Both were later to be rewarded for their unequivocal loyalty by being promoted to vice-presidents of Maxwell's Macmillan empire. And they were to be joined by Ellis Freedman, an American lawyer of Whitman & Ransom, on whom Maxwell relied greatly for most of his legal requirements in the United States. They were a formidable team. And they were there at the end when Maxwell was desperately trying, with their help, to keep his empire afloat.

On our visits to Moscow during the last few years of Maxwell's life I watched like a hawk to see if I could detect any KGB-related activities between Maxwell and the numerous Russians who would come and see him in his suite. But it was impossible. Sometimes he would go on his own to visit the authorities, not saying whom he was going to see. Sometimes I think he did act suspiciously in Moscow but it may have simply been unfair interpretation on my part. It seemed to me on some occasions that many of his Russian visitors acted suspiciously, seasoned by years of living in a Communist state, looking over their shoulder to see who else was about before uttering a word.

I remember being in the Oktober Hotel in 1989 when guests arrived. I was in the suite with Maxwell and met the two Russians who were involved in Maxwell's joint plan with Viniti, the information division of the Soviet Academy of Sciences, to put on to computers the results of Soviet chemical research of the previous twenty years. After introductions we all sat down and the two Russians, and the interpreter, kept looking from Maxwell to me and back again. 'Oh, don't worry,' Maxwell said after a few moments of silence, 'you can talk in front of Mr Davies. He is one of us.'

I don't know what Maxwell meant but it was obviously an invitation for the Russians to stop playing around and get on with the business. On that occasion we talked for an hour about the project. Maxwell said that he would provide computers and new printing equipment to the tune of £1.2 million and Viniti would provide the information and the input of all the research material. Maxwell kept telling the Russians that they had to get a move on because the Americans were very keen to distribute the information worldwide.

I could see the glint in Maxwell's eye as the talks progressed. He loved the idea of being given all this information which he would then pass on to one of his American companies, on this occasion Molecular Design, which Maxwell was determined to build into one of the biggest scientific data bases in the world. By 1991 it was the fourth biggest and making good profits, growing at the time of Maxwell's death at more than twenty per cent a year!

However, this was another Maxwell–Soviet project that never got off the ground. A year later the project was abandoned and the joint venture officially wound up. Maxwell had produced about £500,000-worth of computer equipment, and delivered it to Moscow, but the Russians never began work on inputting the material. Understandably, Maxwell decided to pull the plug and the equipment was never recovered.

One of Maxwell's biggest projects in the former USSR was in connection with the Kondapoga newsprint plant near the Finnish border. Already the giant mill had ten newsprint lines and Maxwell wanted to add another one. The deal was struck that Maxwell would pay £160 million for the line but that payment should be made over a period of five years as he purchased newsprint for his Mirror Group newspapers at low rates. A Finnish consultant was brought in and was paid £300,000 for a feasibility study. The Soviets promised to produce bank guarantees to cover all costs but they never produced the guarantees.

This total lack of efficiency would infuriate Maxwell. I remember him letting fly at the Soviet delegation which should have produced the guarantees. We were in his suite and these five Russians, and an interpreter, were left standing while Maxwell sat at a desk berating them in a mixture of Russian and English. It became near farce as Maxwell kept forgetting his Russian – for he was never as fluent in that language as he claimed – and would repeatedly stammer over the Russian, break into English, and then never let the poor interpreter get a word in. The Russian delegation stood there, perplexed, not really knowing what was going on as Maxwell raged on at their incompetence. He knew as he watched their stony faces that he would never see the guarantees and suddenly he gave up, flopped his hands down on the table and looked at them; while they in turn stared at him. He got up, said a perfunctory 'Goodbye,' and walked out of the room leaving them standing and staring at each other. I showed them out.

Later that day I walked into Maxwell's suite and heard him in a rage on the phone to London: 'The whole country is fucking useless . . . nothing ever happens . . . I might as well be speaking to a brick wall . . . nothing ever happens, nothing, absolutely nothing. I'm coming home.' And he slammed down the phone.

It was during discussions with Alexander Yakovlev, an influential member of the Politburo and Mikhail Gorbachov's closest and most influential adviser, that Maxwell offered to launch a cultural foundation. He offered to contribute £500,000 a year to the foundation and suggested a good beginning would be to launch a distinguished, high-profile, classy magazine to be called *Our Heritage* as a flagship for the foundation. It would highlight Soviet history and culture. Maxwell invited Gorbachov's wife, Raisa, to sit on the editorial board to make sure he achieved the maximum political prestige for his money. Maxwell ordered me to get involved, telling me to report to the Soviet Embassy in London for the pre-launch meeting, attend the launch of the glossy magazine and write reports for the *Daily*

Mirror. The Soviets provided all the editorial matter and the expensive art paper and Maxwell paid for the printing and production costs.

I was introduced to Alexander Yakovlev at the Soviet Embassy in London and we talked. I asked him about Maxwell's projects in the Soviet Union.

Yakovlev replied: 'He is a very good friend of the Soviet Union, one of our best friends in the Western world.'

I asked him if Maxwell was a friend of Comrade Mikhail Sergevich (Gorbachov) and he replied: 'No, he cannot be. They are acquaintances but not friends. Mikhail Sergevich is the General Secretary of the Party. Mr Maxwell is a businessman.'

I realized I was getting the official line, but it was 1989. I replied: 'But Mr Maxwell has been a friend of the Soviet Union for many, many years.'

Yakovlev was not to be drawn, replying: 'Yes, but he is still a businessman.'

It was sometimes surprising that Maxwell kept up his interest in Moscow, because he was constantly frustrated and consequently infuriated by the lack of action by any of the authorities he ever became involved with. In 1988 I flew to Russia with him, only to find that nothing had happened since the last time he had been there more than a year before.

Unusually for Maxwell, he spent a lot of time outside the hotel in Moscow, at meetings and dinners, often going alone. He would always go to the Kremlin to see someone; he would attend meetings at Viniti and NAUKA, at Novosti and at *Moscow News.* But he never seemed happy or relaxed in Moscow, finding the place so frustrating that no matter how hard he tried, how much he shouted, how he flattered and cajoled, nothing ever seemed to get done. To make matters worse, and importantly for Maxwell, he hated the food the Russians provided. So, from 1988 onwards Maxwell arrived with his own food including salmon, cheeses, tins of tuna and soup as well as his own excellent bottles of wine and port to supplement the basics sent up from the hotel kitchens.

Our Heritage was a well-designed, classy magazine but it didn't sell. It was more a Russian version of American coffee-table magazines, to be given away or placed in Soviet embassies around the world. It was another loss-leader for Maxwell but he hoped it might be worth the candle to catch bigger, and more profitable, fish. For one, it drew him closer to the ultimate Soviet powerbase, the Politburo and Gorbachov, which was Maxwell's ultimate target.

Fed up with nothing happening, Maxwell approached the Soviet authorities to find someone to replace the ailing Victor Louis and his son Nicholas who were primarily involved in producing *Information Moscow*, a directory full of information and telephone numbers for Westerners – a sort of *Yellow Pages* – which became a must for everyone in Moscow. The directory made Victor Louis a small fortune. The Russians came up with Felix Sviridov, an efficient former Communist Party tactician who knew how the Kremlin worked. He was made a director of MCC and began to pull the strings Maxwell demanded.

Things began to improve. On arrival in Moscow there wasn't just one man to meet Maxwell's private jet, as in the past, but a host of smarter, well-dressed bureaucrats, who smiled and bowed as they shook Maxwell's hand. Our passports were taken from the plane and we sat and waited for them to be quickly inspected, stamped and returned so there would be no interminable queueing; the soldiers on duty now saluted as we passed; doors were opened; we swept through Customs without stopping; everyone in Sheremetyevo airport realized a VIP had arrived. And there were now highly polished, large Zil limousines waiting at the airport steps to carry us in style through the grey streets to our hotel.

But access to Gorbachov, the prize Maxwell so desperately sought, still eluded him despite the pressure he put on Sviridov to arrange a 'summit'. Maxwell realized he had to pull something out of the hat. He believed finance was the key. So he decided to try and arrange, secretly, a massive $4-billion-dollar emergency private loan to try and make sure that the people of Moscow didn't starve through the winter of 1989–90 and blame Gorbachov and his perestroika ideas. There was real concern that winter that Gorbachov could be brought down if starving Russians took to the streets and food riots broke out. Maxwell contacted Karl Pohl, president of the Bundesbank, and Hans Dietrich-Genscher, Germany's influential Foreign Minister, with whom Maxwell was on good terms, to try and put together the huge loan on Gorbachov's behalf. Maxwell in fact never managed to provide the loan but his efforts did result in a meeting with Gorbachov.

That was in February 1990, when Maxwell went to Moscow with a heavy Israeli team, with novel ideas to help the crippled Soviet economy. Maxwell was becoming more involved in Israel by then and had been pushing Israel's interests in the Soviet Union for two years. The team included the wealthy Israeli industrialist Shoul Eisenberg and David Kimche, director of International Relations for Eisenberg and former senior adviser to Israel's Prime Minister Yitzhak Shamir. For more than a decade Kimche had been one of Mossad's senior directors. Sir John Morgan and I also went along.

Ever since his teenage years Maxwell had problems confronting his Jewish background. He would not deny that he was born Jewish but he would make odd comments that he attended Church of England services and read the lesson in C of E churches. Even in 1964 Maxwell wrote to the

261

Jewish Chronicle in London explaining that he was 'now a member of the Church of England'. In his later years, however, when he managed to confront his Judaism, he became zealous in his championing of the Jewish and Israeli causes.

It was in 1986 that Maxwell 'came out', owned up to his Jewish background and began the psychological process of embracing Judaism once again. He told the *Jewish Chronicle* then: 'My family were observant and I was given a traditional Jewish education. I ceased to be a practising Jew just before the war when I left home. I still believe in God and Judaism's moral education which teaches the difference between right and wrong.' But he added: 'I don't believe in any Church – just God.' The *Jewish Chronicle* tried to persuade Maxwell to be interviewed in depth about his religion but he refused to be drawn further.

It was Betty Maxwell, a devout French Huguenot with a Catholic mother, who helped her husband face up to his past and his religious roots. She once explained: 'As a Protestant Christian married to a Jew, I see my task as making Christians aware of the relevance of the Nazi holocaust for them. If Christianity hadn't created a climate in which anti-Semitism could progress as it did, and if so-called Christian Europe had done what Jesus had asked it to do, there would have been no holocaust, not anyway in such frightening dimensions.'

Mrs Maxwell remembered Gestapo raids on the Jewish ghetto in Paris near where she lived. 'One day after a raid,' she recalled, 'all the tenants in the building except for me and another gentile family were taken away. It was a trauma I never forgot.'

In total, Maxwell and his wife knew 635 Jews who perished during World War II, murdered by the Nazis. In the 1980s Mrs Maxwell spent three years organizing a week-long conference in Oxford on the holocaust called 'Remembering for the Future'. The conference, which brought together six hundred survivors, was opened by Maxwell. It was to be the turning point in his attitude to his own Judaism and subsequently to his attitude to Israel. He broke down and sobbed during his opening speech at Oxford Town Hall; could not continue and Betty Maxwell had to finish his speech for him.

Later, as the conference was virtually ignored by the British press, Maxwell lashed out, saying: 'As a publisher, as a journalist, but above all as a British citizen who lived through Nazi tyranny, I am outraged at this indifference. If evil comes when good men do nothing, then this silence contains the seeds of evil. When Hitler embarked on his murderous course, the world's press – with a few honourable exceptions – said nothing. The British press was guilty then, it is still guilty today.'

It was from this time on that Maxwell began pushing Moscow hard to help the Jews of the Soviet Union. By the late 1980s Israel did succeed in establishing an official consulate in Moscow after decades of being denied any official status, or any representative in the Soviet Union. And yet, even then, the Israeli Consul was treated with hardly any respect or even acknowledgement that he was there. He was, to all intents and purposes, virtually ignored. Infuriated by this, Maxwell took decisive action.

I was with him when he set up an elaborate dinner in Moscow for more than fifty people, which he organized and paid for. He invited a number of dignitories and senior Communist officials and bureaucrats, including leading figures of Comecon, of NAUKA and of Viniti, as well as Soviet parliamentarians. What he didn't tell the Soviet guests was that the guest of honour was the Israeli Consul, who had never previously met any of those at the dinner. And, to prove his point further, he sat the secretary-general of Comecon next to the Israeli Consul!

In the Oktober Hotel later, Maxwell was jubilant: 'That will show the buggers,' he beamed, 'that will make them sit up and take notice.' On that occasion Maxwell had gone out of his way to help the Jewish state, probably infuriating his Soviet contacts and doing himself no good whatsoever in Moscow. Indeed, the dinner caused hostility among his enemies in the Soviet capital, who accused him of meddling in domestic Soviet politics, something that was none of his business.

He talked to Gorbachov, with the KGB chief General Vladimir Kryuchkov and Alexander Yakovlev as well as members of the Foreign Affairs Committee of the Central Committee, about increasing the number of Jewish refugees allowed to leave the Soviet Union for Israel. He helped persuade the Soviet authorities to allow the refugees to fly directly to Israel rather than being processed through Vienna. Without recourse to Israel or the Israeli government, Maxwell appointed himself the unofficial 'Israeli Ambassador to Moscow' and he pursued the role with vigour and remarkable success.

It was Maxwell who persuaded the Soviet authorities to fly to Israel three hundred Russian children who were suffering the effects of radiation years after the Chernobyl disaster. The children, of no particular religious denomination, were flown to Israel, examined and treated in Israeli hospitals. The entire cost, amounting to more than £100,000, was paid by Maxwell.

In May 1989 Maxwell called me to his office and said he had a most important, and unusual, task for me that he hoped I would accept. He told me that three hundred members of the Women's International Zionist Organization were to tour Poland, visiting every one of the Nazi concentration camps and death camps in which the Jews had been gassed and slaughtered. It was the first time ever that WIZO had been allowed to visit Poland because no Zionist organization had been allowed there while the Communists were in power.

The three hundred young woman, from all over the world, were warned of the horror of their visit by WIZO president Raya Jaglam, a woman of remarkable courage, when we all met up in Paris. The tour through Poland was incredibly emotional and I shall never forget the day we spent at Auschwitz when many of the young women broke down, unable to continue, as we saw the horror of the camps and walked through the museum where their parents and relatives had been incarcerated and murdered.

In his later years such thoughts were never far from Maxwell's mind but he never let them interfere with business. One of Maxwell's most ambitious business plans was a massive joint venture involving the Soviets, the Americans, the Israelis and himself. The idea was born in 1990 at a meeting between Shoul Eisenberg, of Israel Corporation, and Maxwell, after Maxwell had held talks in Moscow with directors of Aeroflot, the Soviet airline. The joint venture only came about because of Maxwell's political clout in Moscow, and this was accepted by the Americans and Israelis involved. Maxwell set up a company in America called Aviation Venture International, with Eisenberg, Armand Hammer and Albert Reichmann, the Canadian property developer. If successful, it would have created a serious competitor to the world's hard-pressed aviation manufacturers, including giants like Boeing, McDonnell and European Airbus.

The plan was to take the latest Soviet Ilyushin wide-bodied jets and transport them to Israel, where Israeli Aviation Industries would lengthen the fuselage to carry another 70 passengers, producing an airliner capable of carrying 375 passengers. Technically, the Ilyushin fuselage and the wings were comparable in design to the Western jets. However, the engines and the avionics were a generation behind Western technology. So, the Ilyushin would have been fitted with the latest fuel-efficient American Pratt & Whitney engines and the latest state-of-the-art avionics provided by Israeli subsidiaries to American firms. A deal was signed in Moscow to manufacture and produce an initial 150 aircraft which would have been sold at prices between thirty and forty per cent less than their Western counterparts.

The gem of the deal was how the project was to be financed. By using the Ilyushin fuselage and wings, the Soviets could fund their fifty per cent of the costs using Russian roubles while the Western industries would provide the other fifty per cent. In that way the Soviets would not need to raise US dollars, or any foreign finance, for the project to go ahead. Sales would bring in much-needed US dollars to the Russian economy. Unfortunately, in 1991, Aeroflot went bust and it could not raise the amount of money in roubles needed to fund the project.

Whenever Maxwell flew to Moscow during the last two years of his life the Soviets went out of their way to help him, promptly laying on whatever meetings Maxwell requested. Senior Comecon directors began to work more closely with Maxwell and other Soviet agencies were in closer contact at a senior level. On one occasion in February 1990 Maxwell and Eisenberg, Kimche, Sir John Morgan and myself were invited to a quite remarkable lunch, something which seemed more akin to the hospitality of Russian tsars than the Communists of the Kremlin. It consisted of eight courses, all served with different wines and of course vodka; a meal fit for a visiting head of government. Maxwell enjoyed himself because it proved to him that Gorbachov had finally realized his importance.

In a private meeting, Gorbachov had given Maxwell what he wanted, a personal message for Prime Minister Margaret Thatcher. So pleased was Maxwell that he told no one, not Sir John, myself or Andrea Martin. That was a mistake. After we flew back to Britain, Maxwell secretly phoned Downing Street and asked for an appointment with the Prime Minister to pass on a personal message from Gorbachov. The meeting was arranged for 9 p.m. on the Saturday night. But Maxwell went to sleep in the early evening and totally forgot. At 8.50 he suddenly remembered and raced around to Downing Street in record time, arriving at 9 p.m. exactly. But it had been a close shave. He told me about it later. He said: 'We had a Scotch together and Mrs Thatcher told me that she thought I was really one of them. She had a soft spot for me.' In April 1991, Maxwell offered Mrs Thatcher a remarkable $8 million for her memoirs, but she turned it down. He also tried to persuade her to write a column for the *European*, but she never did. On his next visit to Moscow he expected to be given another important message, but this time for President Bush. It was not to be.

Having been unable to provide a $4 billion loan Maxwell proposed to set up a small, secret, on-screen make-up printing plant for Gorbachov, using the latest technology, in a room in the Kremlin. The idea was that Gorbachov might be faced at some future date with an emergency where the TV, radio and newspapers were held by those opposed to him, glasnost and perestroika. He would then need a way of telling the people what was really going on. And one way would be to produce his own four-page instant news sheets which could be distributed instantly on the streets of Moscow. Gorbachov was keen, plans were drawn up but, once again, nothing came of it, though it was not Maxwell's fault for Gorbachov became engulfed in the political crisis that was to end with the ill-fated coup against him in August 1991. Ironically, the coup by the Old Guard Communists was just such an eventuality that Gorbachov had envisaged when he welcomed the secret printing-plant project.

In October 1990 Maxwell was again privileged to hold another 'summit' with Gorbachov. Again it was in private. Maxwell was thrilled, mainly because Gorbachov had given him two hours of private talks.

Maxwell phoned me afterwards and said: 'I'm sorry you

couldn't be here with me and Gorbachov. I know I promised you would be but he wouldn't allow anyone in the meeting. He gave me the same treatment, and time, as he would give a head of state.' So self-satisfied was Maxwell at this show of indulgence that he was on the phone to everyone during the next few days boasting of his 'excellent' meeting with Gorbachov.

And there was more. Two days after the meeting Maxwell wrote to Israeli Prime Minister Yitzhak Shamir, enclosing a photograph of Maxwell sitting next to Gorbachov at another meeting. He wrote: 'As you can see from the enclosed photographs, I received an extremely warm and friendly reception. This is evident by the fact that he sat me down next to him and made his number-two man, Baldin (who replaces Mr Alexander Yakovlev), and Kryuchkov, the Chairman of the KGB, sit on the visitors' side.'

The letter continued: 'Until last Friday, at the request of President Gorbachov, I transacted all my business through Alexander Yakovlev and everything Gorbachov had to say to me he communicated through him. At our meeting he invited me in future to deal through Mr Kryuchkov, the Chairman of the KGB.'

Maxwell also revealed in the letter that he had delivered a message from Shamir to Gorbachov concerning a timetable for the restoration of full diplomatic relations between Moscow and Jerusalem. In reply Gorbachov had said, 'Please tell Prime Minister Shamir to let us move consistently towards the normalization without any preconditions.'

General Vladimir Alexandrovich Kryuchkov was sixty-four when he took over as head of the KGB in 1988. A tough, unsmiling Tartar, he was renowned for having a tough, unsmiling character as well; a humourless workaholic with enormous energy, self-confidence and single-mindedness. When Andropov became head of the KGB in 1968, Kryuchkov became head of his secretariat. Three years later he was moved to the KGB's First Chief Directorate as deputy head, responsible for European Intelligence, including Britain. He had known Maxwell for years.

After his celebrated meeting with Gorbachov, Maxwell was not to visit Moscow again. But Kryuchkov's career was to end with ignominy when he took part in the flawed attempted coup against Gorbachov in the summer of 1991. As a result of that, Kryuchkov was arrested and was still in jail awaiting trial a year later.

Perhaps one of Maxwell's most public failures involving the Soviet Union was his attempt to 'sell' the Soviet Union and glasnost to the West when he decided to support Gorbachov's reforms by publishing in English the ill-fated *Moscow News*. Maxwell spent about £500,000 launching and running *Moscow News*, sending teams of managers, computer experts as well as senior *Mirror* editorial executives to design and produce an English version of *Moscow News* which he wanted to circulate in the English-speaking world. Yegor Yakovlev, of Novosti Press Agency and a close ally of Gorbachov's, launched *Moscow News* to explain perestroika to the Soviet people. This was to be a different newspaper, a paper that would explain Gorbachov's new ideas for the Soviet Union to the Soviet people as he tried to break down the old Communist ways which were rapidly bringing the country to its knees. Yakovlev became editor-in-chief, and was won over by Maxwell's charm and his idea that *Moscow News* should also be printed in English and sold throughout the English-speaking world. It was another bold Maxwell idea, which in the early days of perestroika was imaginative, though speculative. In Moscow, at a meeting with Yakovlev, I recall Maxwell warmly embracing Yakovlev, telling him they would make a great team together, telling him the circulation would be a million within a few years.

Maxwell did keep his part of the bargain. The first English editions rolled off the antiquated *Pravda* presses in 1988. But

Moscow News had to be totally revamped to have any chance of selling in the West. Maxwell agreed to provide computers, a telephone link and production facilities in London to make the monthly news magazine a success. The fact that it never could make money didn't seem to worry Maxwell.

Alan Shillum, put in charge of the operation, asked Maxwell one day: 'Why are you spending all this money? Every way we examine this project it will never make money. The best will be a loss of £350,000 a year.'

Maxwell replied: 'Mind your own business . . . get on with the job . . . and fuck off.'

For once, Maxwell did provide all he had promised plus a professional team of experienced *Mirror* journalists who produced a bright, good-looking and interesting newspaper. *Moscow News* began selling in earnest in London in May 1990 with a circulation of 25,000. Six months later, with the circulation down to 2,000 copies per issue, Maxwell pulled the plug. The loss of circulation was an excuse, for he had fallen out with Yegor Yakovlev who had realized the political climate had changed and that Gorbachov was being challenged from all sides. Maxwell would not hear of it and ordered Yakovlev to support the Gorbachov line 'come what may'. Yakovlev refused to obey and printed a vicious anti-Maxwell article in the *Moscow News*. The two men never spoke again.

Whenever Maxwell travelled overseas he always kept in close contact with headquarters in Holborn. When Peter Jay was chief-of-staff he was ordered to fax Maxwell an a.m. and p.m. report of everything going on in London, politically, financially and throughout his business empire. And the reports had to include the latest MCC, and latterly, the *Mirror* share prices. He always travelled with a fax machine or two; it was his lifeline to the world.

Another order was to his editors. The *Mirror* and *Sunday*

Mirror editors were under strict orders to make sure he was faxed the leaders for approval before they were put in the paper – under pain of death! And they always were. And yet when overseas Maxwell would nearly always ask me to check the leaders that were faxed to him from London. It was obvious from my experience that he didn't really want to read the leaders most of the time; he just wanted to remind the editors and leader writers who was in command. I would read the leaders, tell Maxwell the subject, and change them if I thought it necessary. Every night Maxwell would tell me: 'Change what's necessary and fax it back with the alterations.' The only ones he insisted on seeing were those with reference to Israel and important political ones. Most of the time he didn't want to know. Indeed, sometimes he would ask a secretary to check it and, if it looked fine, approve it.

One of my other tasks was to rewrite speeches for him – at a moment's notice. He would never bother to read the speeches people had diligently worked on for hours, if not days, before he left London. He would only glance at them an hour or so before he was due to speak. Then he would call me: 'Nick. Have you read this?' he would ask. 'Read it; it's crap.'

I would read it as quickly as possible.

'How long will it take you to rewrite it?' he would say, then add: 'You've got one hour.'

I knew what he wanted. When he wasn't speaking off the cuff, Maxwell liked short, sharp, tabloid-type sentences, nothing convoluted. So, with a secretary typing, I would rewrite a speech, a speech which someone had probably sweated hours over, usually reducing its length by fifty per cent. Most of the time I needn't have bothered. When he made the speech he often took not the slightest notice of the prepared script and would only use a few sharp sentences from the speech I had sweated over. Most of the time he just spoke off the cuff, and did so very well.

271

Maxwell was always paranoid about people knowing too much about him and his various worldwide interests. He took great exception to anyone listening to telephone calls or reading faxes that would come in for him. And yet he never showed me the least paranoia in that respect. When travelling with him I would often get the incoming faxes for him as they came off the machine in his suite, and I would read them before handing them to him. He would say to me: 'Who's read this fax?' And I would tell him: 'No one, only me.' And always Maxwell would say: 'That's all right, then, what's it about?' And I would read it to him or simply paraphrase the contents. And it was the same with phone calls. If he was speaking on the phone when I entered I would signal to him, wondering if I should come in or go away and, without fail, he would always signal for me to come in and sit around while he completed the call.

Maxwell began investing heavily in Israel, and not just in State of Israel Bonds, in the last few years of his life, principally after his dramatic speech in 1988 when he broke down and cried.

It was in 1988 that Maxwell became a substantial investor in Ma'ariv-Modi'in, which published *Ma'ariv*, the country's second-largest circulation newspaper, buying a thirty-three per cent interest for around $10 million. Later, in April 1990, Maxwell acquired an additional twelve per cent of *Ma'ariv*, boosting his share in the company to forty-five per cent. In September 1991, just two months before his death, Maxwell acquired full control, holding eighty per cent of the shares.

It was also in 1988 that Maxwell, using Mirror Group funds, purchased $30 million worth of shares in the Israeli pharmaceutical company Teva. In September 1991, in his desperate bid to raise cash, he announced a formal offer for the Teva shares but the sale had not gone through when he died.

In January 1989 Maxwell bought a thirty per cent stake in Scitex, for $39 million, which turned out to be one of the most successful acquisitions he ever made. Scitex, a leading manufacturer of colour-processing systems for the publishing industry, specialized in computer-imaging equipment. As his financial troubles mounted in 1991 Maxwell was to sell his shares in Scitex for a remarkable profit, selling his stake in the company for $234 million!

Maxwell also merged the Israeli interests of Maxwell–Macmillan with the Israeli publishing house Keter and owned fifty-one per cent of the merged company. He had also announced plans to publish two local weekly newspapers in Israel, one for Russian Jews who were arriving in their thousands every month.

In May 1990 he began consultations with the Israeli government to buy from them a twenty-six per cent stake in the Israeli Discount Bank. All the requisite forms were forwarded to him in London. But when it came to filling in the forms, Maxwell, for some unknown reason, decided to change tack and he put forward Mirror Holdings as the twenty-six per cent stakeholder, rather than himself. Probably due to his desperate situation, he pulled out of the deal altogether a few months before his death.

During the last few months of his life Maxwell became even more involved in Israeli politics, trying to find ways of funding the $10 billion loan guarantee Israel needed to finance the arrival and housing of the thousands of Russians arriving each month. As a way of putting pressure on the right-wing Likud government to thrash out a Middle East peace agreement, the United States had repeatedly put off supplying the loan guarantee they had promised. This infuriated Maxwell who tried all he could to persuade the American administration to change its attitude and give the guarantees. When it appeared these would not be forthcoming he phoned Pohl at the German Bundesbank and Genscher, as well as making contact in Japan in an effort to put together a consortium to provide the necessary guarantees. But to no avail.

In a remarkable speech in the summer of 1991 during a visit to Israel, Maxwell castigated President George Bush and Secretary of State James Baker for withholding the guarantees that he said were necessary to house and find jobs for people emigrating from the Soviet Union. He went on: 'I want to remind the President that the people who carried the burden of the battle for human rights in the Soviet Union and went into Siberian jails and who fought when it was dangerous for human rights were the Jewish people in the Soviet Union in their thousands.'

At the end of the speech, which he made while his own empire was crumbling under a mountain of debt, Maxwell concluded: 'We, the Jews, as well as the people of Israel, are willing to hock ourselves to fund them to give them the jobs and houses.'

Since revelations of the enormous amount of money that disappeared from the Maxwell empire in the last six months of his life, many have wondered whether Maxwell pumped some of the missing millions into the Jewish state. But it is mere conjecture. There is no proof of this and it cannot be taken too seriously.

But it wasn't only politics and business which Maxwell became involved in. Aren Meir, a close business associate of Maxwell's in most of his Israeli dealings, recalled: 'It wasn't only his investment in Israel that people will remember about Maxwell. On one occasion he gave $100,000 to an institution in Tel Aviv for the treatment of autistic children. And he gave substantial donations to other children's charities. And, what is more, he wanted no publicity about the donations.'

It was back in the early 1950s that Maxwell first travelled to the United States and began forming private companies there which were owned by the Liechtenstein trusts he had set up previously. It was an ideal set-up, especially for a man living in Britain with its tough tax laws and far tighter company laws than the United States. In 1952 Maxwell established Pergamon Press Incorporated. Almost immediately, the company began putting together American editorial boards for Pergamon's scientific journals and even bought a few established technical magazines.

It is difficult to imagine that a totally inexperienced young man, with no formal education, brought up in the backwoods of Czechoslovakia before spending six years in the British Army, mainly digging ditches, would have had the knowledge to construct a remarkable network of inter-related companies in Britain and America based on foundations and stiftungs in Liechtenstein. Allegedly, this is what Maxwell did – all on his own – within a few years of leaving the Army. And all in an industry, scientific publishing, in which he hadn't any background or experience, and very little knowledge.

There are those who believe that Maxwell's empire was a classic Intelligence service set-up.

In the United States Maxwell formed a clique of loyal men who were to spend their lives working for him, and who were to be with him at the end as he battled to save his crashing empire. Laszlo Straka, an accountant who joined him in 1952, was to run PPI – Pergamon Press Incorporated – from 122 East 55th Street and later at Pergamon House in Elmsford, New York. There was Sheldon Aboff who also joined Maxwell in the 1950s and was there at the very end. And Ellis Freedman, the New York lawyer who advised Maxwell for decades and knew every detail of his American set-up.

Maxwell formed many companies in the United States during the first twenty years of trading there. America was a safe haven for Maxwell because the banking laws there allowed for remarkable secrecy; but that only held good until 1982, when America changed its banking laws to make them more open to scrutiny. To maintain the secrecy, Maxwell transferred the companies' ownership to his trusts in Liechtenstein.

Throughout the years and decades, the steady, highly profitable, very successful work of Pergamon, in publishing scientific books, journals and papers, many of the highest calibre, continued apace, whatever else was going on in Maxwell's complicated business world.

It was not until 1987, as Maxwell watched with envy his arch-rival Murdoch make successful acquisitions around the world, that he tried to emulate him with a massive purchase in the United States. Harcourt Brace Jovanovich, an American educational publisher, seemed ripe for the picking. Its shares were standing at about $30 when Maxwell pounced, offering $44 a share, a $2 billion bid which he believed would immediately win the day.

However, William Jovanovich, the chairman, had other ideas. He looked into Maxwell's background and spoke words Maxwell did not want to hear.

He said: 'Mr Maxwell's dealings since he emerged from the mists of Ruthenia after World War II have not always favoured shareholders.'

A few days later Mr Jovanovich renewed his attack, accusing Maxwell of being unfit to run America's largest textbook publishers because 'he was not only a Socialist with good connections in Eastern Europe but was also tainted by hidden sources of income'. Within three months of making

276

the bid Maxwell conceded defeat. His background, his reputation and his secret trusts in Liechtenstein had caused him yet another failure.

Two British companies, the news agency Extel and John Waddington's, the printers and games firm, were also companies that played the Liechtenstein defence against the predatory Maxwell and both were successful. Liechtenstein had become a severe embarrassment to Maxwell and yet he stuck to it as the ultimate headquarters of his empire to the bitter end.

It was not until November 1988 that Maxwell was to 'arrive' in the United States as a big player in the big country. In the space of five days Maxwell bought the Official Airline Guides from Dun & Bradstreet for $750 million, a deal which he never thought he was going to win, despite the fact that he was offering more than the real worth of the company.

At the time Maxwell was in New York awaiting the nailbiting ruling from the Delaware Supreme Court on his bid for the mighty American publishers, Macmillan Inc. He had thrown everything possible into winning Macmillan, determined that no one else should top his bid. Each time Maxwell spoke to Robert Pirie, President and Chief Executive of Rothschilds in New York, he would say to him, 'Listen, I'm in it to win it.' Pirie had been advising Maxwell throughout. When the Delaware court decision neared, Pirie ordered some black T-shirts to be made with the words 'I'm init to winnit' written in white. In that ruling, Justice Moore declared the Macmillan auction process was fatally flawed, that the management had favoured the other bidders, Kohlberk, Kravis, Roberts & Co (KKR), over Maxwell; and they had tipped off KKR regarding the bidding. Game, set and match to Maxwell.

Pirie went out and produced new black T-shirts with the words 'We wonnit' emblazoned on the front. There was champagne all round for the bankers and lawyers who had crowded into the presidential suite at the Waldorf. Maxwell was cool as a cucumber.

Someone asked him: 'It's fantastic! Why aren't you celebrating?'

Maxwell replied: 'There's too much work ahead, we must get on.'

But he did enjoy the following day when he marched with his victorious team into Macmillan's Madison Avenue headquarters just before lunch. The chairman Ned Evans was still clearing his desk when Maxwell, unannounced, walked into his office. Neither spoke. Hurriedly, Evans finished collecting his belongings and walked silently out. Maxwell moved behind the desk and sat down, beaming. Then he summoned Macmillan's executives to come and meet him.

In his determination to win control of Macmillan, Maxwell had offered $90 a share, valuing the company at $2.6 billion. Before the takeover battle began, Macmillan's shares were languishing at around $50. Most analysts believed Maxwell had paid an incredible $1 billion more than the company was worth. In the space of five days Maxwell had accrued debts of a staggering $3.3 billion!

But he had finally arrived. And he made his presence felt. Until that time Maxwell had been operating in a low-key manner in the United States, though not from want of trying. For years Maxwell had usually stayed in Elmsford, New York, in the large, four-bedroomed apartment on the top of Pergamon House. It was here that his children would come and stay during vacations.

Whenever Maxwell flew into New York there had been the usual ritual. He would demand a senior Pergamon executive be on hand with his cash. He would be given $2,000 in $100 bills, always crisp and new and in sequence so he had no need to count them. He would just check the first and last numbers on the bills and put them in his trouser pocket.

After taking the money Maxwell's next question would be: 'Have you got my bottles?' which he would ask quietly and discreetly. 'Of course,' the Pergamon man would reply. 'Good,' Maxwell would answer. Maxwell would be inquiring about the twenty-four bottles of Vitalis hair lotion that he would take back to London. It was the basis of the hair lotion his personal hairdresser made up to keep Maxwell's hair a uniform colour.

Accountants at Pergamon told of millions of dollars of borrowing that went on all the time at Pergamon between the public and private side of Maxwell's empire. There were rents paid for private apartments; payroll bills sent to help out private Maxwell companies – all of which came out of Pergamon profits.

From his first involvement in America, Maxwell had remained remarkably low key, not throwing his weight around the city or society and for decades he was happy to stay in the Pergamon company apartment whenever he visited New York. But when he moved into the bigtime he never stayed there again. Now it was the presidential suite in the Waldorf-Astoria, and later the Helmsley Palace. Maxwell quit the Waldorf after a disagreement. Because he was staying there every couple of weeks he arranged with the management to install separate phone and fax lines, at some considerable expense, which would be permanent. One day, in November 1988, President Reagan moved into the suite for a short stay and, quite understandably, his security experts ripped out all Maxwell's private lines. The next time Maxwell stayed the lines hadn't been put back and he demanded they should be – at the Waldorf's expense. They refused. When he left after that visit he refused to pay the bill. Lengthy legal arguments followed but Maxwell never returned.

Having purchased Macmillan, Maxwell decided to repeat what he had done in London: build a palatial apartment above the shop and convert the top floor of the Macmillan building, with its sensational views over New York, into his private suite of rooms. He had the entire top floor cleared and called in Jon Bannenberg, the consultant who designed his London apartment and the interior of the *Lady Ghislaine*, to draw up plans. But it was not to be; too many other matters began crowding his brain and he hadn't the time to concentrate on his new luxury apartment.

In New York Maxwell's mind was never far away from food. For lunch, he would order two or three hamburgers and a mountain of chips from room service – just for himself. And he would wash that down with a couple of pints of buttermilk! For his weight, his girth and his heart, Maxwell ate all the wrong food whenever he visited New York. He loved it.

Whenever Maxwell jetted into New York, Pergamon staff were given detailed instructions of how to stock the refrigerator before he arrived. And for the return overnight flight back to London in his Gulfstream, Maxwell would order a huge menu of takeaway Chinese food which filled two or three shopping bags.

Maxwell always had problems with the American secretarial staff he demanded come to the suite and answer phones, take messages, take dictation, etc. Before every visit he would phone Pergamon or Macmillan and demand two secretaries be put at his disposal at the hotel. They hated being assigned, not just because of his temper and his style of living but because he expected them to work as slaves and carry out his impossible demands.

David Adler, vice-president of Corporate Communications at Macmillan, recalled watching Maxwell at work and the demands he made on some of the secretaries: 'Having dictated a letter he would stand over them saying,

280

"Type faster, type faster," which would put off anyone. He demanded they clean up the floor, clean up the suite, get him food from the refrigerator, serve him drinks, treating them all like his personal slaves. They hated working for him and I couldn't blame them. He was tough on them. As a result he would tell me to get rid of girls, send them back to the offices and get another one. Most of the secretaries lasted only a day or so, many for just a few hours before he would dismiss them. He was awful like that, totally unforgiving. He just wouldn't give them a second chance, ever.

'I remember talking to an irate Maxwell one day from London. He was in a foul mood: "It's no good trying to contact me over here because these so-called secretaries are fucking useless. How long ago did you call?" I told him about an hour. Then I heard him shouting at some poor secretary, demanding why the fuck she hadn't told him I had phoned; why the fuck did she never use her brain. Then he returned to me saying he thought all American secretaries were born with their heads in their bums.'

Adler recalled some of Maxwell's other demands: 'Watermelons were a must. He seemed to love them. I was often to see him eating the melons with two hands, taking great bites and then spitting out the pips all over the carpet. It was positively disgusting to see him eating the melons. And he made not the slightest effort to pick up the pips; that was left to the secretaries or whoever else he told to remove them.

'Another Maxwell must was deli chickens, not barbecued ones; and pink Dom Perignon champagne, not the ordinary bottle; Beluga caviare only and a variety of cheeses, as well as fresh orange juice. And when he arrived at the hotel he would ask whether the refrigerator had been filled and would then go and inspect it, to check.'

As ever with Maxwell there had to be the ritual firing, this time of a longterm, stalwart Pergamon secretary, Beth

281

Mauser, who, by accident, had purchased a barbecued chicken for the great man, instead of a deli chicken. In anger Maxwell threw the chicken against the wall, splattering the whole room – and fired Beth Mauser on the spot.

Adler recalled the first time he ever met Maxwell. He had been phoned saying Maxwell was arriving at the National Airport in Washington and he had despatched two cars to meet him and his entourage. When he arrived at the hotel Adler was there to meet him.

'Why didn't you meet me at the airport?' were Maxwell's first words on arrival. Before Adler could reply, however, Maxwell added: 'Don't you realize I am the most important person in your life? Never forget it.' It was not an auspicious start.

Adler recalls that Maxwell's main preoccupation whenever he was in America was to try and meet as many important people as possible. 'He seemed to measure the success of his visits by how many VIPs he met. He seemed far more concerned with that than making sure his various business interests were working profitably. There was never any attempt to manage the businesses; he would simply rely on people making verbal reports, and submitting accounts to him.'

However, shortly after Maxwell took control of Macmillan, he came across what he described as a 'major fraud which reached to the very highest people in the company'. Maxwell was determined to crack down hard, telephoning the chief executives of various departments demanding a 'full investigation'.

Throughout Macmillan the fraud became more of a joke and was known as the 'pastry scandal'. Maxwell's major scandal actually involved a few people in the supply department ordering too much pastry and other food stuffs from wholesalers, which they would take home for their own use. Maxwell's claim that it had 'reached the very highest in the company' was made because some of the directors had eaten some of the pastry! But Maxwell demanded that heads roll and people be fired – and some were sacked.

Maxwell's takeover of Macmillan also meant that he got his hands on the charitable 'Macmillan Foundation' which in 1989 had an accumulated balance of around $2 million. This was yet another useful source of income for Maxwell for furthering his own reputation among America's top people. And he used it like his own private piggy-bank. For example, he happily paid $100,000 for a table at the 1989 Winston Churchill Foundation dinner in Los Angeles – although he didn't actually sit next to the former US President. That money came from the Macmillan Foundation.

He attended the Trilateral Commission dinner in 1989 with such important people as David Rockefeller, Henry Kissinger and the chairmen of a number of US companies. That cost the fund another $15,000. Maxwell decided that he should sponsor the Literary Lions dinner at the New York Public Library, at a cost of $75,000. Once again the fund paid up. Yet Maxwell only remained at the dinner for seven minutes. He welcomed some of the diners, decided those attending weren't important enough for him, and left, driving back to his hotel to spend the evening watching television!

Sometimes Maxwell really did put his foot in it, despite his boasts of being one of the world's greatest diplomats. I remember time and again Maxwell would tell the same stories, crack the same jokes, at speeches he made at lunches and dinners around the world. This particular joke, which he loved, I must have heard in five or six world capitals. This time in New York, when he was attending the Anti-Defamation League dinner, it went down like a lead balloon.

Expansive and in good humour, Maxwell told the hundreds of guests his favourite joke: 'What would have happened,' he asked, 'if Lee Harvey Oswald had shot Krushchev instead of President Jack Kennedy?' After a pause, Maxwell continued: 'I don't know, but I can tell you one thing, Aristotle Onassis would not have married Mrs Krushchev.'

Maxwell burst out laughing at his own joke, but there was an intake of breath from around the room. No one laughed. The reason: sitting near Maxwell was Ethel Kennedy, to whom he had been chatting, and there were other members of the Kennedy clan at the dinner. At the end of his speech the applause was short and muted. Maxwell didn't understand until it was pointed out to him later that night when he asked why no one had laughed at his Krushchev–Kennedy joke.

What Maxwell yearned for was a meeting with the President. Everything was subservient to that. Somehow he achieved it in 1987, due entirely to the good offices of Robert Gray, the influential chairman of Hill & Knowlton, the PR consultants with access to Capitol Hill and the White House. Maxwell was thrilled to have a one-on-one lunch with President Reagan at the White House. It was a private meeting of which Maxwell never spoke.

Immediately after the election of President George Bush in 1988 Maxwell put pressure on everyone he knew in an effort to meet Bush and begin a dialogue with him. Adler recalls: 'We received a message from the White House saying that when we asked for a meeting with the President, his aides came back and asked: 'Who's Bob Maxwell?' But no one ever had the courage to relate that reply to Maxwell.'

However, despite paying large sums of money to many people, ostensibly described as consultants, Maxwell did not manage to meet President Bush until after he had bought the *New York Daily News*. A Pergamon accountant said: 'We would receive invoices through the mail from well-known, important politicians for either $50,000 or $100,000 for consultancies of which we knew absolutely nothing. We would have to wait until Maxwell returned to New York to ask whether the payments should be made. On every occasion he would just say, "Pay it." It was remarkable.'

Those who Maxwell brought on board included, among others, Senator John Tower whom Maxwell expected, as a friend of George Bush's, would bring him the President. He was to be disappointed. Adler said: 'Tower never delivered and that made Maxwell mad. He was being paid $200,000 a year and not performing. Maxwell said to me on one occasion: "What the hell is that man Tower doing for his money? I'll tell you; he's doing nothing; he must be made to produce the goods, to deliver."'

In Britain, however, Maxwell always made a fuss of Senator Tower. I was deputed by Maxwell to take care of Tower during one of his visits. We had breakfast together one day and dinner at night. From my viewpoint it was very useful talking to the man so close to Bush and the American defence chiefs, but I'm not sure what the late Senator Tower gained.

I remember talking to Maxwell following the air crash in which Senator Tower died. He was reminiscing at the time. He said: 'It was a great shame Senator Tower died like that. He was doing some very useful work for us.'

I asked him: 'What do you mean by that?' and Maxwell said: 'No one knows everything in these situations. He may have been killed.'

I didn't really believe, from what I had read of the crash, that it was anything but a genuine accident and told Maxwell so.

'Don't ever jump to conclusions,' Maxwell said, 'things never look the way they seem.'

We continued: 'Do you really believe he was killed?' I asked.

'No,' Maxwell replied, 'I'm not saying that. But you never know.'

Since Maxwell's death I have reflected many times on

Maxwell's comments at that time, especially as month by month more of Maxwell's murky past has been revealed.

He hired the Washington law firm of Senator Howard Baker to handle the public offer of shares in Berlitz, just so that he could get close to Howard Baker; and for no other reason. He tried to get close to Walter Mondale, the lawyer who was the former Vice-president to President Jimmy Carter, just because of the position he had held ten years before.

However, Howard Baker did come up trumps. It was Baker who twisted arms to get Maxwell accepted, almost immediately, into the influential Gridiron Club, within days of Maxwell buying the *New York Daily News*. Many sceptics in New York believe one of the principal reasons Maxwell bought the *Daily News* was because of the number of doors that would then be opened to him. And it worked, but only for six months.

Adler is convinced that Maxwell's deal with former Secretary of State George Shultz to write his memoirs for Macmillan was a further effort to cement good relations with the Republican party. Adler commented: 'Maxwell offers Shultz an amazing $2 million for his memoirs, so of course he's going to get the contract. At the same time as making the announcement in 1990 Maxwell stupidly declares the book will be on sale within one year and available in ten languages. At that time Shultz hadn't written a line.' Eventually, after Maxwell died, the book was rescheduled to be on sale at the end of 1992!

Adler however knew his job was on the line when Maxwell began blaming him for any incident that went wrong. Adler recalls: 'I remember receiving a phone call from Maxwell one day. He was angry. I had received a phone call from the White House telling me that there was no possibility at that time of a meeting between the President and Mr Maxwell. Nothing else, just that. So I telephoned the news through to London and, as Maxwell was busy, left a message with his secretary.'

Maxwell later boomed down the line: 'Never, never give a message from the President of the United States to a secretary. Only give such messages direct to me. No one should know of these things. Do you understand?'

Adler used to watch Maxwell 'seducing' journalists. 'I would introduce Maxwell to the journalists. If they were women he would simply try to charm them, and many were very happy to be charmed by this man about whom they had only heard brutish, awful stories; a real-life Citizen Kane. They thought they had succeeded in winning him over. The male journalists he would also seduce but in a different way. He would offer business deals to them; asking them to write special articles for him; inviting them to London; and nine times out of ten they would all go away and write glowing reports about him. He had them eating out of his hands. And he succeeded on nearly every occasion.'

One journalist he did not succeed in charming was Martha Smilgis of *Time* Magazine who spent an entire week with Maxwell in 1989, travelling with him, watching him at work, in meetings, entertaining, and even eating with him. She said: 'The one thing that hit me straight away was the way he ate. He was an obsessive, compulsive eater. I watched him eating grapes; he ate everything, including the stems of the bunch of grapes, but without realizing it; they just disappeared into his mouth. On several occasions I watched his approach to food and it seemed as though food was his turn-on, his sexual kick.

'And then of course there was the level of his bullshit. He told me he was worth $5 billion but from everything I had read, the maximum would have been $3 billion; and that was probably too high. So I wrote he was worth just $3 billion but he never commented on it when he read the final article. He would boast about his contacts, the numbers of world leaders who called him. I'm sure most of it was bullshit.

'What I couldn't understand was the way Maxwell talked to and bullied his senior staff back in London. Employees seemed to cringe subserviently before him, like whipped dogs. I found that very sad.'

In the days that Smilgis was with him she formed a harsh opinion. 'I believe he was very lonely, despite being married for so long and having such a large family. And he was extraordinarily vain and he never seemed happy, never happy in himself. I thought he was a genuinely evil man and very mean; mean towards his wife and children and the staff. He seemed to be genuinely wicked, his moods changing for no reason but to crush and humiliate people in public. I thought him like a dictator, very Stalinesque in the way he dealt with everyone. Thank God he never had any political power.'

Maxwell came to New York in the late '80s believing he could buy his way into society through the age-old method of spending lavishly on charities. And spend he did; but only in words, and virtually never in deeds.

Robert Gray was involved in a number of Maxwell charity ideas that never saw the light of day: 'Maxwell wanted to be loved by everyone and I am convinced that is why he made so many extraordinary pledges. I know that he pledged $75 million for a Maxwell centre for discovering a cure for AIDS and for research for a cancer cure vaccine. He promised the money to Dr Robert Gallo, the blood-screening expert and co-discoverer of the AIDS virus. Time and again he promised the money but nothing was forthcoming. People were standing by in New York waiting to begin work on hiring staff and equipping laboratories with the money he had pledged.

'So I flew over to London to confront him. I told him that he had to be fair and honest to all those waiting in New York to start work. If he was going to give the money then I told him to give me a cheque or, if he wasn't going to come up with the money then he had to be honest and tell the truth – that he wasn't going to give the promised money. Looking miserable and defeated, he told me he couldn't provide it at that moment and it was therefore better to let the people know, so they could look elsewhere for the funds.'

There were other pledges, too. Perhaps the most famous was his promised $50 million as the half share towards the high-flying environmental research institute for Minnesota which was to be called the Gorbachov–Maxwell Institute. The State of Minnesota was to provide the other $50 million. From Maxwell's viewpoint the whole idea went brilliantly, for he was able to arrive in Minnesota as the guest of Governor Rudi Perpich, bringing with him one of the world's most famous leaders, Mikhail Gorbachov. Here was a splendid occasion where Maxwell could be photographed with Gorbachov, shaking hands and allegedly donating $50 million towards an environmental centre based in Minnesota. As Gray said: 'No money ever came from Maxwell. Never. After the pictures and the celebrations I never heard a word about the pledge.' Nor did Minnesota.

Maxwell also promised a 'generous donation' to Hastings College in Hastings, Nebraska when he was awarded a Doctorate of Communications there. But nothing was ever received.

Gray believes that Maxwell wanted to fulfil all his pledges, primarily because he wanted to be loved by everyone for his generosity. He also believes that Maxwell wrongly thought he did have access to 'unlimited funds' to give to charities. But the reality was that he didn't.

Yet Governor Perpich and Maxwell were to remain acquaintances. When he lost the governorship the courageous Perpich decided to go and help his fellow Croatians as they battled to keep their homeland from the invading Serbians in his native Yugoslavia as it began to be torn apart by civil war in 1991. Perpich answered the appeal of Croatian President Franj Tudjman and offered to help bring much-needed foreign investment to bolster the Croatian economy.

Governor Perpich called Maxwell and told him there was a strong possibility he could purchase a major newspaper group in Croatia for around $100 million. Maxwell was immediately interested. But as the two men tried to put together a deal Croatia came under escalating attacks from the Serbian-dominated Federal Army and Serb guerrillas. Maxwell sent me over to Zagreb and I held talks with Perpich and President Tudjman and the defence chiefs to see whether there would be any newspapers or TV stations still in existence as the war closed in on Zagreb. Every week the war continued, the price of the newspaper group dropped $10 million. One night Maxwell said to me: 'When you went over there the group was worth $100 million. Now it's down to $50 million. Soon I will be able to purchase it for just $10 million.' And laughed. Living among the suffering Croatians I thought this was no laughing matter, for the wretched people were having to live through the hell of day and night shelling and sniper fire as they watched their towns and cities reduced to rubble.

It was ironic that Maxwell should spend his last few working days in New York among that older generation of men with whom he had worked for decades – his confidential lawyer Ellis Freedman, and his close lieutenants Laszlo Straka and Sheldon Aboff. They were the men who had shared many of Maxwell's secrets; they knew how Maxwell moved his money around his business empire and they knew that money moved from private to public companies non-stop. And they knew about his secret source in the tiny principality of Liechtenstein.

TEN

'They'll wish they'd never been born.'

The seeds of what became known as Mirrorgate were sown many years ago in the early 1980s when I received a phone call out of the blue from a visiting Israeli by the name of Ari Ben Menashe. He said he was from the Israeli government on a visit to London and could we meet. It was not unusual for me to hear from foreign government officials visiting London as I was foreign editor of the *Mirror*.

Menashe was unlike any other Israeli government official I had met; he was young, scruffy and not very articulate. He explained that he was an Iraqi Jew, still only in his thirties, who had been brought up in Teheran. He spoke Arabic, Hebrew and Farsi.

The conversation got off to an awkward start because it transpired Menashe was not in fact looking for me but for a namesake of mine, another journalist who had joined the *Mirror* training scheme in Plymouth but had left the group and worked on the *Guardian* and the *Observer*.

Menashe explained that he could act as a contact back in Tel Aviv where he worked as a desk man in one of the government offices, but not directly employed by the information service. We exchanged numbers. During the next few weeks and months he made contact, giving me information which had the ring of truth about it but which

291

was of little interest to a tabloid like the *Mirror*. He seemed to have his finger on the pulse, particularly in reference to Iran, which was at that time one of the world's number-one foreign stories.

Whenever he came to Britain, which was two or three times a year, we would meet. The only son of a family which included two older sisters, after graduating from university he had settled in Tel Aviv. His father had died and he lived with his mother in their Tel Aviv apartment.

He told me that he worked for the Israeli government first as a junior clerk in Washington, flying back and forth to Israel every two weeks carrying papers; then he had quit, and claimed he had lived in Nicaragua and worked closely for a year with the Sandanista leader Daniel Ortega. He said he had been married but his wife had walked out on their honeymoon because he had been called up at a moment's notice to fly out with the Israeli forces that freed the aircraft passengers in the famous Entebbe raid.

He said that he had carried out the assassination of a Palestinian in Beirut, one of the gang of Palestinians who had taken part in the 1972 Munich Olympics massacre. He claimed that he and the girl with whom he had carried out the murder had made love the night before, while in their Beirut hotel. It sounded too much like James Bond.

But the information he provided through the years was mostly accurate, particularly concerning Irangate, the sup-plying of arms to Iran in exchange for hostages. He would feed me tit-bits which turned out to be true but I was never totally satisfied that his information was always on the level.

We became friends; he came to dinner; at his request he stayed at my house; he met my then wife, Janet Fielding, the actress who made her name as a Dr Who assistant, but she took an instant dislike to him. And he certainly had ambition. He was determined to make money, to make something of his life, to be successful. He greatly admired Maxwell for the success he had made of his life. He repeatedly told me that he did not want to remain a civil servant.

After a year or so he told me that there was an arms dealer in London who, he understood, was providing arms to the IRA. If true, this was a first-rate story for any British newspaper and Menashe hatched a plan to make contact, pretending he wanted to buy some Soviet AK-47 rifles, arranging for me to go along.

In the summer of 1984, during one of Menashe's visits to London, he arranged a meeting. I informed a senior member of the *Mirror* newsdesk, a colleague of mine for many years, Robin Parkin, that I was looking into what could be an explosive story, but I gave him no clue as to what it might be. Before handing the whole story over to the newsdesk I wanted first to check it out.

But as soon as we arrived at the dealer's office my heart sank for on the coffee table were all sorts of military hardware magazines – the man was obviously an arms dealer. So I asked him straight out: 'Do you mainly deal in arms?'

He replied, 'Yes, pretty well exclusively.'

Our explosive story had blown up in our faces. If he was so open about dealing in arms it was obvious the authorities would know all about him, and had probably checked him out. Here was no secret dealer supplying arms to the IRA. No story. I told him I was the Foreign Editor of the *Daily Mirror* and gave him my card. He did look a little perplexed that a *Mirror* man should be dealing in arms.

Menashe spun a story that he wanted to buy 20,000 AK-47 rifles for some Third World country, which for security reasons he did not wish to name, and they haggled about prices. As far as I know nothing whatsoever came of the alleged deal. That series of events put a question mark over Menashe's credibility.

In January 1985 Janet Fielding left for Stockholm to appear in a three-month-long play. The day before she was due to fly back to London I arrived home to find a 'Dear John' letter on the breakfast-room table. There had been no arguments, no discussions, no complaints – nothing to suggest she wanted out of the two-year marriage. She had returned a day early and taken everything out of the house that belonged to her. Two days later divorce papers arrived through my letterbox. I never spoke to her again. A wily old decorator who had been working on the house for a year, suggested I change the locks on the front door and I agreed to his suggestion.

I needed a holiday, the shock of my wife of two years, my second wife, walking out without a word, even a disagreeable word, had knocked the wind out of my sails. I wanted to get away, to be alone. I needed to do something, not lie on a beach somewhere thinking. At about that time the newspapers were full of stories and articles about the Amish people, who had come into the limelight because of the brilliant film *Witness*. Two years earlier I had been to the States to tour the battle sites of the American Civil War, which had always fascinated me; so I decided once again to go off to America to get away from work and worries – the Amish people would perhaps give me an interest, something totally different.

I mentioned to Menashe that I was going to take off for a week, go to the States and study the Amish people. He told me he had a friend, Ben Kaufmann, who lived in Smithville, Ohio, near where the Amish people live, whom I should look up. I took his number, phoned him and told him I was arriving and on which flight. He met me with his wife at the airport and drove me to a local motel where I booked in. They invited me to their home and I went along a day or so later.

Their home was a small, detached, clapboard house and outside was a sign, 'Custom Camo' – 'camo' I later learned was short for 'camouflage'. Under their home was their business, a shop hewn out of the ground, where they sold army surplus gear, and in a tiny barred room were some guns, mainly hand guns, rifles and shotguns. It was a typical smalltime American backwoodsman operation. They were both kind and considerate and I had a meal there. They told me they wanted to break into the bigtime and become international arms dealers and we talked about it. They told me they had talked to Menashe about it. I also thought that this young couple were far too innocent and naïve to even try to get involved with international arms dealing. I told them I was a journalist in London and that's how I had met Menashe. One morning Ben Kaufmann, who was a good shot, took me rabbit shooting in the woods a few hundred yards from his home, but I refused to shoot the rabbits, instead I took potshots at treetrunks.

The Amish people fascinated me. I spent most days driving and walking around their land, their workplaces, their shops, seeing their way of life, so very, very different from London. Their simple life, which to a great degree is lived the same as when their forefathers arrived in the New World three hundred years before, provided me with something totally different and absorbing, away from London, women and disillusionment. The Kaufmanns were forgotten.

It was around this time that Menashe asked if he could use my home as an accommodation address. I told him I wasn't keen and suggested he go and find a place in London's West End. He said that wouldn't be suitable as he would have to pay and he only expected the occasional letter to arrive. He told me it was Part One of his plan to make a new start in life, leave the government and make his mark in the world.

He had no idea what he was going to do but if successful he wanted me to join him. Maxwell had taken over the *Mirror* only a few months before and I was looking to get out. As time went on, Menashe's plans became more ambitious; one plan was to start a leasing company for big civil jets, another was to lease satellites to international companies, a third was to take over Pearson, publishers of *The Financial Times*. Every time I asked him where the huge amounts of money were to come from he told me that he had backers in Israel and the United States who would fund him once he came up with the right idea; money was no object.

In 1986 Menashe told me that he was going to meet some arms dealers in Vienna who had been responsible for channelling arms to Iran during Irangate and he offered to take me along. I jumped at the idea. Here was a chance to meet the people the world's press had been writing about but had never contacted. I checked our library at the *Mirror* and could find nothing. Because of the alleged IRA story that had collapsed earlier I told no one at the *Mirror*. In Vienna we stayed at the Hilton and met six or seven men, alleged arms dealers; two turned out to be Austrian car dealers in financial trouble; one was an American hippy, a leftover from the '60s who lived in France; another was a Polish smalltime currency dealer; and the most respectable was a retired Austrian engineer who claimed he had contacts in the Austrian government. All, without fail, said they were keen to be involved in arms dealing especially if that meant providing arms to Iran and being paid by the American government. But all said they had never sold any arms to anyone anywhere.

The Pole told me that he could introduce me to the major-general in the Polish army who was responsible for overseas sales of Eastern bloc arms, from AK-47 rifles to MiG 27s and tanks. All he had to do was make a few phone calls to Warsaw. Within twenty-four hours he told me all was arranged and we took off for Warsaw. I had my Sony tape recorder with me. On landing we were interviewed by a senior army officer but the general we had come to see never showed up. I was politely refused entry and took the next plane back to Vienna. The next day I flew back to London, not very happy with Menashe and his world-shattering stories.

It was after this episode that Menashe claimed that one of his duties, on behalf of the Israeli government, was to keep a watch on possible arms dealers in Europe to see that no deals by freelance arms dealers ever took place to hinder whatever the Israeli government wished to carry out in conjunction with the United States.

During the next two years I saw less of Menashe but we continued to speak on the phone. He told me during this time that he had been appointed Number Three at Mossad, a piece of news that surprised me; then months later he said he had been promoted to Number Two and, finally, after several meetings with Prime Minister Yitzhak Shamir he said he was then Head of Mossad. Later he told me that Shamir had appointed him Special Foreign Adviser inside the Prime Minister's office, directly responsible to him. I just didn't believe him.

When I moved house to south-east London in 1987 Menashe asked if he could use my place once again for mail and I refused. I told him that I didn't want to know. However, letters that were to surface when Seymour Hersh published his book *The Samson Option* showed my address in south-east London, which was a surprise to me. Without permission, Menashe had seemingly had a letterhead printed and continued to use my new address.

It was in 1989, after a gap of about six months, that Menashe surfaced again and said he had a book proposal to put to Maxwell. He knew that Maxwell had recently taken over Macmillan, the New York publishing house, and asked if I could get him an interview. Menashe said that he wanted to write a book about Irangate showing that President Bush was involved with Irangate and that Israel had been the supplier and shipper of all the US arms to Iran during the Irangate period. I told him that I would approach Maxwell for an interview.

It was on a Saturday in May, 1989 that I took Menashe to Maxwell's suite of offices and we were ushered in and offered coffee. Menashe appeared highly nervous. Also there was Eve Pollard, then editor of the *Sunday Mirror*. We all sat spellbound as Menashe outlined his plan for the book. His idea, as his English was not brilliant, was that I should ghost-write the book and with Maxwell's authorization Macmillan in New York would publish it. To my surprise he then told Maxwell he wanted a $750,000 advance! Maxwell replied: 'You're talking telephone numbers.'

Maxwell said he could make no such decision. He suggested we go away, prepare a summary of the book which he would send to Macmillan for their decision and he would be in touch. Two weeks later I heard directly from Maxwell that Macmillan didn't want to know, the project was of no further interest to him. I telephoned Menashe and told him that neither Maxwell nor Macmillan was interested and suggested he try to sell his idea somewhere else. I didn't hear anything from him for six months. I have no idea whether Maxwell ever did get in touch with his editors at Macmillan. I suspected, but never told Menashe, that Maxwell probably picked up the phone to the Israeli Embassy in London, or to friends in government in Jerusalem and sought their advice. But I have no proof of that. Knowing Maxwell, however, I believe that's what he did, which was why he was so negative in his reply. Three years on, the possibility of President Bush's involvement in Irangate was still the subject of speculation in Washington. Menashe did subsequently testify to the Judiciary Committee of the House of Representatives investigating allegations that release of the US hostages in Iran was delayed in 1980 in order to assist President Ronald Reagan's election. Menashe told the committee that at the time of Irangate he had been a mid-level member of the Intelligence service of Israel.

From affidavits Menashe produced at the time *The Samson Option* was published, it seems that he had been employed in the External Relations Department of the Israel Defence Forces for ten years but left the department in September 1987. He did not tell me he had left government service but I did know that during 1988 and 1989 he spent months in Peru, with the Maoist terrorist organization Sendero Luminoso – Shining Path. I have no idea what he was doing there.

It was some time in November 1989 that I received a telephone call informing me that Menashe had been arrested in California, involved in a scam organized by the FBI, accused of conspiring to sell three Israeli-owned C130 cargo planes to Iran. Menashe told the authorities that he was working on a book commissioned by Maxwell, to be published by Macmillan, and that he was only carrying out research for the book when arrested.

Maxwell, Macmillan and myself were contacted by the District Attorney in charge of the case and asked to verify Menashe's story. Of course it was totally untrue and Mr David Zornow, a lawyer instructed by Macmillan, informed them that such a project had been mooted in May of that year but had not been taken up. Maxwell called me up and asked me what I knew. I gave him a brief outline of my knowledge of Menashe and of his ambition to become a wealthy man. Maxwell knew all about the book deal, but I reminded him again.

I waited for the blast that I believed must come. I deserved one for not warning Maxwell that in my opinion Menashe had Walter Mitty tendencies. Surprisingly, he remained calm, not even getting angry. Instead, he said earnestly: 'You should have told me everything you knew about this man before you allowed me to meet him. You should have warned me about him. You should never have let him meet me.' I apologized.

Maxwell asked David Zornow to check with the US Justice Department, the FBI and the DA's office to see whether I was implicated in any way or whether my name had come up during the FBI scam. Maxwell told me later that Zornow had checked me out and they had never heard my name until after Menashe had been arrested. They said I was of no interest to them. I then received phone calls from apparent friends of Menashe, of whom I had never heard, asking me to go to New York, where Menashe was being held, and back up his story that he was simply researching the proposed book. I couldn't do so and didn't.

Menashe remained in jail awaiting trial for a year. Some of the original charges against him were dropped and he was acquitted of all remaining charges. His defence to the court was that he was acting on behalf of the Israeli government.

Menashe emerged from jail an angry man. He told journalists that he had been betrayed by the Israeli government that he had served so faithfully for ten years. He claimed he had been a member of an ultra-secret committee set up by Israel to sell arms to Iran to help that nation's fight against Israel's enemy, Iraq; then he said he had been a special Intelligence adviser to Prime Minister Shamir. It appears that he was also determined to do all in his power to involve Maxwell and myself. I heard from those journalists, mainly American, who met him that he was determined to 'get' me. He believed Maxwell and I should have backed his story but why we should have done so, Menashe alone knows. After all, his rage was directed at the Israeli government.

He went to newspapers, magazines and the American networks trying to sell his story of Irangate to the US media. I received phone calls from the *Wall Street Journal*, *New York Times*, *Washington Post* and ABC, who all asked me to verify the stories that Menashe was telling them about international arms dealing and Irangate in particular. He had told them that I knew everything and would confirm his high-flying tales. I told them all I knew but added that I could provide no evidence whatsoever to support his stories of massive arms deals.

Around Washington during 1990 Menashe was treated with some respect, tinged with suspicion. He was telling a most convincing story. He obviously knew a lot of facts about Irangate, but the journalists who spoke to me said they were having problems dividing fact from fiction. He told them his main concern was to 'blow the top' on Irangate and, by so doing, cause enormous political damage to President Bush, and to the President's re-election campaign in 1992. I told them I thought Menashe was unreliable and to take everything he said with a pinch of salt.

Time Magazine published a two-page story about Menashe in 1991 – investigating his claims and questioning his credibility. *Time* called him a 'spinner of tangled yarns'. Researchers from the American ABC television network went so far as to test Menashe with a lie-detector machine. The results were astonishingly consistent; on a scale of reliability from zero to minus eight 'on every major question Menashe recorded either minus eight or minus seven – showing he was clearly trying to deceive'.

Seymour Hersh, Pulitzer Prize-winning American journalist, has a distinguished reputation. He asked me if I could verify claims that were being made to him by Menashe and phoned me on a couple of occasions in London. I told him I knew Menashe, had known him for some years but that I could not in any way confirm any of Menashe's claims.

301

He took no notice of my warning signals and went ahead and published *The Samson Option*, relying on some letters produced by Janet Fielding for the single chapter that covered Maxwell and myself.

I never saw those letters from Ohio and did not of course recognize them when the *Mirror* faxed them to me in Harare. It was the most appalling bad luck – for me – that the letterhead, with the name 'Custom Camo' at the top, should have disappeared during transmission because if I had seen those words, I would have remembered my visit to Ohio. Those words weren't on the fax and, as a result, I issued the denial that was to make me look at worst a liar, at best an idiot.

Any journalist worth his salt knows that if I had remembered being in Ohio and meeting Ben Kaufmann I would have been a fool to deny it. Throughout most of the '70s I had been part of the *Mirror*'s investigation team covering the Lucan murder and his disappearance, the John Stonehouse affair, the Wilson slag heaps and the Jeremy Thorpe scandal. I knew that journalists would be sent to Ohio to investigate – and the game would be up. And I would have remembered that photographs had been taken. There is another point; I don't really believe I would have posed for photographs if I had been purchasing arms.

Fleet Street scoured the world trying to discover the arms deals Menashe claimed Maxwell, or myself, or both of us, had been involved in. Maxwell was the man they were trying to pin. Menashe had claimed that I was involved with numbers of huge arms deals, and that I made millions of pounds from such deals. It is odd therefore that Menashe never produced any evidence whatsoever proving a single deal. The reason was that no arms dealing had ever taken place; though there was some circumstantial evidence. And Fleet Street never discovered anything either, though not for want of trying. I know that I have never bought or sold a single bullet, or any other piece of military equipment!

Mordechai Vanunu was a different story. He was the Israeli nuclear technician who brought photographs and details of Israel's secret nuclear weapons facility to *The Sunday Times* in September 1986. The week before *The Sunday Times* printed their story on Vanunu, the *Sunday Mirror* ran a 'spoiler' which alleged Vanunu was a con man retailing false stories about Israel's nuclear secrets. It was a story that I was never involved in, asked about, or told about. At that stage I was not working for the *Sunday Mirror*. And, for *Daily Mirror* purposes, because Vanunu was in Britain, the story was handled by the newsdesk, not the foreign desk, until the time he turned up in Israel, apparently trapped in Rome by a seductive Mossad girl.

Menashe informed Hersh, who wrote in his book that I betrayed Vanunu to Mossad. Allegedly, I phoned Menashe when Oscar Guerrero – a Colombian acting as Vanunu's agent – had come to me at the *Daily Mirror* with the Vanunu story. I never met, saw or talked to Guerrero. He had gone to the *Sunday Mirror*.

The role that Maxwell played in the Vanunu story I do not know and cannot comment on. Hersh maintains that Maxwell was the vital link between Guerrero going to the *Sunday Mirror* and the Israeli Embassy in London being told of Vanunu's whereabouts. As a result, Vanunu was picked up by Mossad, lured to Rome and smuggled back to Israel where he is serving an eighteen-year sentence. I knew nothing about it.

It was because of the Vanunu story of 1985 that Faber & Faber, the British publishers of *The Samson Option*, first offered it to *The Sunday Times* for serialization. Hersh and Menashe were flown to London by Faber & Faber and the

Sunday Times Insight reporter Peter Hounam interviewed them three times. Menashe boasted to Hounam that a photograph of Vanunu that appeared in the *Sunday Mirror* had been specially flown from Israel by him and handed to me. In fact the photograph had been taken by Hounam himself and given to Guerrero. Hounam told Faber & Faber that in his opinion Hersh was wrong, and *The Sunday Times* did not want to serialize the book.

Notwithstanding, Matthew Evans, chairman of Faber & Faber, decided to go ahead and publish the book in Britain. He approached the *Daily Mail* which was most interested in publishing the sensational story.

Understandably, the *Daily Mail* was seriously worried about Maxwell's litigious reputation, and knew very well that Maxwell would throw the libel book at it if it alleged, on the basis of the book, that he was an international arms dealer.

On Sunday, October 20, I was in Harare, Zimbabwe, with other British correspondents, attending the Commonwealth Conference. We had just spent the weekend at Victoria Falls with the Commonwealth leaders and had flown back to Harare when I was approached by an agitated Stephen Doughty, the *Daily Mail*'s reputable Diplomatic Correspondent. He needed to see me urgently about something very, very important. We talked and he told me that the *Daily Mail* was to run the Hersh claims the next day and, understandably, the *Mail* wanted a quote from me.

I told Doughty that I knew about the allegations, that newspapers and TV networks had approached me about the same matters during the past twelve months and that after investigation they had all come to the conclusion that the claims were untrue. I told him that I believed the allegations had come from Ari Ben Menashe, a former Israeli government official, and I gave a little of his background.

Later that evening Doughty informed me the *Mail* was not going ahead with the story.

The following day all hell broke loose. Members of Parliament raised the question of Maxwell and myself in the House of Commons, where they were protected by parliamentary privilege. The result of this was that the *Mail* and every other paper in the land could happily and legitimately reprint the Commons allegations without fear of a libel action. Naturally, every newspaper, the Press Association and the British TV stations all knew I was in Harare and all their correspondents knew me well. The *Evening Standard* was the first on the streets with a front page story; it wasn't long before everyone else followed suit. That day I was rather popular.

The two MPs who revealed Hersh's claims were Rupert Allason, the Tory MP for Torbay who makes money by writing 'spy' books under the name Nigel West, and Labour MP George Galloway, who spent a week in Tunis in 1990 as a guest of the Palestine Liberation Organization. The *Mirror* attacked their allegations, which could not have been based on any evidence, save from those sources provided by Seymour Hersh.

The journalists covering the conference treated me as a colleague and a friend and I have nothing but admiration for their concern, their sincerity and their professionalism. I knew they had a job to do and they didn't appear to relish the task their London desks set them. We all continued to dine out together as we had most evenings and I was, understandably, the butt of a number of jokes.

Everyone kept asking me how I could be so relaxed in the face of such pressure, such damning evidence, such notoriety at being branded a spy, an arms dealer and the man who betrayed an informant. Quite simply, I could because I was innocent of all three charges. I knew that I had never worked for Mossad, never sold a single bullet and

305

did not and could not have betrayed Mordechai Vanunu. All I can say is that it is remarkable, the inner feeling of confidence one experiences from being innocent of serious allegations. Kipling's advice came to me many times during those days:

> If you can keep your head when all about you
> Are losing theirs and blaming it on you.
> If you can trust yourself when all men doubt you,
> But make allowance for their doubting too . . .

I would fall asleep with ease at night reciting those lines.

Maxwell of course strongly denied that he had any links with Mossad, and condemned the two MPs who tabled the motions as irresponsible. Maxwell told the BBC's *World at One*: 'I certainly have no connections with Mossad. It is outrageous that you should use this. It is a ridiculous statement. The allegation is made under the privilege of the House, with no shred of evidence about it.' He immediately issued a writ for libel from Mirror Group Newspapers, from himself and myself against Seymour Hersh and Faber & Faber.

Yet there was worse to come. I shall never know how I came to forget about Ohio, except to add that I had deliberately put out of my mind everything that had happened to me at that time – the time of my second divorce. When asked whether I have been to some place or other I always try to place it in work terms. During the last twenty years at the *Mirror* I had spent about three months of every year overseas in various places. I went over in my mind all the stories that I had covered in America and Ohio didn't figure. In Harare my colleagues were keeping me briefed of everything their offices were discovering – and the word from Ohio was that the alleged letter-writers didn't recognize me when showed a photograph. I was much relieved. I knew that if the Ohio letters were forgeries the entire arms scandal would be seen for what it was – the work of a man with a grudge.

I issued my statement to the British press, TV and radio denying categorically I had ever been to Ohio, and remember adding jocularly after some of the interviews, 'Well, I don't think I've been there.'

In telephone conversations with *Mirror* editor Richard Stott during those two days before flying back to London I told him everything I had said before; told him what Maxwell had known from the days when Menashe had been arrested in November 1989, and told him I had not been to Ohio. However, I urged him not to go overboard with denials until I had returned to London, gone through my expenses, my diary and, I used the phrase, 'got my head back into 1985'. When I flew back to London I was dismayed to learn the paper had gone ahead with a denial.

I was sitting in Stott's office when the news editor Steve Lynas came in with information that the *Daily Mail* intended to publish a colour picture the next day – Friday, October 25 – showing me with Mrs Kaufmann at their home in Smithville, Ohio. I was dumbfounded. In a flash it all came back and I could see myself posing with this small thirtyish woman with short hair standing on the balcony of her clapboard home. I felt an absolute idiot. The *Sun* epitomized what the world thought of me the next day with two headline words – 'You liar'. It is something which I will probably never live down, yet it was simply a slip of the memory.

After that brilliant journalistic coup by the *Mail* things moved fast. Back in London I was in contact by phone with Maxwell who was in New York. He assured me that he was one hundred per cent behind me and knew that I was absolutely innocent of the charges made against me. He told me he had once again been in touch with the US Administration of Justice who had repeated they had no knowledge of any alleged involvement by me in arms dealing. I shall never forget the phrase Maxwell used about the Ohio débâcle: 'Don't worry about Ohio; that doesn't matter two fucks.'

He ordered me to change my office car for another one and go into hiding somewhere so the press couldn't find me. He also instructed me to give my new telephone number to him, and to him alone, saying: 'We can't trust everyone at the *Mirror*; they're after us.' Ever since my return from Zimbabwe there had been a number of reporters and photographers almost permanently camped outside my house and Maxwell had told me to say nothing more to them. 'We shall see them all in court,' he proclaimed.

On Monday, October 28, I went to work as usual and was asked to attend a meeting upstairs some time later to thrash out the whole thing. Stott's secretary said that, if I liked, I could ask a colleague to accompany me to take notes. At no stage was I informed this was a disciplinary hearing. I assumed they wanted to find out the truth for the sake of their own information, the good name of the paper and Maxwell. At the meeting, which was held at around noon, were Stott, Haines and Charles Wilson, the group's editorial director. We went through everything for nearly two hours. Wilson hardly ever spoke but Haines and Stott could not, would not, believe I had forgotten I had been to Ohio. They accepted I was not an Israeli spy and that I had nothing at all to do with the Vanunu case. I knew that what worried Stott was that the *Mirror*, of which he was the proud editor, had been made to look foolish in its forthright defence of me, and I had let the paper and him down with an horrendous bump.

I left the meeting and, taking Stott's advice, went home for the rest of the day. I went to the garage to collect my car and was told by the long-serving 'Dickie' Bird, the garage attendant, that I couldn't take my car because that morning he had been told by management to return the car to the transport department. It didn't matter because I had my other car, so I took that home.

Within a few hours Stott phoned asking me to come in and see him. As I entered the room, Stott and Haines were laughing out loud, and I heard Stott say, 'Balls to suspension.' Their mood changed immediately. Stott informed me that as a result of the investigation of that morning it had been decided to fire me, effective immediately, for 'gross misconduct' in lying to the paper about the Ohio trip. He also added that Maxwell had decreed that I had the right of appeal to him, the publisher. I didn't say a word.

I left the room to be met by two security guards who told me that I was not allowed to go to my desk, not allowed to speak to anyone and that they had been ordered to escort me out of the building immediately. I felt I was going to jail.

During the next few days Maxwell phoned frequently. He was still in New York. He kept telling me: 'Don't worry about a thing, I will work everything out. You must write your appeal to me immediately, so that I can have it on my return.'

I asked him: 'Why did you let them fire me?'

He replied: 'I had no alternative. I was informed that if I didn't go along with the plan to sack you I would find myself without an editor; and that would have made it seem we were guilty of this Mossad rubbish. But there is no need to worry, you still have a job. Just keep your head down and say nothing to anyone till I sort it out.'

In another phone call from New York I asked Maxwell if there was any truth whatsoever in Hersh's allegations against him. He wasn't at all angry at my question, rather amused.

He replied: 'You know that you and I have never dealt in arms and we have never discussed the matter except in relation to Menashe. Hersh's allegations are a complete

309

fabrication. He cannot have a shred of evidence. But it will cost him and Faber & Faber a packet. They'll wish they'd never been born.' And he laughed.

Two days later Maxwell flew into London, stayed less than twenty-four hours and, complaining he had a cold and felt exhausted, flew to Gibraltar for a few days alone on his yacht. He took with him a mass of documents, including my appeal letter and my company file, the notes that management kept on every employee.

On Monday, November 4 I received a phone call from one of Maxwell's secretaries in London telling me that Maxwell would be returning to London on Wednesday, November 6 and wanted to see me at 10 a.m. on Friday, November 8. It was not to be.

It was a week after Maxwell's death at sea that Faber & Faber and Seymour Hersh attempted to substantiate their claims and put some flesh on their allegations against Maxwell and myself. Matthew Evans, chairman of Faber & Faber, called a press conference on Tuesday, November 12 to 'prove' that I was personally involved with the betrayal of Vanunu to Israel in September 1986.

Evans read out to the assembled journalists, who crowded into the room, a statement from Seymour Hersh that they had 'documentation' showing Davies had, under a false name, met secretly in a Geneva hotel in September 1986 with Israeli Intelligence operatives and an unnamed private detective in an attempt to arrange for the wiretapping of the home and office telephones of the senior *Sunday Times* reporter working on the Vanunu revelations . . . the detective also supplied them with logs of Davies' telephone calls from the hotel . . . a Luxembourg bank, one of whose major customers was Robert Maxwell, had requested the detective's services . . . Davies and another *Mirror* journalist, Frank Thorne, had arrived at the hotel . . . they were later joined at the Cornavin Hotel by three Israelis including an attractive woman named Cheryl or Cindy Hanin (the Israeli Mossad spy who allegedly seduced Vanunu to Rome).

The night before this statement was made by Matthew Evans I was phoned at home by Seymour Hersh and asked about the Geneva story. I told Hersh: 'All I can say is be very, very careful. I don't know anything about this. What you're saying is absolute hogwash.'

After the press conference Rupert Allason claimed that three days before dying at sea Maxwell knew that I had been involved in betraying Vanunu. Allason also claimed that one of the phone calls from the Geneva hotel was made to Maxwell, although he was unable to say where. Allason also said he understood the calls had been recorded and there were also still photographs taken from videotapes of the Geneva meeting.

Within seventy-two hours of their celebrated press conference Seymour Hersh and Matthew Evans were at the mercy of Fleet Street, described by the *Mirror* as 'a pair of suckers' in showing such naïvety. They had fallen for one of Fleet Street's old con men, a trickster by the name of Joe Flynn, who admitted to the British press: 'It was all a sting – a one hundred per cent pack of lies.'

It was Matthew Evans himself who went to Amsterdam and met Flynn at the airport, handing him £500 for the initial information. Flynn eventually received £1,200 from Evans. Evans, however, refused to believe he was duped, but Seymour Hersh eventually admitted to *The Sunday Times* that he had been conned by Flynn.

As the *Daily Mirror* wrote on Monday, November 18 – three weeks after I had been sacked for allegedly lying and two weeks after Maxwell died – 'The ease with which Hersh was stung casts doubt on his other allegations against Davies and former *Mirror* publisher Mr Maxwell.'

ELEVEN

'If there is a way back after death, then I will be the one to find it.'

His Serene Highness, Prince Hans-Adam II von und zu Liechtenstein, rose with a smile and stretched out his hand as Maxwell walked into the room. 'Good morning,' he said as Maxwell gripped his hand and shook it warmly before motioning him to sit down in the drawing room of his apartment on the top of Maxwell House.

Prince Hans-Adam II, the Head of State of the Principality of Liechtenstein, had come to visit Maxwell, the man who was the largest single investor in the principality, as the tiny fifty-six-square-mile European enclave is officially described. Maxwell had sent his helicopter to Heathrow to fly the Prince to Maxwell House.

Maxwell was putting on the charm, smiling, being polite and very amicable to him as they sat and chatted together. Coffee and orange juice were served. It was the spring of 1990. Early in the conversation Maxwell said that he believed that he was the largest single investor in Liechtenstein.

The Prince, speaking perfect English, replied: 'Yes, that is so, I believe you are. You know how much we value your investments in the principality and we hope you are happy with everything.'

Maxwell answered: 'I think it is right to say we are very

happy and I must tell you that we intend to go on being the largest investor there,' and he laughed. The Prince, then forty-five, immaculately dressed, bright and intelligent, and every inch a gentleman, was being diplomatic and very polite, so he laughed too, but not so loud.

The amicable meeting continued for about fifteen minutes. Maxwell went on to say how important his involvement was in Liechtenstein and repeated that the Maxwell Foundation had been based in the principality for decades and he assured the Prince that he would never dream of moving it. 'The sensible arrangements in Liechtenstein suit the Foundation perfectly,' Maxwell added.

It would be extraordinary for the Prince, Liechtenstein's royal head of state, to fly to Britain to visit Maxwell unless Maxwell was indeed a substantial investor in the principality. In 1988 Maxwell maintained that his Foundation was earning an annual income of £25 million. He claimed in 1990 that he was worth approx £2.5 billion! He boasted that the Maxwell Foundation had made charitable donations of nearly £2 million. It is true that a number of Maxwell's pledges, particularly in the United States, were never made. But was it all a charade? Was it all lies? If Maxwell had not been a substantial investor in the principality I don't think Prince Hans-Adam II would have graced Maxwell with a royal visit. His advisers would have known the facts.

On a few occasions through the years Maxwell went on the record to explain his Liechtenstein trusts. He always maintained that all the Pergamon–Maxwell group of companies, including Mirror Group Newspapers and his holding in Maxwell Communications Corporation were owned and controlled by the Maxwell Foundation, which had earlier been known as the Pergamon Foundation, and others, such as the Pergamon Holding Trust and the Pergamon Media Trust.

Maxwell had always vehemently maintained that the

Liechtenstein foundations were 'entirely independent' of him. That was a lie.

Every few months a mysterious 'Dr R.', as Maxwell always referred to him, would arrive unexpectedly, and with no appointment, at Maxwell House. Dr R. would go in to see Maxwell and they would talk privately for perhaps thirty minutes. They nearly always spoke in German. Then Dr R. would go upstairs to Maxwell's small private study and be left there alone for perhaps two or three hours. He was never given a secretary, or anyone in Maxwell House, to help him. He would usually be given a Wang to write reports and letters. He would then see Maxwell again and leave. He was in fact Dr Werner Rechsteiner, a Swiss lawyer who was responsible for carrying out Maxwell's orders in relation to the Maxwell Foundations.

To sustain the secrecy of Dr Rechsteiner's existence and importance Maxwell ordered his telephonists and receptionists never to announce Dr Rechsteiner if he ever phoned. In case Maxwell was on the loudspeaker, and there were people in the room, the telephonists were told to say: 'There's a personal call for you.' Maxwell went out of his way to keep Dr Rechsteiner very much in the background.

Dr Rechsteiner was also responsible for carrying out Maxwell's orders concerning any secret anstalts (part company, part foundation) and stiftungs (tax-free trusts) Maxwell held in Liechtenstein, Switzerland and Gibraltar. There were many, all with unusual and exotic names, and names which Maxwell kept in his remarkable memory. Maxwell went on to control these trust direct by fax. Then the faxes would be destroyed in the office shredder. Simple, direct and efficient.

On one occasion in April 1987 Maxwell called Dr Rechsteiner to the *Lady Ghislaine* when it was moored in Palma, Majorca. For hours Maxwell and Rechsteiner were closeted together, then Rechsteiner used the on-board Wang to type a document. The document decreed that on Maxwell's death, his son Kevin would take over the foundations. Rechsteiner also flew to London to discuss the chapter in the Haines biography which concerned Liechtenstein.

The same working relationship took place with Dr Walter Keicher and, after 1986, with his son Werner, both Swiss lawyers who represented Maxwell's interests in Vaduz, the Liechtenstein capital, and had done so for more than thirty years. Officially Keicher was the 'director' of the Maxwell foundations. But it was Rechsteiner who conducted nearly all the work for Maxwell in Liechtenstein, not Keicher. Only once or twice a year Keicher would visit London, and Maxwell hardly ever spoke to him on the phone, but Rechsteiner was phoned frequently.

Occasionally, perhaps once a year in the late 1980s, Maxwell would visit Liechtenstein and he would see both Keicher and Rechsteiner, but always in private with no one else present. Rechsteiner was a slim, smart, intelligent and charming man with a ready smile who was always happy to chat and pass the time of day, but nothing more.

The secrets of Maxwell's extraordinary life lie in the offices of Keicher and Rechsteiner in Vaduz. All the other trusts, foundations and companies that Maxwell owned throughout the world probably end up back in one place – Liechtenstein. And it is unlikely that those secrets will ever be fully revealed. It is probable as the international political pressure mounts, the demands from the banks increase and the pensioners' voice grows louder, that some information will be given. It is probable that Keicher and Rechsteiner, in consultation with those who control the trust laws in Liechtenstein, will find it necessary to reveal some of the secrets of those trusts; but it is unlikely that the trusts and foundations will be thrown open for lawyers and bankers to sift through at will. For that would break the Liechtenstein code of secrecy and, in a trice, the principality's main source of income would be destroyed; for no one wanting to hide their secrets would ever again place their trust, or their money, in Liechtenstein.

It is almost certain that Maxwell was the ultimate beneficiary of the foundations and trusts despite all the denials that he made throughout his life whenever he was challenged. But the way the foundations were formed made it legally possible for Maxwell to deny the fact. For the reasons Liechtenstein is so beloved and used by those seeking anonymity is that in Liechtenstein law, the creator of a trust does not need to identify the intended beneficiaries, and the founder himself can sign in a nominee name. Maxwell knew that whatever anyone discovered in Liechtenstein, legally or illegally, his involvement would still remain a secret. And so would the identities of anyone or any government agencies that might be involved. It was watertight.

As Maxwell said after taking over Mirror Group Newspapers: 'I am not the proprietor; I am the Publisher.' Legally, the owner of MGN was the Maxwell Media Trust, based in Liechtenstein.

Since his death there are those who wonder why Maxwell continued to use Liechtenstein for his base. Since the middle of the 1980s Britain's tax laws have been reasonable, even for really wealthy men, and favourable, making it profitable for companies, domestic and international, to base their headquarters in London. Indeed, some international accountants have described Britain of the late '80s as a 'tax haven'. Maxwell's Liechtenstein connections were also proving highly embarrassing for him, used as defences by companies Maxwell was trying to take over. By keeping the ultimate ownership of his empire a secret in Liechtenstein, Maxwell was always open to criticism and suspicion. It was to prevent him taking over various companies in Britain and the United States. As Victor Watson, chairman of

Waddington's, asked about Maxwell's Liechtenstein connections when he successfully fought off a Pergamon takeover: 'If it was all as clear as Mr Maxwell says, then why does he keep it so secret?'

Why? What was Maxwell hiding? It could well have been his connection with the KGB. From the evidence emanating from Moscow during 1992 it does seem conclusive that Maxwell was working in one capacity or another for the KGB. In private, many believed Maxwell was a tool of the Soviet Union and some people said so in public, referring to his European connections as 'from the East', a euphemism for the Soviet Union. Following the collapse of Communism and the end of the Soviet Union, the so-called 'evil empire', it is difficult today to remember the hostility and censure there was towards Moscow throughout the years of the cold war.

Since Maxwell's death on November 5, 1991, evidence has come to light proving that his empire was crumbling under massive debt. There is no doubt that in the last few months of his life Maxwell plundered nearly £1 billion from Maxwell Communications Corporation, Mirror Group Newspapers and the various pension funds in one of the greatest frauds in modern times, much of it to repay money owed to banks.

But that is not the whole story. Nor do the figures seem to add up. The highly respected *Financial Times*, the newspaper of the City Establishment and arguably the most prestigious newspaper in Britain, spent a fortune investigating the fraud. For months, a highly talented team of twelve *FT* journalists followed every possible lead, interviewed more than 150 people in thirteen countries and produced a remarkable six-part dossier, 'Inside Maxwell's Empire', which they headlined 'The Big Lie',

The *FT* pinned everything on Maxwell: 'The Robert Maxwell story is about the vanity, brutality and delusion of one man, and how he persuaded others to believe him. He

317

borrowed £3 billion from the world's biggest and most respected banks to build an empire that was doomed to failure. As it tottered he stole more than £900 million from his companies and their pension funds, most of it in just 10 months as he made a futile effort to pacify the banks. All he bought with the stolen pensions of 30,000 past and present employees – many of whom now face destitution – was a few more months of life at the cost of £3 million a day.'

The *FT* continued, however: 'No one stopped him committing one of the biggest business frauds of the century. One after the other, the lines of defence failed: directors, banks, trustees, pension regulators and the Bank of England.'

Maxwell was able to carry out his wholesale theft of so much money with remarkable ease. He was able to seize the money, from his companies and from the pension funds, because of the sweeping powers he had deliberately secured for himself as chairman of those companies, and by securing control of the pension trustee committees. Throughout his seven years at Mirror Group I don't think Maxwell ever missed a meeting of the pension trustees. He may have skipped hundreds of appointments, meetings, dinners and other commitments but he never missed a meeting of the trustees.

His policy of divide and rule, his policy of never letting anyone, not even his sons Kevin and Ian, know the whole picture, enabled Maxwell to act virtually unchallenged. Indeed, Maxwell had the most enormous powers. He had the right to sign cash out of MCC's bank accounts or sign away MCC assets on his signature alone, although two signatures were necessary for Mirror Group deals. But then his sons were on the board.

It was back in 1989 that Maxwell put into operation the means whereby he could plunder the pension funds. He first pooled all the assets, amounting to about £700 million, of the pension funds of all his companies. Then he formed a company, Bishopsgate Investment Management, with himself as chairman. All but one of BIM's directors were directors of his private companies, including Kevin and Ian. From then on BIM controlled the pension investment policy so that the trustees of the individual pension funds could no longer see what was happening. BIM also took physical control of many of the actual share certificates.

This was in total disregard of and against the spirit of IMRO, Britain's pension regulators and pension management watchdog. Then Maxwell went about getting BIM licensed by IMRO. He did so with just days to go before the laws were changed. IMRO went ahead and licensed BIM under the Financial Services Act 1986, despite the fact that the BIM set-up was unique. It was the vital step in allowing Maxwell access to the pension millions. Worse still, IMRO licensed BIM under its rules for Occupational Pension Schemes, which do not have to submit audited financial accounts for inspection. It was because IMRO, set up by the Government, failed the MCC and *Mirror* pensioners so badly, that the Government looks morally responsible for what happened (although investigations are not yet complete) and will have to come to the rescue of the pensioners if not enough of the stolen pension funds are recovered.

In the light of what has been revealed since Maxwell's death the way in which Maxwell reacted to any suggestion of fraud among his employees is extraordinary. Indeed, one of the reasons he bugged his directors and accountants was because he feared they were embezzling money. He insisted, against tough opposition from union representatives, that any employee at Mirror Group Newspapers fired for fraud of any kind would automatically lose his pension entitlement. Maxwell insisted on going further, decreeing that relatives of fund members were not entitled to pension payments if

319

the member had committed a fraudulent or negligent act. On one occasion in the late 1980s a clerk in the pension department was found to have embezzled £23,000 from the *Mirror* pension fund. Maxwell was informed. He never saw the young man. But the police were immediately called, the man was arrested and charged with fraud and he was fired. Maxwell also fired the man who had hired the fraudster, because, Maxwell claimed, he should have known the man might have embezzled the pension funds!

Betty Maxwell was to be caught by the same rule. Her pension rights, which could have amounted to £250,000 a year, were stopped by the trustees when Maxwell's frauds surfaced. And it would seem very unlikely that she would ever share any of the £20 million which the family believed they should be entitled to under the insurance policy taken out on Maxwell's life. There seems very little possibility that she will receive anything from his Will, because others will have first call if any monies are discovered.

And yet Betty Maxwell found it difficult to believe her husband could have been the monster he turned out to be. She said, some time after his death: 'If some of the things that appeared to have happened in the last months of his life actually happened, they can only have been the acts of a desperate man.' They were.

Many financial analysts, including the *FT* experts, believe most of the £900 million Maxwell stole from his companies and the pension funds was recycled to other banks in a desperate attempt to shore up his tottering private empire. And that £200 million of the stolen money went into a massive, illegal, secret share-support scheme – with Maxwell madly buying shares in MCC and MGN to stop the price falling. Because if the price fell Maxwell had to provide more shares to banks as collateral for the money they had loaned him.

Allegedly, the other £700 million disappeared like this: about £550 million was paid back to the banks during the summer of 1991, and £150 million went in trading losses of his hundreds of private companies, like the *European* and the *New York Daily News*.

What the companies, the banks and particularly the pensioners want to know is whether there are any hidden pots of gold. There does seem to be a great deal of money, perhaps as much as £500 million, unaccounted for. Some, perhaps most, of that £500 million, could have gone to repay further debts and in servicing his loans, but not all of it.

We also know that Maxwell paid considerable sums of money to his aides, advisers and directors of various companies in the last nine months, to those who left his empire, like Peter Walker, Lord Donoughue, Jean-Pierre Anselmini and Mark Booth. But those payments would barely have made a dent in the total.

In 1991 Maxwell sold the jewel in his crown, Pergamon, the cornerstone of his business empire, which he founded in 1948. That was sold to the Dutch publisher Elsevier for a remarkable £440 million. Maxwell floated forty-nine per cent of Mirror Group Newspapers in May 1991, raising another £250 million. And there was more. Maxwell sold Scitex for £120 million, the French TV channel TF1 for £80 million, Britain's Central TV for £30 million and MTV Europe for £40 million; making a total of £960 million.

On top of that, Maxwell received a dividend from MCC of £90 million, making a grand total in cash of £1.14 billion.

One of Maxwell's success stories throughout the 1980s was playing the foreign exchanges. Bankers have reported that, remarkably, Maxwell was capable of keeping currency parities in his brain at all times. He needed to, the amount he played the foreign exchange markets, gambling on whether currencies would move up or down. It is accepted that he made another £50 million on foreign exchange deals in the summer of 1991, bringing the total to virtually £1.2 billion.

On top of that enormous sum it has been proved that

he stole around £900 million from his companies and their pension funds. That means that Maxwell must have gone through a huge cash mountain of over £2 billion in a matter of a few months.

So what happened to that cash mountain? Some of the money from the Pergamon sale went to pay short-term MCC debts. As a result, in May 1991 MCC was solvent, making profits, and had £240 million in the bank on deposit. It still had a debt mountain, but MCC had to pay only £400 million by October 1992 and the next payment, of £600 million, was not due until October 1995. Its principal bankers and directors were confident in the summer of 1991 that MCC would make those payments comfortably. It was in good shape. So was Mirror Group Newspapers. It was making good profits – £80 million a year – and had money in the bank on deposit too.

Bankers who talked to Maxwell on a regular basis throughout 1991 seemed happy enough until a month or so before his death, whatever they may have said since. The regular meetings were normal, as they had always been, with Maxwell explaining the current financial position of MCC or MGN, or of Robert Maxwell Group, the private side comprising about four hundred companies.

Indeed, an MCC director who attended some of those meetings with various bankers opined, 'In my view, the meetings were normal with no fuss or bother. None of the bankers at those meetings seemed to show any concern or fears that things were going wrong. Indeed, some were rather jokey meetings right up until the end. He answered whatever questions they asked quite easily, and fully. There seemed to be no arguments, no rows, no demands, no tough questioning by the bankers at any of those regular meetings. Maxwell was his charming self, but he always was at any of those meetings.'

However, since Maxwell's death the banks have told their

side of the story. Several UK clearing banks, as well as many others, maintain they were aware that the creditworthiness of the private side was deteriorating in May 1991 after the MGN flotation. One UK clearing bank told the *FT*: 'The picture began to change so fast that we would need new projections of where the cash was coming from nearly every fortnight.'

Yet the bankers seem to have done very little to determine what was happening throughout the last six months of Maxwell's life. The banks appear not to have asked any questions when they did receive money due to them or when they were handed over share certificates as backing for loans. For many of those share certificates, amounting to £200 million, were shares belonging to the pension funds of MCC and Mirror Group. Many of those share certificates handed over to the banks still had the name 'Bishopsgate Investment Management' written on the top. The banks knew that BIM was a Maxwell company which he had founded to take control of all of his companies' pension funds from the trustees of the individual pension funds. BIM had also taken physical control of many of the actual share certificates. The banks were aware that the only reason for the existence of BIM was to manage pension funds throughout the Maxwell empire. Did they raise the question of any of the BIM share certificates during meetings with Maxwell and other directors during the spring and summer of 1991?

And it isn't just the banks who should shoulder a share of the problem of what happened to the money, and the funds of pensioners. There are the merchant bankers who advised Maxwell. There are the auditors and accountants. Nearly a year after his death Coopers & Lybrand Deloitte, MCC's accountants, have argued they had no knowledge of what was going on. And then, of course, there are the stockbrokers. Still there is nothing from them but silence. All of them took Maxwell's money, charging fees for their advice;

and they all seem to have been deceived by Maxwell. Now, they should put their hands in their pockets and provide the necessary funds for the innocent pensioners.

The principal fear of the banks seems to have been that the private side of the Maxwell empire was in deep trouble. It comprised a tangled web of nearly four hundred companies, many no more than brass plates in offshore tax havens, which was run by Maxwell, his sons and a few trusted aides in London and New York. It held Maxwell's investments in property and foreign newspapers as well as the solid assets, shares in MCC and MGN. The web was under three parent companies: Headington Investments, owned by a Gibraltar trust company, the Robert Maxwell Group and the Maxwell Foundation, his Liechtenstein-based charity.

How severe was the crisis on the private side? In the summer of 1991, about seventy per cent of MCC, worth about £700 million, and fifty per cent of MGN, worth about £250 million, were owned by the private side. And there were certainly other assets around the world amounting to perhaps £1 billion. The private side probably had between £1.5 and £2 billion-worth of assets. In the great majority of cases, that would be fine, when fifty per cent of the assets were making profits. It certainly wasn't a situation for which the only solution was the wholesale plunder of £900 million. But very few people, perhaps only Maxwell himself, knew the whole truth about the private side. And maybe his brain, addled by years of taking the sleeping pill Halcion and increasing amounts of hard liquor, was beginning to forget.

His faithful hairdresser George Wheeler had noted a change: 'During the last few sessions with him during 1991 I recall him drinking a bottle or two of vintage port during the ninety-minute chemical process, the time I needed to colour his hair.' And it was only in the last months of his life that he began knocking back bottles of Chivas Regal.

So why did Maxwell perpetrate his gigantic fraud, a fraud which he must have known would be revealed sooner or later, which would bring nothing but shame, vilification, anger, humiliation and a long, long jail sentence? As the Watergate Deep Throat advised: 'Follow the money. Only then will you find the truth.'

The administrators of MCC and MGN, and their huge staffs, the Department of Trade and Industry and the Serious Fraud Office with fifty-five lawyers, accountants and police officers, sifted through tons of paperwork for months on end trying to piece together the jigsaw, trying to find out what happened to the £2 billion which disappeared in the last six months of Maxwell's life.

There are three men who I believe, should give them the answers to many of their questions. Between them, these three men may know where *all* the money went. They may also know if there are any hidden pots of gold.

The three are: Dr Werner Rechsteiner, Maxwell's Swiss lawyer; Mr Ellis Freedman, his ageing American lawyer; and Vladimir Alexandrovich Kryuchkov, the former Chief of the KGB who is now in a Moscow jail awaiting trial for the attempted coup against Gorbachov.

Despite all the evidence of Maxwell's fraud the questions still remain: did Maxwell commit suicide? Was he murdered? Or did he simply fall overboard?

Many arguments can be made for the likelihood that Maxwell was murdered. In the last few months of his life there were very good reasons why either the KGB or an organized crime syndicate in New York may have decided to kill him.

During 1990 and 1991 the KGB had become increasingly unpopular in Moscow in particular, as well as other cities and towns throughout the crumbling Soviet Union. Attacks were being made on the KGB and its operations in the Soviet parliament, an unparalleled occurrence in the history of the USSR's Intelligence-gathering organization, which had far greater political clout than any other Western organization doing the same job.

Senior KGB officers were very well aware of what had happened to secret Intelligence officers of all ranks in Eastern European countries when their Communist regimes had been overturned and thrown out of office. Not only had some been chased, beaten up and killed by angry mobs seeking vengeance, but many had been thrown out of their jobs and left penniless and friendless. In Moscow many decided they needed to protect their futures and the best way to do so was to make sure they had overseas bank accounts in hard currencies, preferably US dollars.

Even today, a year after the collapse of the Soviet Union, investigations are continuing into reports that senior KGB officers feathered their overseas nests around the time of the August 1991 coup against Mikhail Gorbachov, the coup that precipitated the disintegration of the USSR.

The KGB had always been responsible for the movement of overseas currencies and it was responsible for investigating and bringing to justice those Soviet citizens who broke the strict currency laws. It was also responsible for checking payments to overseas companies.

Maxwell's relationship with the Soviet Union had been strange, even remarkable, to say the least. It had begun in the late 1940s and then, in 1954, Maxwell arrived in Moscow, allegedly for the first time since World War II. He came with his confidante of that time, his PA, Anne Dove. He walked into the magnificent British Embassy building in Moscow and asked to see the commercial counsellor. At that time in fact Britain didn't have a commercial department at the Embassy, so Maxwell went to see the chancery department. He said he was a stranger in Moscow but had come to the

USSR with the idea of reaching an agreement with the Russians to publish their scientific journals in the West. He was also hoping to reach an agreement for access to all Soviet scientific publications.

Maxwell was in luck. At that time the Russians had an enormous stock of scientific material which they were very keen to see published in the West to show their prowess and achievements in many different scientific fields. The British sent him off to the prestigious Soviet Academy of Sciences and suggested he should contact officials at NAUKA (new science), the publishing house of the Academy of Sciences. So successful was Maxwell's visit that he left Moscow a few days later armed with a mass of Soviet publications, 'to publish as much as he wanted' in the West.

Maxwell was to become a frequent visitor to Moscow during the next four decades and on the surface it was inexplicable that a printer and publisher of Soviet scientific journals and papers should be treated with such respect and privilege in the Communist state.

For, during the long relationship with the Soviet Union, Maxwell did not in fact publish a great many Soviet scientific journals at all, nor was much money involved. Over the years Maxwell only printed, through Pergamon, about thirty Soviet journals, all provided by NAUKA, and a few hundred papers. Indeed directors at Pergamon complained to Maxwell time and again in the 1960s and 1970s that Pergamon lost money on the Russian scientists' books because after expensive translation and a small print run no one ever wanted to buy them! A former Pergamon employee, Richard Newnham, realized the Moscow books were 'an albatross' and yet Maxwell was very happy, and appeared privileged to publish the scientific books while the Russians continued to treat Maxwell as a VIP when they were earning nothing from their published works in the West.

And yet this curious commercial relationship with Moscow,

which seemed to be based on losses for Maxwell and no profits for anyone, was to lead to the very highest in the land. The man responsible for Maxwell's remarkably close relationship with the Kremlin over many of those years was Yuri Vladimirovich Andropov, who was destined to become the most powerful man in the Soviet Union when he was appointed General Secretary of the Communist Party's Central Committee in 1982.

But it was in Andropov's capacity as chairman of the KGB, which he took command of in 1967, that he enabled Maxwell to become an important contact for the KGB, though it seems that Maxwell was never a spy, never a secret agent. As explained earlier, he was a 'banker' for the KGB and an agent of influence.

Andropov remained head of the KGB until 1983, the longest-serving head of the Soviet's Intelligence arm in its entire history. Andropov's mission in the 1970s was to bring the KGB closer to the Central Committee, so that the two most powerful branches of the Soviet system worked together as two arms of the same organization. Andropov was also to become a senior member of the Politburo, almost ensuring that one day he would succeed to the top job as General Secretary. Undoubtedly Andropov was the most successful of all heads of the KGB – and probably the most powerful.

It was as a result of Maxwell's relationship with Andropov that the publisher was treated with such respect in Moscow, almost as a VIP. Quentin Peel, the *Financial Times'* well-informed man in Moscow from 1987 to 1991, was mystified at the remarkable respect, if not awe, which the most senior bureaucrats in the Kremlin gave to Maxwell whenever he was visiting Moscow, or even when his name was mentioned. Peel, a highly intelligent, perceptive journalist, commented: 'Maxwell was treated like no other visiting head of an international business empire. He seemed to command far greater respect and treatment than one would have expected as a publisher of books, magazines and newspapers. The mention of his name would invoke unease among those bureaucrats to whom one was speaking.'

But with glasnost and perestroika, with the collapse of Communism and the disintegration of the Soviet Union, with the West urging the International Monetary Fund and other Western agencies to help the nations that have emerged from the Soviet empire, the KGB had no further need for Maxwell, especially when he failed to deliver what they demanded.

And there are those in Moscow who believe Maxwell could have been got rid of by the hardline KGB men – to stop those senior members of the Communist Party who had smuggled out millions through Maxwell's Liechtenstein connection from collecting their ill-gotten gains.

And the Soviet scientific authorities had no further need for Maxwell – he had sold Pergamon.

There are other conspiracy theories. It must be accepted that Maxwell's connection with the KGB was known to Western, and particularly British, Intelligence, but there does appear to have been a quid pro quo that Maxwell should not be touched, for some reason or another. By the end of 1990, however, the international political climate had changed so dramatically that Maxwell's 'protection' was no longer valid.

And then there were Maxwell's newfound enemies – the mobsters of New York who for decades had been plundering the *New York Daily News* and did so throughout the months before his death when Maxwell owned the paper. It was typical Maxwell that he decided to try to end the Mafia's stranglehold on the *Daily News* and went to the Manhattan District Attorney's office to ask for advice and an investigation into racketeering at the *Daily News*.

After months of investigations, reports from the DA's

office in the summer of 1992 revealed the control Mafia bosses exercised on the New York newspaper scene. The Bonano family controlled the *Daily Post*, the Lucchese family the *Daily News*.

When police, federal labour racketeering agents and investigators from the Manhattan DA's office swooped on the home of Robert F. Perrino, who ran the newspaper delivery office at the *Post*, they found a mini arsenal including Berettas, Lugers, two revolvers, two 12-gauge shotguns and two switchblades. As well as $100,000 in cash and three dozen pieces of expensive jewellery, they found manuals on how to kill people. Perrino had disappeared. The evidence the DA's office uncovered showed that Maxwell had cut across the most ruthless mobsters in America.

It is little wonder that Maxwell was reportedly so nervous whenever he visited New York in the last few months of his life, so very different to the showman who had taken over the *Daily News* in the spring of 1991.

Carolyn Hinsey was a secretary at the *Daily News* when Maxwell came across her as he toured the newspaper office after winning control in March, 1991. He stopped at her desk.

'Young lady,' he asked, 'what do you think of me?'

Six-feet-tall Carolyn stood up and looked him in the eyes. 'I think it'll be great to have a boss bigger than I am.'

Maxwell roared with laughter, and the following day told Carolyn that she would be his new assistant. Typically, he nicknamed Carolyn 'Tiny'.

After his death eight months later, Carolyn said: 'His temper was as bad as I feared, but he also had a sense of humour that surprised me. He could be a gluttonous pig when eating alone but charming at public dinners.'

And she was totally surprised at how Maxwell spoke to people. She recalled: 'Those who angered him were "clowns", "dogs", "children", "dickheads" and "idiots". No one was spared. Once in a while he would call someone a genius, his voice dripping with sarcasm. Yet when he was in a good mood he could be very funny. He delighted in throwing faxes in the toilet and then telling the person who had sent them, "Oh yes, I am reviewing them now."'

Carolyn was amazed at Maxwell's appetite. Despite the fact that his empire was collapsing around him, that he feared the Mafia were threatening his life and he knew the KGB weren't happy with him, Maxwell never stopped eating. Indeed, according to Carolyn Hinsey, his appetite seemed to have increased, as though food was his sole comfort. During those last few days in New York Maxwell started his day with two or three bowls of cereal, a pot of coffee and a whole watermelon. Throughout the day he ate fresh fruit, chicken soup (which he always called Jewish penicillin), cheeses and chocolate bars. For dinner he usually enjoyed $200-worth of Chinese food. In New York $200-worth of Chinese food would usually be enough to feed four people!

Carolyn Hinsey reported that the last day she saw Maxwell, Saturday, October 26, he was in the worst mood she had ever seen him in. 'He was very angry about the Seymour Hersh book and the allegations that he was linked to the Israeli Intelligence agency, Mossad. All day he screamed at me, "Get that dickhead on the phone." I would ask him which "dickhead" and he would tell me which one. At one point he took the phone when trying to contact the editor of the *Sunday Mirror*. He failed so I volunteered. He literally picked up the phone and threw it at my head shouting, 'You are a fucking idiot; you can't do anything.' Fortunately I caught it. Maxwell stormed upstairs and ordered Joseph, his butler, to bring him a bottle of Chivas Regal, ice and tonic. Hours later he phoned downstairs and told me I could go home. It was the last I saw of him.'

*

The last time I spoke to Maxwell was during that weekend before he flew back to London en route to the *Lady Ghislaine*. In every conversation I had with Maxwell he was never angry, nor did he raise his voice. Indeed, though he didn't like the allegations in the Hersh book, he did also joke about it, telling me how much he would make Hersh and Faber & Faber pay for their 'stupid libel'. But he was very conspiratorial, telling me to stay in hiding, to lie low, to speak to no one and to keep in direct contact with him the whole time, giving him my phone numbers whenever I moved. But he was also remarkably supportive, telling me he knew I was not guilty of any of the allegations made in the Hersh book and emphasizing that he would sort out everything on his return. In all the conversations over that weekend, and I think there were four, Maxwell sounded very together, under no stress or strain, and not at all angry. I know he was an accomplished actor but I would have thought that I might have detected something strange if he was in fear of his life or seriously contemplating suicide.

In those last few days before he died Maxwell was still furiously borrowing money from banks, 'borrowing' money from the *Daily Mirror*, acting, as always, as if he owned everything and he had the absolute right to do as he wished with any of the companies, public or private, of which he held the stewardship. He had never changed; he had never learned. To the last, Maxwell was as guilty as the DTI reports of the 1970s had reported; he was 'an unfit person to run a public company'.

When Maxwell flew to New York at the end of October he had taken with him £50 million, a loan from Bankers Trust in the name of Mirror Group Newspapers. He handed over the money to the *Daily News*, which was losing money like water in a sieve. The last loan ever made to Maxwell was announced by Lloyds Bank and Barclays Bank on October 28, an extension of a longstanding loan, £80 million advanced to Maxwell's private companies, backed by a charge against Maxwell House, his empire's Holborn headquarters, which was one of the last assets he hadn't mortgaged to the hilt.

For how long Maxwell knew the die had been cast is impossible to tell. Perhaps, in his arrogance, he never realized that he couldn't, Houdini-like, perform a miracle escape until the last moment. But that was fast approaching. On the morning of Tuesday, October 29, the US bank, Shearson Lehman, informed Maxwell that because of failure to repay its loans it was going to seize collateral: shares in Berlitz, a MCC subsidiary. If Shearson Lehman carried out its threat, that would block the proposed sale of Berlitz, a sale which Maxwell hoped would give his empire some much-needed breathing space.

The following day, however, Goldman Sachs, the US investment bank which had been one of Maxwell's most staunch supporters for years, delivered a formal warning that unless it was paid £10 million owed for foreign currency dealings in forty-eight hours it would sell the collateral Maxwell had handed over – a block of MCC shares. Maxwell knew that a sale of MCC shares by Goldman Sachs would spell disaster, for Goldman had been the biggest buyers of MCC shares in the company's history. If Goldman sold, every holder of MCC shares would turn seller and MCC would be doomed. As the *FT* wrote: 'That would trigger the meltdown that Maxwell had always feared; bank loans throughout the empire were backed by the value of MCC shares, and if the price fell, the empire would crash.'

There were just three weeks to go before MCC's half-yearly figures were due to be announced. They would reveal lower profits and, as a consequence, the share price would drop. And Maxwell, who now owned seventy per cent of the shares, hadn't any more cash left to secretly purchase more shares through private companies to keep the price steady.

Before flying to the yacht Maxwell summoned Bob Cole, who recalls: 'He put his arms on my shoulders and kissed me on the cheek. He had only done that twice before. My father, who was Jewish, used to hug me like that. At the time I thought it strange. Now, I wonder if he was saying goodbye.'

Early the next morning Maxwell climbed the stairs to the roof of Maxwell House for the last flight aboard his helicopter – with the insignia of the MGN lion that Maxwell had chosen to be the group's emblem on the side. He flew to Luton Airport where his latest Gulfstream IV was waiting to whisk him to Gibraltar and the *Lady Ghislaine* which was there waiting for him.

However, what was unusual about Maxwell's last flight to the *Lady Ghislaine* was that he went alone. No secretary, no valet, no butler. No one. He had never done that before. He said he wanted to rest and shake off a cold. But no one noticed he had a cold. However, he did take with him an enormous amount of papers, five large box-cases full of them.

He left behind troubled Mirror Group directors. Deputy publisher, Ernie Burrington, who was to become chairman of the company after Maxwell's death, and the group's finance director, Lawrence Guest, were worried about £47 million which had disappeared earlier from MGN's bank account. They didn't yet know Maxwell had taken out a further loan of £50 million against the group. Burrington told the *FT*: 'Lawrence Guest was prepared to take on Maxwell and this time I was going to ask the other directors to do it as well. We agreed we would hit Maxwell when he came back from his trip.' He never did.

Meanwhile, pressure was building up at Maxwell House. The *FT* phoned Kevin Maxwell to say it had completed a month-long investigation into the Maxwell empire and was about to publish a report that said hidden debt in the private companies was much higher than the outside world realized. Swiss Bank Corporation, which was waiting for a promised repayment of £55 million, informed Maxwell House that if the money wasn't repaid by Tuesday, November 4 they were going to their lawyers.

As the empire of which he was so proud was about to crash, on board the *Lady Ghislaine* Maxwell seemed at peace with himself, and with the world. The ship's captain, Gus Rankin, was to recall: 'It was as if he had decided to drift, to just let everyone else get on with it. Amazingly, he did no work. He seemed healthy. He ate well and drank well.'

But Maxwell was behaving oddly, even for a man who constantly changed his mind. He told Rankin to head for the Madeira capital of Funchal but the town was besieged with reporters wanting to interview Maxwell about his alleged Mossad connections. So Maxwell told Rankin to go to a deserted island nearby, Desertas, so he could have a swim. On Saturday, November 2 Maxwell decided to return to Funchal and that night 'borrowed' $3,000 dollars and went gambling in the casino.

On the morning of Sunday, November 3 Maxwell told Rankin to drop him off at an airport in the Atlantic between Madeira and Bermuda. Rankin was bemused. He said later: 'It was an extraordinary request. He must have known there were no airports between Madeira and Bermuda, in fact no islands. I told him there was nothing but open sea.'

Once, and once only, Maxwell had discussed with me his fascination with the legendary Bermuda Triangle – that area near the beautiful island where a number of aircraft mysteriously disappeared through the 1940s and '50s. Maxwell had said that he had read a great deal about the mystery and believed it to be true – that there was something about wind currents in the area that forced down aircraft. He believed that was the only explanation for the numbers of aircraft that had disappeared in the Triangle for no apparent reason. That single piece of information from Rankin made me wonder whether Maxwell had thought of disappearing.

He had spoken to Andrea Martin on a number of occasions about disappearing, quitting the ratrace and the pressure and 'doing a Stonehouse', faking his own suicide and beginning a secret life somewhere in South America. He had daydreamed about it, saying: 'I have thought it would be a wonderful way of ending one's life, living in a lovely house with a swimming pool in the middle of nowhere with not a worry, not a thought for all the problems. I would have plenty of money and the telephone would never ring again.' He mused: 'I would be at peace then and happy.'

Maxwell told Rankin to sail to the Canaries and arrived in the morning of Monday, November 4. He spoke to Burrington and apologized for disrupting his lunch; he phoned Dr Pisar in Paris. Pisar recalled: 'We talked of plans for the immediate future, chiefly Maxwell's excitement at being nominated by the Scientific Institute of France to receive the Légion d'honneur, France's highest award, and he was to be made Man of the Year by the Jewish Scientific and Cultural Institute at the Plaza Hotel, New York, later in November. There was satisfaction in his voice. A man that contemplates suicide does not think that way.'

He phoned his son Ian in London. Maxwell drafted the speech Ian was due to deliver on his behalf at an Anglo–Israeli dinner that night. Ian recalls: 'He gave a great belly laugh at a joke about Yasser Arafat, the Palestinian leader, jumping out of an aircraft mistaking a Jewish prayer shawl for a parachute.'

The log of calls from the ship shows that Maxwell spoke to Kevin a number of times that day, so he would have been aware that the storm clouds were about to burst, for Goldman Sachs had given formal notification that it had sold some MCC shares. At that moment Maxwell knew the game was up.

Maxwell's last night began at the five-star Hotel Mencey after he had showered and changed in his suite on the *Lady Ghislaine* and taken a taxi to the hotel. He wore an open-necked shirt, check trousers and a light summer jacket. He also wore his blue baseball cap, which looked wildly out of place in the sophisticated dining room. He looked nothing like one of the world's wealthiest men as he sat down and ordered three beers one after the other, which he drank quickly. He ate well, having ordered spinach and asparagus mousse, cod in mushroom and parsley sauce and a single pear. From those in the hotel there seemed nothing unusual about Maxwell that night. Surprisingly, that night Maxwell puffed at a Havana cigar, for he was so against smoking he rarely even smoked the Havanas he loved.

He had a coffee and brandy at the Cafeteria Olympus down the road and was driven back to the ship. During his entire last evening he had been alone, a situation which he was used to but didn't like. Back on board Maxwell told Rankin to cruise slowly through the night, to Gran Canaria and back and then head for Tenerife's southern airport where his Gulfstream was waiting to fly him back to London. After Ian phoned to report on the dinner and the speech, Maxwell took his last call at 11 p.m. from Rabbi Vogel, of the Jewish Lubavitch sect, who hoped Maxwell would be able to obtain some religious books from Russian archives. Maxwell said he would ask Gorbachov.

What happened next? Could anyone have boarded the ship that night and murdered Maxwell?

The Spanish authorities have traced every boat in the area that night and accounted for each one. And Rankin has said it would have been impossible. He was on the bridge throughout most of the night and the *Lady Ghislaine*'s radar had picked up nothing suspicious as they cruised at a steady fourteen knots. Naturally, suspicion also rested with the crew. All eleven crew were interviewed more than once by Spanish police, by insurance investigators and again after Interpol requested further interviews. Rankin said that at the approximate time of death he and two other crew were on the soundproof bridge and heard and saw nothing. An engineer was in the engine room out of sight and earshot. All other members of the crew were sleeping and said they heard nothing unusual.

Maxwell was seen walking on deck at about 4.25 a.m. by a member of the crew and at 4.55 Maxwell phoned the bridge to ask that the air-conditioning be turned down. That was the last time Maxwell was seen or heard. On the previous evening, however, Maxwell had ordered a stewardess to lock the main sliding doors to his quarters from within, leave the key with him and make her exit through the outer bathroom door, leaving it unlocked behind her. On the morning Maxwell died the main sliding doors were found locked from outside, and the heavy steel-framed doors leading to the deck were closed. Maxwell's key was missing and Rankin had to use the master key.

Maxwell could not have left through the bathroom, which had access to the outer deck. It could not be opened from the outside. What was so unusual was that Maxwell had closed doors behind him, because he never did, let alone lock them. The locking of the doors was a deliberate act and yet was not included in the Spanish police report.

It seems, from all the evidence, that Maxwell did not fall overboard despite the original theory that he had collapsed from a heart attack and fallen over the 3ft-6in-high wire barrier. Conditions were good, the sea calm. The most plausible theory is that some time after 5 a.m., as dawn was breaking, Maxwell decided to take his own life. Naked, he left his suite, locked the door and threw the key overboard. Gently, so as not to make a noise or a splash, he eased himself into the water and held on with his left hand, tearing the muscles in his shoulder. Then it seems from the autopsy reports that he swam, and he kept on swimming until he suffered a heart attack. He didn't drown, because not sufficient seawater was found in the lungs; but he did suffer a mild heart attack.

On the eve of Maxwell's celebrated funeral on the Mount of Olives in Jerusalem, his personal doctor for many years, Dr Joseph Joseph, went on record as saying he did not think Maxwell had died of natural causes, believing his death was suspicious. He denied Maxwell was suffering from a heart condition.

Following so hard on the heels of the allegations that Maxwell was a Mossad agent, many people believe the incredible funeral Maxwell was given in Israel, more like that of a head of state than a foreign businessman, gave credence to the theory. More than that, the style of the funeral led people to believe that Maxwell had played a far more important role in Israeli international diplomacy than had hitherto been hinted at. It is true that in the last few years of his life, Maxwell, having rediscovered his Judaism, did all in his power, in Moscow in particular, to help the Jewish cause, taking on the role of the unofficial Israeli ambassador to the Soviet Union. But that was pure Maxwell.

President Chaim Herzog of Israel, who attended the funeral, said: 'He scaled the heights. Kings and barons besieged his doorstep. Many admired him. Many disliked him. But nobody remained indifferent to him.'

The former Israeli Prime Minister Shimon Peres, who knew Maxwell for many years, said: 'Here on the Mount of Olives eternity will absorb one of its greatest sons. He deserves not only freedom but rest.'

And the Israeli Premier Yitzhak Shamir commented: 'I knew him, especially in recent times, as a person who invested money in Israel and who put his wide contacts on the international arena at Israel's service.'

The world responded to Maxwell's death with the most remarkable outpourings of praise for the penniless peasant boy from Czechoslovakia who ended his life an alleged billionaire at the head of one of the world's great media empires. It was ironic that Maxwell should have responded to a journalist who came to compile his obituary with the words: 'Go and write God's obituary first; it will be shorter.'

But the world was fulsome in its praise of Maxwell. Margaret Thatcher, who had called him 'one of us', the greatest compliment Thatcher gave to people, revealed that Maxwell had always kept her informed with what was going on throughout Eastern Europe; Edward Heath talked of his help towards the European cause; Neil Kinnock spoke of Maxwell's steadfast support of the Labour Party and genuine commitment to the advancement of the British people; John Major believed Maxwell would not want the world to grieve at his death but marvel at his extraordinary life; and Mikhail Gorbachov spoke of Maxwell's great contribution to the improvement of relations between nations in mass media management and publishing.

Those early epitaphs were the nearest Maxwell ever came to earning respect. He tried to buy respect by appealing to the common man, saving British football clubs, but most supporters of the clubs he owned ended up booing him; he tried the same tactic with the 1986 Commonwealth Games in Scotland; he hoped to win respect by becoming one of the great media moguls of the twentieth century but didn't succeed there; and he believed that by promising millions of pounds to charities he could buy the respect which eluded him throughout his life.

It was all to change with such lightning speed. His own paper, the *Daily Mirror*, the paper that praised Maxwell as 'the man who saved the *Mirror*' and 'a soccer saviour', turned against him with a vengeance; other newspapers recorded the legacy of a corrupt man, a bully, a thief, a spy, a fraudster, even a monster. These were not the epitaphs Maxwell would have wanted. Understandably, with the appalling revelations that he had plundered the pension funds, the world turned against him.

Maxwell would sometimes say to me, and to others: 'If there is a way back after death, then I will be the one to find it.' If he does find that way, administrators, bankers, policemen and thirty thousand pensioners will be waiting.

INDEX

Aboff, Sheldon, 255, 275, 290
Adler, David, 85, 280, 282, 286–7
Aeroflot, 265–6
AIDS, stories warning of, 123
Allason, Rupert, 305, 311
Amish people, 294–5
Andropov, Yuri, 252–4, 328
Anselmini, Jean-Pierre, 222–3, 227, 321
Arafat, Yasser, 336
arap Moi, Daniel, 219–21
Argentina, Maxwell dealing with, 239, 241
Asscher, Professor William, 189
Astone, Vincenza, 102–3
Auxiliary Power Corps, 19
Aviation Venture International, 265

Baddeley, Jean, 74, 91–5, 99, 103
Baker, James, 274
Baker, Senator Howard, 286
Bankers Trust, loan from, 332
Bannenberg, Jon, 280
Berlin Wall, tearing down, 57–8
Berlitz, 333
Bermuda Triangle, 335–6
Bernstein, Sidney, 238
Bird, Dickie, 238
Bishopsgate, Investment Management, 319;
    pension funds, managing, 323
Bishopsgate Investment Trust, 223–4
Bonano criminal family, 8–9, 330
Booth, Mark, 192, 240, 321
Bouygues, François, 243–4
Bower, Tom, 22, 90, 249
Bradbury, David, 175
Bramhall of Bushfield, Lord, 237–8
Brassey's, 33, 237
British Airways, helicopter division, 96
British Book Centre, New York, 27
British Printing Corporation, 32–3
Brumback, Charles, 147
Bryant, John, 144
Bulgaria: Balkan Film Enterprises, 226;
    Communists, 227; European Bank, 231;
    foreign debt, 223–4; Lyudmila Zhivkov
    Foundation, 221; Maxwell Bank of
    Bulgaria, 223, 227; Maxwell Foundation,
    231; Maxwell Management School, 222;
    Maxwell wooing, 221; Maxwell's projects in,
    224–5; Opposition leaders, talks with, 226;
    president's palaces, 225; printing works,
    contract to build, 228; proposals for, 228–32;
    Rodina complex, 228; Scitex, purchase of,
    228; Zhivkov, deposing of, 223
Burrington, Ernie, 63, 334
Bush, President George, 149–50, 267, 274,
    284–7, 298
Butterworths–Springer, 26

Cable News Network, 3, 57, 187
Callaghan, James, 159
Carpenter, Leslie, 43
Carr, Sir William, 35–6
Carter, Jimmy, 286
Carter-Ruck, Peter, 198
Cashmere, 216
Cathew-Yorkstoun, Brigadier M.A., 20
Caviare, 13–15
Caxton Holdings, 29
Central TV, 33, 321
Chalk, Clive, 198
Cheesman, Martin, 86
Cherkasky, Michael G., 9
Chernenko, Konstantin, 253–4
Chicago Tribune Group, 10, 146–7
Chirac, Jacques, 243
Churchill, Winston, 90
Clackson, Stephen, 129–31, 167–8, 175
Cole, Bob, 75–7, 149, 182, 334
Cole, Brian, 226–8
Commonwealth Games, 168–70
Corsan, David, 210
Croatia, 290

Daily Herald, 34
Daily Mirror: circulation, 121–2; drugs and
    AIDS stories, 123; editorial comment,
    Maxwell approving, 121; Ethiopian
    campaign, 45; foreign bureaux, closing,
    123–4; foreign news in, 55–7; guard,
    appointment of, 127; leaders, Maxwell
    approving, 270–1; Lithuania, story on,
    125; low pay at, 52; Maxwell running, 45;
    Maxwell's interference in, 126–7; new boss,
    employees meeting, 43–4; newsdesk, 155;
    retainers, Maxwell banning, 124; stories in,
    picking, 55; turning against Maxwell, 341
Dean, Brenda, 51
Denning, Lord, 159
Der Telegraph, 21
Derby County, 241
Diamond, John, 60
Dines, Debbie, 94–5
Dinkins, David, 151
Doi, Madame, 215
Donoughue, Lord, 159, 321
Doughty, Stephen, 304
Dove, Anne, 32, 90–1
DTI reports, 30–1, 158–9
du Cann, Sir Edward, 210
du Maurier, Ivan: Maxwell (Hoch) becoming, 20

East Germany, Maxwell in, 233–6
Edwards, Bob, 47
Eisenberg, Shoul, 261, 265–6
Elsevier, 79, 321
Embarrato, Al, 8

Index

Encyclopedias, sales of, 29–30
Ettington Park, 128
European, 1–9, 9, 59, 114–15, 118; American market, launch on, 152–3; changes to, 141; concept of, 132–3; editor-in-chief, Maxwell as, 134–5; European Commission, Maxwell talking to, 218–19; financing, 133; launch of, 136–40, 170; plan for, 218–19; *Sunday Correspondent*, plan to merge with, 144
European Periodicals, Publicity and Advertising Corporation (EPPAC), 23
Evans, Harry, 134
Evans, Matthew, 304, 310–11
Evans, Ned, 278
Evening News, 132
Extel, 277

Fauré, Edgar, 243
Ferguson, Jack, 129
Fielding, Janet, 292, 294, 302
Financial advisers, 322–4
Financial Times, fraud investigation by, 317–18
Finland: Maxwell in, 232–3; newsprint deals, 232–3; saunas, 233
Flying, regulations on, 203
Flynn, Joe, 311
Forbes, Malcolm, 192–3
Foreign exchanges, Maxwell playing, 321
France: Agence Centrale de Presses, 242, 245; bicentenary celebrations, 242; Maxwell's forays in, 241–5; Provençal newspaper group, 243–4; Rights of Man exhibition, 243; TF1, 243–5, 321
Freedman, Ellis, 256, 276, 290, 325

Gallo, Dr Robert, 288
Galloway, George, 305
Genscher, Hans Dietrich, 261
Gillespie, Bill, 130
Goldman, Sachs, 333–4
Gorbachov, Mikhail, 107, 125, 145, 213, 232, 253, 259–61, 264, 340; coup against, 173, 269, 326; *Daily Mirror* letter to, 53–4; General Secretary, election as, 254; Maxwell, welcoming, 254–5; printing plant for, 267; private summit with, 267–8; Thatcher, sending message to, 266
Gorbachov, Raisa, 258
Gorbachov–Maxwell Institute, 289
Gordievsky, Oleg, 255
Gough, Brandon, 210
Gradov, Yuri, 249
Gray, Robert, 284, 288
Great Britain-Sasakawa Foundation, 210
Greenslade, Roy, 52, 59–64, 111–13, 124–6
Gregory, Robert, 77
Gridiron Club, 286
Gridiron dinner, 149–50
Grigg, Simon, 13, 15, 68, 98, 154
Guerrero, Oscar 303–4
Guest, Lawrence, 334

Hagerty, Bill, 64
Haines, Joe, 64, 97, 227, 308–9; biography, writing, 49; editor-in-chief, coveting job of, 59; Greenslade, enemy of, 59; Maxwell,

working for, 46–9; Poland in, 238; retirement 60–1; weekends, Maxwell interrupting, 200
Halcion, 188–90, 324
Hambro, Sir Charles, 25, 90
Hammer, Armand, 255, 265
Hans-Adam II of Liechtenstein, 312–13
Harcourt Brace Jovanovich, 276
Hastings College, Nebraska, 289
Headington Hill Hall, 29, 71, 73–4, 87, 229
Headington Investments, 324
Heath, Edward, 340
Heathfield, Peter, 123
Hendry, Tom, 139
Henry, Wendy, 47–8, 64
Hersh, Seymour, 11, 297, 301–6, 309–11, 331–2
Herzog, President Chaim, 339
Hewlett-Davies, Janet, 130
Hill & Knowlton, 284
Hinsey, Carolyn, 330–1
Hoch, Ludwig, Maxwell born as, 17
Honecker, Erich, 57, 233–6
Hounam, Peter, 304
Hussein, Saddam, 145

Ilyushin aircraft, 265–6
IMRO; Bishopsgate Investment Management, licensing, 319
Information Moscow, 260
Insull, Mike, 201
International Foundation of St Cyril and St Methodius, 228
Irangate, 292, 298
Israel: Israeli Discount Bank, negotiations for, 273; Maxwell investing in, 272–4; politics, Maxwell's involvement in, 273–4; publishing interests in, 273; Scitex, investment in, 273; Teva, purchase of shares in, 272–3

Jackson, Jesse, 198
Jackson, Professor Derek, 35
Jaglam, Raya, 265
Jane's Publishing, 32–3
Japan, Maxwell in, 205–12, 214–15
Jarratt, Alex, 40
Jaruzelski, General, 218, 233, 236–9
Jay, Peter, 55, 76, 97–8, 107, 157–8, 160–2, 165, 169–71, 176–7, 199–200, 204, 270
John Waddington's, 277, 317
Jones, Leslie, Maxwell becoming, 20
Joseph, Dr Joseph, 339
Journalists, Maxwell's attitude to, 120
Jovanovich, William, 276

Kaifu, Prime Minister, 215
Kaufmann, Ben, 294–5, 302
Keicher, Dr Walter, 315
Keicher, Werner, 315
Kennedy, Ethel, 284
Kenya, death threat, 219–20
Keys, Bill, 33
KGB: currency, movements of, 326; dossiers on Maxwell, 249–50; funds, Maxwell as conduit for, 7–8, 252–3; increasing unpopularity, 325–6; Maxwell's involvement with, 7–8, 247, 317; secret service collaborators, 250

Kimche, David, 261, 266
King, Cecil, 34
Kinnock, Neil, 340
Kissinger, Henry, 212–13, 283
Kohlberk, Kravis, Roberts & Co, 277
Koinkov, Colonel Alexander Yevgenovich, 250
Kroll, Jules, 11
Kryuchkov, Vladimir, 264, 268–9, 325
Kurenkov, Colonel Serge Alexandrovich, 250

Lady Ghislaine, 6, 8, 77, 87, 97, 151, 186,
    191–201, 225, 243, 314, 332, 334-5
Lamyatin, Leonid, 173
Leasco Data Processing, 30–1
Leigh-Pemberton, Robin, 160, 172
Lemaine, Pierre, 67
Liechtenstein, Maxwell investments in, 7,
    276–7, 312–17
Linklater, Magnus, 131
Lithuania, troops in, 125
London & Bishopsgate Holdings, 166
London Daily News, closure, 131–2; concept of,
    128–30; launch, 130; morning meetings, 167
Louis, Nicholas, 260
Louis, Victor, 249, 260
Low-Bell Ltd, 23
Lucchese family, 9, 330
Lukanhov, Andrei, 223, 225
Lyudmila Zhivkov Foundation, 221

Ma'ariv, 272
Ma'ariv Modi'in, 272
MacDonald, George, 147–8
MacKichan, Robin, 139–40
Macmillan Foundation, 283
Macmillan Inc., 79, 143, 255, 277–8, 298;
    apartment above, 280; pastry scandal, 282–3
Macullum, John, 214
Mafia, control of print unions, 10–11
Major, John, 340
Maloney, Mike, 98, 222, 238
Markov, Georgi, 222
Martin, Andrea, 87, 142, 162–3, 165, 196,
    200–1, 225–6, 336; Berlin, missing in, 235–6;
    Maxwell's attitude to, 105–18; Maxwell's
    personal assistant, as, 94–6, 102–5; office,
    charge of, 98–9; Poland, in, 238
Mather, Ian, 145
Mauser, Beth, 281–2
Maxwell, Anne, 84
Maxwell Bank of Bulgaria, 223, 227
Maxwell, Betty, 200; character, 68–9; children,
    65; constituency, running, 32; degree,
    studying for, 72; events, attending for
    Maxwell, 171; functions, attending, 69; Jewish
    cause, work for, 69; lifestyle, 86; loyalty, 70;
    Maxwell falling in love with, 20; Maxwell
    needing, 85, 88; Maxwell's behaviour to,
    66–8, 85–8; pension rights, stopping of, 320;
    reliance on, 89; religion, 263; Remembering
    the Future, organization of, 262–3
Maxwell, Christine, 73, 84
Maxwell Communications Corporation, 165,
    206–7; money plundered from, 317–18, 321;
    sale of shares in, 333

Maxwell, Debbie, 175
Maxwell Foundation, 7, 313–15, 324
Maxwell, Ghislaine, 73; Balliol, at, 72;
    childhood, 81; jobs, 81–2; Pergamon,
    joining, 81; relationship with Maxwell, 81–3
Maxwell, Ian, 13, 45, 156–7, 200; Balliol,
    scholarship to, 72; Bob Cole, relationship
    with, 75–7; fired by Maxwell, 74–5; functions,
    attending, 69; ignorance, kept in, 318; Japan,
    in, 211; last conversation with Maxwell, 336;
    relationship with Maxwell, 75–8; TF1, in, 243
Maxwell, Isabel, 73, 84
Maxwell, Karine, death of, 73
Maxwell, Kevin, 73, 156–7, 165, 200, 334, 336;
    Balliol, scholarship to, 72; character, 78;
    functions, attending, 69; ignorance, kept
    in, 318; Maxwell Foundations, taking over,
    315; New York, in, 79; relationship with
    Maxwell, 78–9
Maxwell, Laura, 77–8
Maxwell Media Trust, 316
Maxwell, Michael, death of, 73
Maxwell, Pandora, 78–80
Maxwell, Philip, 28; Balliol, scholarship
    to, 72, 83; intellect, 83; relationship with
    Maxwell, 83–4
Maxwell, Robert: air travel, 97; Auxiliary
    Power Corps, in, 19; baby talk, 197–8;
    back trouble, 180; background, 246–7; bad
    manager, as, 24; bed, working from, 178;
    Betty, behaviour towards, 66–8; birth, 16–17;
    boredom, sense of, 202; Britain, defence of,
    252; Britain, escape to, 18–19; British view of,
    41; brothers and sisters, 17; business career,
    start of, 18; business papers, attitude to,
    164; cash mountain, disappearance of, 322;
    change in drinking, effect of, 324; cheques,
    signing, 169–70; childhood, poverty of, 16–17;
    children, 65, 70–84; cigarettes, hatred of, 179;
    colds, catching, 1–2, 178–9; death, mystery of,
    325; discussions with, 5; eating habits, 177–8,
    180–3, 194–5, 209, 280–2, 287, 331; editors,
    clashes with, 123; education, 17–18; empire,
    construction of, 275; enemies, 326–7; final
    change of name, 20; fraud, perpetration of,
    325; friends, lack of, 6; funeral, 339; gambling,
    198–9; hair, colouring, 185–6; Halcion, taking,
    188–90, 324; Hersh's allegations against,
    303–10; host, as, 172–4, 184; information,
    seldom giving, 15; Intelligence officer, as,
    21; invitations, acceptance of, 69, 171; Ivan
    du Maurier, change of name to, 20; Jewish
    background, confronting, 261–3; journalists,
    attitude to, 120; KGB having no further need
    for, 329; KGB money, laundering, 7–8, 252–3;
    Kremlin, visits to, 253–4; *Lady Ghislaine*, on,
    191–201; languages, 18; last night, 337–9; last
    trip, 334; lateral thinking, 55–6; Leslie Jones,
    change of name to, 20; lung cancer, 179;
    marriage, 20; meetings with, 166–9, 174–6;
    memos, not responding to, 164; Military
    Cross, receiving, 20; money men, meeting,
    165–6; money, borrowing, 25; mood swings
    and paranoia, 191; Moscow, in, 259–61;

Mossad agent, accused of being, 11–12; mother, execution of, 20; murder, possible, 6–7; New York, in, 11; obesity, 180–4; overseas travelling entourage, 222; paranoia, 272; parenthood, attitude to, 70; parents, 89; Paris, in, 67; payments to aides, 321; people, approach to, 4; phones, bugging, 107, 111–12; pledges, unfulfilled, 289; political career, 31–2; powder puff, 186; Publisher, addressed as, 120; publishing, *see* Pergamon Press, Mirror Group Newspapers, etc., restlessness, 190–1; Saturdays, on, 3–4; secretaries, attitude to, 99–101; security, paranoid about, 201; senior management, treatment of, 162–3; sexual peccadillos, 101–3; siestas, 178; sisters, finding, 21; sixty-fifth Birthday Book, 74; sleeping habits, 154, 187–90; Solotvino, return to, 253; sons, paying, 80–1; speeches, rewriting, 271; storytelling, 70; suicide, whether committing, 6; telephone calls, taking, 163; tidiness and cleanliness, obsession with, 183; travelling, 202–5; *see also* Soviet Union, etc., twenty-four-hour paper, dream of, 127; vanity, 185–7; women, and, 89–119; World War II, in, 18

Maxwell Trusts, 33

Maxwell's Fall, 52, 59

Maxwell: the Outsider, 22, 90, 249

McCaffrey, Sir Thomas, 159

Meir, Aren, 274

Menashe, Ari Ben, 291–304, 307, 309

Menem, Carlos, 239, 241

Meynard, Elisabeth *see* Maxwell, Elisabeth (Betty)

Michele, Anthony, 9

Microfirms International Marketing Corporation, 31

Millar, Peter, 141

Miners' strike, Maxwell attempting to settle, 123

Mirror Group Newspapers: colour printing, 49–50; employees, reduction in number of, 10, 51; flotation, 40–2, 321; journalists, 41–2; Maxwell acquiring, 4, 42–3; Maxwell Media Trust as owner of, 316; money plundered from, 317–18, 321; papers in, 39; pension trustees, Maxwell at meetings of, 318; profit levels, 122; profit, in, 51; sale of part, 147; staff, reduction in, 122; women editors, 63–4

Mirrorgate, 291

Mitterrand, President François, 13, 242–3

Molecular Design, 257

Molloy, Mike, 42, 46, 52–4, 58–9, 123–4, 133–4, 175

Mondale, Walter, 286

Mongolia, 215–16

Montgomery, Field Marshal, 20

Morgan, Sir John, 98, 216, 222, 235, 237–8, 240, 261, 266

Morgenstern, Philip, 198

Morgenthau, Robert M., 8–9

Moscow News, 269–70

Mossad, 220, 297, 305–6, 331, 339; Maxwell accused of being agent of, 11–12; Vanunu, picking up, 303

MTV Europe, 321

Murdoch, Rupert, 34, 44; acquisitions by, 276 British newspapers, breaking into, 36; party Maxwell attending, 192

National Enquirer, 146

National Graphic Association, 50

Nesterenkov, Vladimir, 250–1

New York: Maxwell in, 148–53; Maxwell spending in, 288–9; Maxwell's nervousness in, 327; mobsters of, 329; print unions, control of, 10–11; Waldorf-Astoria, 279

New York Daily News: crime syndicate controlling, 7–9; *European*, distribution of, 152–3; Mafia, control by, 152–3; Maxwell buying, 9–10, 146–53; money, losing, 332; New York, as part of, 146; purchase of, 286; staff, sackings, 151–2; unions, 9–10

Newnes, subscription book division, 29

Newnham, Richard, 327

News of the World: Maxwell, attack on, 35–6, takeover battle, 35–7

O'Gara, Paddy, 40

Odhams Press, 33, 38

Official Airline Guides, 277

Ogilvy, Sir Angus, 210

Ortega, Daniel, 292

Our Heritage, 258–60

Owen, Dr David, 210

Paris, 67

Peel, Quentin, 328

Pension funds: employees losing right to, 319–20; money plundered from, 317–21; share certificates belonging to, banks accepting, 323

People, the, 47–8, 53, 58

Pereira, Joseph, 103

Peres, Shimon, 172–3, 339

Pergamon Foundation, 313

Pergamon Holding Trust, 313

Pergamon Media Trust, 313

Pergamon Press, 26, 28, 207, 248; editorial board, 248–9; Philip Maxwell, instructions to, 84; poor management of, 49; profits, inflation of, 30–1; sale of, 147, 321, 329; Soviet journals, publication of, 327; success of, 28–30, 42; UN papers, publishing, 248

Pergamon Press Incorporated, 275; borrowing, 279

Perpich, Rudi, 289–90

Perrino, Robert, 9, 330

Petrov, General Vitaly, 251

Pirie, Robert, 277

Pisar, Dr Samuel, 67, 189, 238, 336

Pohl, Karl, 261, 274

Pohl, Ulrika, 118–19

Poland: Maxwell's involvement in, 236–9; Women's International Zionist Organization, tour by, 264–5

Pole, John, 107, 111–12

Pollard, Eve, 64, 298

Popov, Dimitar, 229

Print unions: Maxwell taming, 44; New

York, in, 147–8; printing outside London, reaction to, 50; redundancies, 122; sharp practices, 39–40
Prior, James, 210
Private Eye, 149
Prunskiene, Mrs K., 142–3

Racing Times, 153
Reagan, Ronald, 149, 279, 299
Rechsteiner, Dr Werner, 314–15, 325
Reed International, 33, 38; Mirror Group, sale of, 38–9
Reichmann, Albert, 265
Retainers, 124
Rhodesia, 212–13
Richardson, Sir Michael, 160
Rippon, Lord, 159
Robert Maxwell and Pergamon Press, 84
Robinson, Peter, 32–3
Rockefeller, David, 283
Ronson, Gerald, 210
Rosabaud, Dr Paul, 26, 248
Rothermere, Lord, 129
Rothschilds, 35, 277
Ryzhkov, Nikolai, 253

Samson Option, The, 11, 297, 299, 302–3
Sasakawa, Ryoichi, 209–12
Scargill, Arthur, 123
Schalit, Jean, 133–4
Schmidt, Helmut, 133
Scholz, Arno, 21
Scientific Advisory Committee, 26
Scitex, 228, 273; sale of, 321
Scottish Daily News, 37–8
Shamir, Yitzhak, 261, 268, 297, 300, 340
Shearson Lehman, 333
Shillum, Alan, 270
Shultz, George, 286
Simkin Marshall, 26–7
Smilgis, Martha, 287–8
Smith New Court, 160
Smith, Andrew, 166
Smith, Ian, 212
Somerfield, Stafford, 35
Soviet Union; Academy of Sciences, 256; children suffering from radiation effects, treatment of, 264; collapse of, 8; cultural foundation, projected, 258–9; Gosbank, 251; Israeli interests in, 261; Jews, Maxwell helping, 263–4; Kondapoga newsprint plant, 257–8; Maxwell's involvement with, 246–7; Maxwell's relationship with, 326–7; Maxwell's status in, 249; Moscow, loan to, 261; projects with Maxwell, 256–7; publishing deal, 249, 252, 327; transfer of money from, 251; Western technology, acquisition of, 255
Sporting Life, 50, 63
Springer, Ferdinand, 22–3, 25–6, 248
Steinberg, Saul, 30
Stott, Richard, 50, 53, 55–8, 64, 307–9
Straka, Laszlo, 255, 275, 290
Sunday Correspondent, 143–4
Sunday Mirror leaders, Maxwell approving, 270–1

Sviridov, Felix, 260–1
Swiss Bank Corporation, 335

Tanaka, Itaru, 211
Taylor, Elizabeth, 192
TF1, 343–5; sale of, 321
Thatcher, Margaret, 160, 172, 206, 340; Gorbachov, Maxwell delivering message from, 266–7
Thompson, David, 125
Thorne, Frank, 310
Thornton, Clive, 39–40
Times, The, 35, 63
Tower, Senator John, 285
Trachtenberg, Larry, 166, 216
Trump, Donald, 82
Tudjman, Franj, 290
TV Times, 33

Ulan Bator, 215
United States; banking laws, 276; development of business in, 255–6; important people, Maxwell meeting, 282–3; Maxwell in, 278–80; Maxwell travelling to, 275; private companies in, 275–6; secretarial staff in, 280–1

Van der Byl, Piet, 213
Vanunu, Mordechai, 11–12, 303, 306, 310–11
Vogel, Rabbi, 334

Walesa, Lech, 236
Walker, Al, 8
Walker, Peter, 321
Watson, Ian, 9, 138–41, 144–5, 152–3
Watson Victor, 316
Welsh, Judy, 99, 165, 171
Wheeler, George, 185–6, 324
Whittam-Smith, Andreas, 134
Williams, Charles, 159
Williams, Les, 182
Wilson, Charles, 63, 308
Wilson, Harold (Lord Wilson of Rievaulx), 46–7, 159, 210
Wilson, P.J., 55
Women's International Zionist Organization; Poland, tour of, 264–5
Woodward and Bernstein, 6
Workers' co-operatives, 37–8
World Economic Forum, 216–18
World War II, Jews murdered in, 262–3

Yakovlev, Alexander, 258–9, 264, 268
Yakovlev, Yegor, 269–70
Young & Rubicam, 170

Zhivkov, Lyudmila, 221
Zhivkov, Todor, 221, 223, 225
Zornow, David, 299–300